Visions and Revisions

in

Modern American Literary Criticism

Visions and Revisions
in
Modern American Literary Criticism

EDITED, AND WITH AN INTRODUCTION, BY

Bernard S. Oldsey

AND

Arthur O. Lewis, Jr.

A Dutton **dep** *Paperback*

NEW YORK

E. P. DUTTON & CO., INC.

1962

ACKNOWLEDGMENTS

Grateful acknowledgment is made to the following for permission to
quote copyright material:

Joel E. Spingarn, "The New Criticism," reprinted from *The New
Criticism*, by permission of Columbia University Press. Copyright,
1911, 1939, by Columbia University Press.

H. L. Mencken, "Theodore Dreiser," reprinted from *A Book of
Prefaces* by H. L. Mencken, by permission of Alfred A. Knopf, Inc.
Copyright, 1917, 1945, by Alfred A. Knopf, Inc.

Van Wyck Brooks, "Sherwood Anderson," reprinted from *The
Confident Years: 1885-1915*, by permission of E. P. Dutton & Co.,
Inc. Copyright, 1952, by Van Wyck Brooks.

Vernon L. Parrington, "Victorian Realism," reprinted from *Main
Currents in American Thought*, Volume III, by Vernon L. Parrington, by permission of Harcourt, Brace & World, Inc. Copyright,
1930, by Harcourt, Brace & World, Inc.; renewed, 1958, by Vernon
L. Parrington, Jr., Louise P. Tucker, and Elizabeth P. Thomas.

Paul Elmer More, "Modern Currents in American Literature,"
reprinted from *The Demon of the Absolute*, by permission of
Princeton University Press. Copyright, 1928, 1956, by Princeton
University Press.

T. S. Eliot, "Tradition and the Individual Talent," reprinted from
Selected Essays: New Edition by T. S. Eliot, by permission of
Harcourt, Brace & World, Inc., and Faber and Faber, Ltd. Copyright, 1932, 1936, 1950, by Harcourt, Brace & World, Inc.; copyright, ©, 1960, by T. S. Eliot.

Allen Tate, "Techniques of Fiction," reprinted from *Collected
Essays*, by permission of the publisher, Alan Swallow. Copyright,
1948, 1959, by Allen Tate.

Cleanth Brooks, "The Waste Land: Critique of the Myth," reprinted from *Modern Poetry and the Tradition*, by permission of

ACKNOWLEDGMENTS

To ACKNOWLEDGE all the help and encouragement received in putting this book together would be impossible, but the editors want to note especially the contributions of William L. Werner, Professor Emeritus of American Literature, and Henry W. Sams, Professor of English, both of The Pennsylvania State University. Each, in his own way, helped bring this book to completion.

PREFACE

IT IS assumed, in the making of a book such as this, that there is a body of literary criticism, properly set off as Modern American, which has become an influential, symbiotic, almost (some would have it) self-sustaining form of literary expression; that this body of criticism acts as a cultural index to our society; and that, in its various guises, it deserves representation in a form of publication readily available to the general reader as well as to the student of American literature.

The essays presented here are meant to reflect a spectrum of critical thought expressed in this country during the twentieth century—or to be more exact, between 1911 and 1960, the publication dates of Spingarn's "The New Criticism" and Young's analysis of "Rip Van Winkle." Arrangement of the essays is roughly chronological; but even though this arrangement and the introduction partake of the historical view, the guiding principle of the book is one of comparison and contrast—a reaching back and forth across temporal lines to disclose what might be called the statement and counterstatement, or the visions and re-visions, of American criticism.

Three main criteria were applied in selecting the essays in this volume. It was asked of each piece that it be representative of a major approach or individually refined viewpoint significant within the field of American criticism; that it sustain itself as a piece of writing, in terms of style and force; and that it be capable of throwing some light on the problems encountered by the modern reader—problems often created, frequently sustained, and sometimes solved by criticism itself.

The editors of this collection, like all anthologists, were faced by the severest restraint and harshest decision—space and the exclusion of writers who, taken together, might make up as good a book as the present one, though certainly a different one in emphasis. It is particularly hard to omit such a figure as John Crowe Ransom, who is in a sense the father of the new New Criticism, and whose limpid expository prose with touches of Latinate thunder has had the admiration and respect of the editors for many years past. However, Mr. Ransom is not a critic who "anthologizes" so easily and well as others of his school, which has been fully represented by such kindred figures as Tate, Cleanth Brooks, Burke, Blackmur, and Yvor Winters. Another critic difficult to pass by without a word of acknowledgment and respect is Malcolm Cowley; his essays in clear explication and fine appreciation of various American authors have become a byword of popular criticism. Perhaps his only peer in this area is Edmund Wilson.

After Ransom and Cowley such a list of regrettable omissions might be extended to some length. The names of many writers—R. P. Warren, F. J. Hoffman, W. K. Wimsatt, for example—suggest themselves immediately; and certainly no companion volume could afford to ignore their contributions. But there is no end to this sort of naming of worthies: to name some and ignore others would in itself be an act of critical injustice. Thus the present collection must be regarded as merely an introductory display of the rich and many-layered fabric of modern American literary criticism.

CONTENTS

O = to read
O = already read

"A culture is not a flow, nor even a confluence; the form of its existence is struggle, or at least debate—it is nothing if not a dialectic."

—Lionel Trilling in *The Liberal Imagination*

INTRODUCTION

I

IT HAS often been said, with some accuracy, that one of the earliest signs of maturity in literature is the appearance of large numbers of literary critics. With this standard, it is not difficult to demonstrate that American literature reached full maturity in the twentieth century, for seldom has literary criticism been so various and fruitful.

Modern American literary criticism began as a reaction against the genteelly romantic work of James Russell Lowell and his followers—Stedman, Taylor, Aldrich, and others—of the late nineteenth-century New England tradition. The concern of these critics had been largely with matters of taste and decorum, resulting more often than not in a concentration on the "safe" literature of the past and a failure to recognize the merit of contemporary writers. True, with Whitman, Howells, James, and a few college professors of the nineties like Woodberry, Matthews, Boyesen, and Gates there had been a readier appreciation of contemporary, less genteel writers, but at the turn of the century it was still more likely than not that such a book as *Sister Carrie* would be suppressed.

Lacking any strong native critical tradition to which they could appeal, American critics of the twentieth century have turned elsewhere—to classical Greece: Plato, Aristotle; to Italy: Vico, Croce; to France: Taine, Sainte-Beuve, Brunetière; and especially to England: Coleridge, Bentham, Arnold, Hulme, Richards—for direction and standards. What might be called "schools of criticism" have formed and dissolved almost as quickly as discerned, and individual critics have shifted and revised their views in such a way as often to defy classification. Nevertheless, a number of general groupings, some of them lasting for several decades, can be observed.

In the first thirty years of the century three groups were reasonably strong: the Impressionists—Huneker, Mencken, Nathan—called for immediate, almost sensory appreciation of the new writers; the Humanists—Brownell, Babbitt, More—

insisted on the need for fixing standards against which the new writers could be measured; a kind of nationalistic group —Bourne, Brooks, Mumford—led a search for a specifically *American* pattern for the new writers to follow. Although these three approaches continued to be represented, after about 1930 the major critics fell into three other groups: the leftists—Parrington, Hicks, Calverton—often Marxist, insisted upon the sociological utilitarian aspects of literature; the psychological critics—Krutch, Troy, Wilson—variously Freudian, Jungian, and Gestalt, attempted to explain literature in terms of the writers' personalities; the New Critics—Ransom, Blackmur, Brooks, Tate—industriously examined the *language* of poetry. The two chief developments of the fifties have been the emergence of the myth critics—Chase, Fiedler, Young, Fergusson, Wheelwright—who have brought a new synthesis of biographical, psychoanalytic, and folkloristic materials to bear on the work of art; and the Chicago Critics—Crane, Olson, McKeon—who have attacked the New Critics as undisciplined and irresponsible in the interpretation of literature.

Such groupings as these are at best superficial, and it should be noted that those critics whose work is likely to last longest—Eliot, Wilson, Burke—have generally availed themselves of more than one approach.

II

It would be an exaggeration to claim that all modern American criticism has evolved from one essay by Joel E. Spingarn (1875–1939) called "The New Criticism" (1911). But there would be less exaggeration in saying that this piece constitutes a landmark in American criticism, ranking with the publication of Eliot's "Tradition and the Individual Talent" (1919). Spingarn, whose total output was slight, was fortunate enough to find the right time and approach for summing up one age of criticism and announcing another. His preparations for this task consisted of having been trained by Lewis E. Gates and Benedetto Croce ("under his banner I enrolled myself long ago"), and of having written *A History of Literary Criti-*

cism in the Renaissance (1899). Although later he edited an excellent collection of contemporary essays, *Criticism in America* (1931), his own major contributions were encompassed in a single volume, *Creative Criticism* (1917, 1931).

Often referred to as an impressionistic critic, Spingarn might be more accurately described as an *ex*pressionist. It is true that he partly agreed with Anatole France's idea that a critic need only "have sensations in the presence of a work of art"; and it is likewise true that he fought on the impressionist side in the "battle of the books" (replying, in *A Spingarn Enchiridion*, 1929, to attacks from Paul Elmer More). But the key word in "The New Criticism" is *expression*, both in its precise sense as Spingarn would apply it to art, and in its limited, or corrupt, sense as applied by factional schools of criticism. It is also the clue to his culminating statement that "taste must reproduce the work of art within itself in order to understand and judge it; and at that moment aesthetic judgment becomes nothing more nor less than creative art itself."

The achievement of Spingarn's essay is that it summarizes Western World criticism, defines both the impressionistic and (in the Crocean sense) expressionistic view, and looks forward to what we now construe as *the* New Criticism, in respect to isolating a piece of literature for close textual, aesthetic analysis. So that criticism might attain its proper function —discovering what the author has tried to express and how well he has expressed it—Spingarn, in his essay, clears away what he considered to be deadwood. We have done with all rules, he declares—with literary genres, with vague abstractions about the comic and tragic, with theories of style, with moral judgment (thus eliminating the question of "Was it worthwhile expressing?"), with techniques as separate from art, with the sociological determinism of Taine, and finally with the separation between genius and taste. Obviously, we have not "done" with a number of these critical aspects, or roughly half of the essays in this collection would not be here. But Spingarn sharpened our sights, made us aware of a new vision, and while not producing much specific criticism on his own, cleared the way for Eliot, Ransom, Tate, Blackmur, Burke, and others—by calling for close attention to the work of art itself, and by insisting that criticism is itself an art.

The most exciting criticism of the early part of the century came from the Impressionists. Where the Humanists were concerned with the comparatively dry establishment of standards, and the "Nationalists" with a discouraging search for merit in earlier American literature, the Impressionists were discovering and offering help to the new American writers like Dreiser, Sandburg, Lewis, Cabell, and Sherwood Anderson. In their journals, most notably in *Smart Set* and in the *American Mercury*, they printed essays of praise as well as the work of many writers who have now come to be recognized as major figures in American literature. Because impressionistic criticism is of the moment, it is perhaps more ephemeral than other kinds; nevertheless, the writings of James Huneker, George Jean Nathan, Paul Rosenfeld, and H. L. Mencken, at least, often overcome this handicap.

If Huneker was the early leader of this group, Mencken (1880–1956) was assuredly the best, as he was the most colorful, of the disciples. His major contributions appear in *A Book of Prefaces* (1917), in the six volumes of *Prejudices* (1919–27), and in the scholarly *The American Language* (1919–48). *A Book of Prefaces*, from which the essay in *Visions and Revisions* has been drawn, was not, by a considerable margin, Mencken's first critical book, nor did it differ in any major respect from either his earlier or later collections. But it is a landmark in American criticism, since in its four long essays resides the essence of Mencken's critical position. In "Joseph Conrad" and in "Theodore Dreiser" he praises what proves to be vital in the work of these two major literary figures: the unflinching view of the world, the sense of man's battle against a hostile environment, and the courage to write the truth. In "Theodore Dreiser," too, Mencken examines the background—literary and domestic—which produced the novels; he pays tribute to Dreiser's "gigantic steadfastness" as he "plods along in the laborious, cheerless way he first marked out for himself"; he attacks Dreiser's enemies. But he also points out the faults—stodginess, prolixity, weakness of plot—as well as any critic has succeeded in doing. In "James Huneker" he is concerned with "the exception . . . the solitary Iokanaan in this tragic aesthetic wilderness, the only critic among us whose vision sweeps the whole field of beauty, and whose reports of what he sees there show any genuine gusto." In "Puritanism as a Literary Force" the conclusions are the logical result for one who could write, and believe in, the first three essays. Puritanism, "the prejudice against beauty as a form of debauchery and corruption," as Mencken called it, stood between Dreiser and success, prevented Conrad's complete acceptance, and posed a threat to the gusto of which Mencken was a much greater exemplar than his master, Huneker.

In many ways the product of a journalist first, a satirist second, and a literary critic last, Mencken's perceptions are clear; and if his conclusions are not always valid, his prose is entertaining, informative, and eminently readable. More than most of his fellows he practiced what he called for in "Criticism of Criticism of Criticism" (1919): ". . . the function of a genuine critic of the arts . . . [is] to provoke the reaction between the work of art and the spectator."

Sometimes close to the Impressionists, and often joined by writers whom the Impressionists were first to recognize, were a number of liberal critics who, following Randolph Bourne (1886–1918), were chiefly concerned with making Americans aware of themselves as Americans. After Bourne's premature death, Van Wyck Brooks (1886–   ) assumed leadership. In works more often manifesto than criticism, like *America's Coming-of-Age* (1915) and *Letters and Leadership* (1918), as well as in controversial studies of Mark Twain (1920, 1933) and Henry James (1925), he led the way toward making America more self-conscious about its intellectual life. American literature was sterile, Brooks declared, because of the longstanding dichotomy between highbrow and lowbrow, between intellectuals and practical men; there had been too little attempt to find a middle way between those concerned only with idealistic theories and those concerned only with making money. Brooks and Lewis Mumford, Harold Stearns, and Waldo Frank, among others, consciously dug through the American tradition in search of a "usable past" that might form a pattern for contemporary artists—who would in turn assume leadership of a new America.

The danger in the approach of Brooks and his associates was that in their emphasis on the frustrations of the American spirit and their attempt to re-evaluate the writers of the past they overlooked positive points of significance to their own cause and failed in the recognition of contemporary writers who had gotten the message (Brooks at first neglected Dreiser). Brooks himself later repudiated much of what he had said in his earlier books, and in the five volumes of his *Makers and Finders* series (1936–52) turned to almost chauvinistic appreciation of writers he had once castigated. Similarly, the best critic among his followers, Lewis Mumford, prefacing a reissue (1957) of *The Golden Day* (1926), assigned to Longfellow the role of pioneer in the movement to which he and Brooks belonged, and admitted his error: "Over my utter neglect of Longfellow . . . I would now smilingly do penance."

But, despite errors, this group of "Nationalists"—for want of a better term—served the cause of American culture well. Brooks' program for a "national culture to come . . . in order that America may be able in future to give something to the rest of the world that is better than what the world too generally means by 'Americanism'" was a needed antidote to national smugness, and bore fruit. One need name only Vernon Louis Parrington, Constance Rourke, and Henry Nash Smith to see the disparate types of critics who have profited from his example.

Irving Babbitt (1865–1933) and Paul Elmer More (1864–1937) are generally regarded as the leaders of the New Humanism in America. Claiming intellectual descent from Matthew Arnold and with the earlier example of William Crary Brownell before them, the Humanists, many of them university professors like Robert Shafer, Norman Foerster, and Prosser Frye, brought to bear on the study of literature some of the keenest intellects and most thoroughly trained minds of the century. They had in common the belief that man, living as he does on the three levels of the natural (or animal), the human, and the religious (or ideal), must "make a resolute distinction between man and nature and between man and the divine." Thus, they objected equally to the attempt of the medieval church to raise man to the level of the ideal to the exclusion of the human and to the efforts of modern biologists, sociologists, psychologists, and naturalistic writers to regard man as on the level of the animals. They called for human happiness as opposed to either divine or animal happiness and proposed that application of standards drawn from the best experience of the past, adherence to what Babbitt called the "inner check," and moderation in all things would produce such happiness. Other critics found this position untenable, and the resulting battle of the books raged for most of two decades. Babbitt in such volumes as *The New Laokoön* (1910) and *Rousseau and Romanticism* (1919) was a redoubtable warrior and the true standard bearer of the humanist cause, but the most sustained statement of their position was made by More as editor of the *Nation* (1909–14), in fourteen volumes of *Shelburne Essays* (1904–36), and in numerous other collections of literary, social, and religious criticism.

Typical of More's approach is "Main Currents of American Literature," first published in *Revue de Paris* (1927) where it had the avowed intention of trying to explain to French readers something about More's contemporaries. The attack on Amy Lowell, Cabell, Dreiser, Masters, Lewis, Dos Passos, and Mencken is perhaps More's severest criticism of modern American writers. But it is worth noting that in this same essay his defense of his humanist colleagues and his call for colleges to teach "the discipline of classical humanism" are worthy statements of a critical position that has much to offer the conscientious reader of today.

Recipient of the Nobel Prize for Literature in 1948, distinguished as poet, dramatist, and literary editor, T. S. Eliot (1888–) is easily the most influential of the critics represented in *Visions and Revisions*. Of his own criticism he has said that "its merits and limitations can be fully appreciated only when it is considered in relation to the poetry I have written myself." Clearly, he is in the direct line of English poet-critics that includes Dryden, Johnson, Coleridge, and Arnold, and, like them, he has been a focus of critical activity in his day. Like these great predecessors, too, he cannot be placed in a particular critical camp: in his insistence on the importance of the work of art as art he is perhaps the last of the great Impressionists; in his concern for applications of standards from past literature he is close to the Neo-Humanists; in his requirement that literature must teach right human action he approaches—if not the utilitarian, sociological critics—the Tolstoyan view of art; in his intensive study of the language of poetry he is godfather, if not parent, of the New Critics.

Descendant of an old New England family, Eliot was educated at Harvard, Oxford, Marburg, and the Sorbonne; among early influences upon his critical thinking were such brilliant teachers as Irving Babbitt, George Santayana, and Henri Bergson. Important early literary influences were Coleridge, Rémy de Gourmont, and his contemporaries T. E. Hulme and Ezra Pound. His formal training has been in literature and philosophy—both Eastern and Western—and he brings to his criticism a remarkable fusion of keen intellect and cosmopolitan learning. He writes with an unemotional, objective style, more often than not tempered by an urbane wit and irony that belie the often journalistic occasion that brought about the writing of a particular essay.

Of the several hundred critical pieces he has published, Eliot has collected a comparatively small number in book form, most importantly in *The Sacred Wood* (1920), *Selected Essays* (1932, 1950), *The Use of Poetry and the Use of Criticism* (1933), and *Of Poetry and Poets* (1957). Although the subjects of these essays are wide in range, they may be conveniently grouped under three general headings: those dealing with poetical and critical principles; those dealing with individual writers (usually poets), such as "The Metaphysical

Poets" and "John Dryden"; and those dealing with the relationship of poetry (and criticism) to other aspects of society, such as "Religion and Literature" and "The Humanism of Irving Babbitt." The first group is of most immediate concern here.

"Tradition and the Individual Talent" (1919) is in many ways a preview of Eliot's later criticism. It is both a statement of the significance of poetry in the whole tradition of culture and a call for impersonality in art. Each new work of art alters the existing order of past works: "the past . . . [is] altered by the present as much as the present is directed by the past." The poet must be aware of the responsibilities this situation produces, must write with "a sense of the timeless as well as of the temporal," must surrender himself to "something more valuable." The poet's mind is in effect a kind of receptacle for storing ideas and impressions which the imagination will eventually transmute into poetry. It is his job to find images which will convey emotion to the reader (in "Hamlet and His Problems" Eliot named this set of images the "objective correlative"). Poetry, then, "is not a turning loose of emotion, but an escape from emotion; it is not the expression of personality, but an escape from personality."

In "The Function of Criticism" (1923) he followed up this attempt to describe the poet's work with a similar attempt to describe what the critic ought to do. Essentially he attacked what he regarded as the too impressionistic criticism of his day, insisting that the critic, presenting facts through comparison and analysis, must be willing to take a stand. The true function of the critic is "the elucidation of the work of art and the correction of taste."

Eliot's own "correction of taste" has been most successful. In "The Frontiers of Criticism," a lecture delivered before an audience of thousands in 1956, he expressed some surprise at being "regarded as one of the ancestors of modern criticism, if too old to be a modern critic myself." But the fact is that his influence has been tremendous, and when he revises his views—compare the statements on Milton in "The Metaphysical Poets" (1921) and in "Milton II" (1947) or on the theory of impersonality in poetry in "Tradition and the Individual Talent" (1919) and in "Religion and Literature" (1936) — there is much soul-searching in academic and critical ranks.

In "The Frontiers of Criticism" Eliot replaced his earlier description of the function of the critic with a new one: "to promote the understanding and enjoyment of literature." Expressing a certain chagrin over some of the criticism that had resulted when others took too literally some of his earlier "phrases which have had a truly embarrassing success in the world," he nevertheless pointed out that "These last thirty years have been . . . a brilliant period in literary criticism both in Britain and America." His own role in whatever brilliance criticism may have had has been second to none.

III

As the battle of the books came to a close and before the New Criticism had fully developed, there arose in this country a considerable body of criticism based on social, economic, and political precepts. This "sociological" criticism was deterministic in attitude and moralistic—sometimes even propagandistic—in aim. Its standards were not so much belletristic as they were social; it dealt not so much with poetry as with fiction, especially the novel of purpose. The left wing of this school was built on Marxist grounds; and a fairly obvious division has always existed between those members who have been Marxist and those who have not—although in this instance, too, the revision principle has operated within the works of Edmund Wilson, Granville Hicks, James T. Farrell, and others.

One of the founders of this school of criticism was the French literary philosopher and historian Hippolyte Taine, who, viewing literature as a product of *race, moment,* and *milieu,* affirmed the position of early naturalists like Emile Zola and the Goncourt brothers. In America, Vernon Louis Parrington (1871–1929), operating on a basis of Jeffersonian monism, produced a home-grown, almost Agrarian, variety of socio-economic literary analysis. Although he began his career with a pamphlet on Sinclair Lewis, Parrington is known as the author of a single monolithic work, never quite finished, entitled *Main Currents in American Thought: An Interpretation of American Literature from the Beginnings to 1920* (published in three volumes, 1927–30). It was Parrington's avowed purpose, as stated in the introduction to this work, to trace the development of "certain germinal ideas" that are considered "traditionally American." Although American letters provided the major grounds for such a tracing, Parrington openly declared his decision to follow "the broad path of our political, economic, and social development, rather than the narrower belletristic" one.

The predictable direction and dangers of Parrington's path have been outlined by Lionel Trilling in his essay "Reality in America," where he credits Parrington with an "informing idea" and "an influence on our conception of American culture not equaled," but eventually describes his as theory-bound and narrowly liberal. Like others who disagree with Parrington, Trilling points to the short shrift accorded such writers as Poe and Henry James because they were, for Parrington, literary freaks who sported outside his deterministic confines. But Parrington himself provided the shock of intelligent questioning—from outside a closed circuit of literary acceptances—that has produced its own effects. In his "Victorian Realism," included here, it is surprising to note how Parrington precedes Richard Chase in announcing that Henry James was not a realist but a romanticist in disguise. The critical distance between the historical determinist and the mytho-symbolic analyst becomes immediately apparent, however, in Parrington's final commentary on James: "His characters are *only* projections of his brooding fancy, externalizations of hypothetical subtleties. He was concerned *only* with *nuances*. Like modern scholarship he came to deal more and more with less and less. . . ." Chase, of course, would delete the word *only,* as well as the last line.

Other sociological critics in America were frankly Marxian in approach, particularly during the Depression. In books like *The Liberation of American Literature* (1932), *The Great*

Tradition (1933), and *Proletarian Literature in the U.S.* (1935), such writers as V. F. Calverton, Granville Hicks, and Michael Gold directly applied the Marxist view to literary history. James T. Farrell (1904–), a novelist turned critic, began with the same view but changed it. His earlier books of criticism, *A Note on Literary Criticism* (1936) and *The League of Frightened Philistines* (1945), consist mainly of essays reprinted from periodicals like *Labor Action* and *The New International*—a Marxist publication in which "Literature and Morality" originally appeared before it became the title essay of a book published in 1947. Reflecting his early position, this essay does two things rather plainly: first, it poses the essential problem of social responsibility or morality in literature; and, secondly, it uses class-consciousness as an analytical wedge. Farrell's later essays, collected in *Reflections at Fifty* (1954), indicate his change of mind; in one of them, "Literature and Sociology," he reveals himself as still sociological in intent, but dissatisfied with the Marxist approach to literature, because of its narrow hardness. "Even in interpreting sociological, economic, and political events," he explains, "it is necessary to develop a conception of multiple causation. This Marxism does not do. My statement requires a revision of some past political and social attitudes of mine, but I reserve for the future an account of this. I have constantly insisted, all during my literary career, that Marxism provides no basis for *judging* literature."

Partly because of his sensitivity, partly because of his wide learning and eclectic turn of mind (he has written on everything from the Iroquois Indians to the Civil War and the Dead Sea scrolls), Edmund Wilson (1895–) has escaped the pitfalls of Marxian criticism, even though he was able to provide one of the finest historical accounts of Marxist doctrine in *To the Finland Station* (1940). There is little doubt that Wilson was influenced by Taine, Marx, and Vico; all three are referred to in "The Historical Interpretation of Literature," where the eighteenth-century Vico is cited at some length, as having fathered "the first social interpretation of a work of literature." Wilson's essay explains sociological criticism as such and identifies its author as a practitioner of the same. It would be unfair, however, to categorize Wilson as simply this and nothing more, since he is perhaps the best balanced, or at least the most catholic, of modern American critics. He might be classed as symbolic interpreter for his work in *Axel's Castle* (1931), where he not only defines and analyzes Symbolism but also makes one of the most important pronouncements of his career: "The literary history of our time is to a great extent that of the development of Symbolism and its fusion or conflict with Naturalism." He might also be classed as a psychoanalytic critic for the series of Freudian essays that make up *The Wound and the Bow* (1941), where he utilizes a theory of psychological compensation in accounting for the literary abilities of writers like Hemingway, Kipling, and Henry James.

Wilson is sometimes disparaged as a literary journalist and surface-scratching popularizer; but most critics of critics find him stylistically clear, intellectually sound, and critically balanced—capable of applying specialized viewpoints and at the same time achieving humanistic and aesthetic breadth. (It is interesting to speculate on whether, in dropping his chapter on Wilson from the revised edition of *The Armed Vision,* Stanley Edgar Hyman has altered his harsh opinion of him.)

Lionel Trilling (1905–   ) is perhaps the only American critic who approaches Wilson in scope and versatility, with the possible exception of Kenneth Burke. A product of the eastern seaboard (born in New York City, educated at Columbia University, where he remains a professor of English), Trilling has fused sociological and psychological elements into a humanistic frame. His essay on "Art and Neurosis" shows continued interest in the psychoanalytical aspects of criticism, indicated earlier in "Freud and Literature." Both essays appear in Trilling's best book, *The Liberal Imagination* (1949), whose title and intent are revealed in the preface: "To the carrying out of the job of criticizing the liberal imagination, literature has a unique relevance . . . because literature is the human activity that takes the fullest and most precise account of variousness, possibility, complexity, and difficulty." This statement is consistent with his idea concerning art, neurosis, and psychoanalysis: he grants that much can be learned about the artist through clinical analysis, but concludes that the essence of art is irreducible, a gift, which can be examined only in and of itself. Such distinctions between related matters, with insistence upon the essentially individualistic and aesthetic properties of literary art, show up in Trilling's later volumes, *The Opposing Self* (1955) and *A Gathering of Fugitives* (1956). His taste and aesthetic inclination are evident in those figures he chose for early biographical studies—*Matthew Arnold* (1939) and *E. M. Forster* (1943). His tone and style, as might be expected, are urbane, intellectual, and incisive.

F. O. Matthiessen (1902–1950) is another academic critic with liberal and sociological tendencies. Two elements which help distinguish his work are its scholarly thoroughness and its demand for wholeness. In fact this one word—"wholeness" —epitomizes Matthiessen's attitude toward life and art. In "The Responsibilities of the Critic" he makes a plea for broadness of learning and experience; he asks that knowledge of the past and knowledge of the present—gained as much as possible through experience—be incorporated in the ideal critic. This is the basis of his argument against a certain amount of New Criticism—it must not shun the whole experience of life, unless it wants to reach a dead end of verbal and technical limitations: "The trouble is that the terms of the new criticism, its devices and strategies and semantic exercises, can become as pedantic as any other set of terms if they are handled not as the means to fresh discoveries but as counters in a stale game." Actually, Matthiessen's essay gives a short account of various critical approaches; what he has to say about the "Kenyon School," as well as sociological and myth criticism, might very well form part of the introduction to this book, and is worth examining for its neat, objective summarizations.

Showing an affinity with William James' pragmatism and with the French Existentialists' concept of *engagement*, Matthiessen committed himself to the idea that "the judgment of art is unavoidably both an aesthetic and a social act." In "The Responsibilities of the Critic" he attempts to demonstrate how this is so even with such writers as Shakespeare and, unexpectedly, Wallace Stevens. For Matthiessen, then, the most mature function of the critic, in making his social-aesthetic judgment and in relating our times to other times, is to "discern and demand the works of art that we need most."

But Matthiessen's demand does not make the critic into a political censor or narrowly utilitarian guide. The subjects of his own study offer proof to the contrary. Very unlike Eliot in politics, he nevertheless established himself as a critic with *The Achievement of T. S. Eliot* (1935, 1947). In addition to editing collections of stories by Henry James and coediting *The Notebooks of Henry James* (1947), he wrote a highly regarded study, *Henry James, The Major Phase* (1944), and a biography, *The James Family* (1947). Through these works, as well as *Theodore Dreiser* (1951), and especially *American Renaissance* (1941), Matthiessen's scholarly-critical contribution has become noted for its historical, biographical, and analytical soundness and objectivity.

Kenneth Burke (1897–   ) moves away from the biographical and historical approaches to literature, except where they contribute some increment of credence to an analytic procedure: as for example in his treatment of the imagery in *1984* as a manifestation of George Orwell's tuberculosis. Burke is primarily concerned with the analysis of symbolic action— and very often in terms of how it operates in respect to audience reaction. In this sense he might be classified as America's pre-eminent example, with one eye on Freud and one on George Herbert Mead, of the socio-psychological critic.

What makes Burke one of the most resourceful, original, and elucidating critics of our time is the fact that he improves, or moves on from, the concept put forth by Sir James Jeans that no man sees the universe except through his own cloud of dust. Burke ramifies this thesis by considering the visual mode as characterized not by a dust cloud but by various lenses, each man being able to view literature (and the universe) through as many different kinds of lenses as he is capable of handling. His criticism thus often appears as new views through lenses sometimes borrowed, sometimes new. In "Literature as Equipment for Living" he takes a microscopic view, reducing literature to the lowest common denominator, seeing it as an elaboration of lines radiating out from the most basic points of communication. Burke has several times stated that a book is but the expansion of a single sentence; in this essay he shows, with deadly playfulness, that it may be the expansion of a grunt, a groan, a smile, a shriek, a gesture. With this article he brings us closer than one might expect toward the literary problem of "theme" and the psychological problem of "effect."

"Literature as Equipment for Living" is representative of Burke's work as a whole, encompassing in short form many of his ideas spent in the search for a "strategy of strategies" (which is his way of saying a theory fit to embrace all symbolic action). Since the publication of his first book of criticism, *Counter-Statement* (1931), Burke has shown constant concern for achieving a dialectic that will explain literature in dramatic terms, through internal structure, act-scene relationships, and affective qualification. "Thus"—he explains at the beginning of *The Philosophy of Literary Form* (1941)— "the reader who wants the specific criticism of books might be more disappointed than the reader who wants a theory of the criticism of books. . . ." Burke's crescent theory often expresses itself in triads—like the three subdivisions he proposes for the analysis of an "act" in poetry: "dream (the unconscious or subconscious factors in a poem . . .), prayer (the communicative functions of a poem . . .), chart (the realistic sizing-up of situations that is sometimes explicit, sometimes implicit, in poetic strategies)." This triadic relationship has been worked out on a much larger plane in *A Grammar of Motives* (1945), *A Rhetoric of Motives* (1950), and *A Symbolic of Motives* (due in 1963). These evolve from Burke's position that any piece of literature functions on a grammatical level (of logic), a rhetorical level (of audience affectiveness), and a poetic level (of self-compensation as symbolic act).

Burke has been criticized as being a philosophical dialectician who turns to literature only by way of exemplification; R. P. Blackmur, in "A Critic's Job of Work," accuses him of utilizing all objects without much concern for literary taste or evaluation. Burke's answer is that he has been working on a large scale, and that eventually a more worthwhile form of evaluation will result, through "differentia." In the meantime, Burke stands as a powerful influence on modern critics and criticism, offering, as he goes, deep insights into works like the *Ancient Mariner* and *The Magic Mountain*.

IV

The battle of the books drew to a kind of official close with the publication in 1930 of Norman Foerster's *Humanism and America* and C. Hartley Grattan's answering *The Critique of Humanism*. Although both collections called on the best talent of their respective sides, little was added to what had already been said. The most important development of this last skirmish was the appearance in Grattan's volume of several younger critics who were to set the literary tone for the next three decades. Some of them, joined with others interested in analytical criticism, have come to be known as the New Critics.

Although most members of the group came to prominence in the thirties and have had their greatest influence in the forties and fifties, it is clear that the New Criticism had its beginnings somewhat earlier. Its final shape, in so far as shape can be determined from such vastly different personalities and critical positions, is an amalgam of the scientific study of language and the analysis of poem *as poem* of which I. A. Richards and T. S. Eliot were the respective exemplars in the twenties.

The followers of Richards and Eliot—most notably the Englishmen Turnell, Empson, Leavis, and Read; the Americans Ransom, Tate, Blackmur, Brooks, Warren, and Winters—have pushed far beyond the beginnings of *The Principles of Literary Criticism* (1924) and *The Sacred Wood* (1920), and often maintain critical positions that seem to bear little resemblance

to their starting point. But a closer look discovers several
common principles upon which the New Critics agree, and
which others—Burke, Wilson, Cowley, for example—have frequently adhered to: (1) the work of art must be treated as an
object in itself, independent of the author's intention and of
the facts of his life and environment; (2) the language of
poetry is a special language, distinguished from the language
of science and ordinary discourse by its ordering of words
and images to create a whole greater than its parts; (3) literary
genres, though recognized, are unimportant; (4) criticism is
itself an art on a par with other creative forms such as poetry
or painting. The object of the New Critics has consistently
been to distinguish the literary, and especially the poetic, use
of language from other ways of using language. They have
been concerned, that is, with the question of *what is a poem?*
or, put still another way, with exploring along the lines established by Coleridge in the first chapter of *Biographia Literaria*
(1817): "In the truly great poets . . . there is a reason as-
signable, not only for every word, but for the position of
every word. . . ."

Most of the group objected, in their early careers, to the
too academic quality of American criticism, but by 1950 the
most important members of the group were professors themselves and had indoctrinated a new generation of teachers
with their ideas. Malcolm Cowley, noting that the New Critics
themselves could hardly qualify as a school, pointed out:
"Where Mr. Ransom and Mr. Tate, for example, are miles
apart in many of their judgments, young Mr. X, who has
listened to both of them and read both of them, seems to be
a conglomeration or coagulation of Ransom and Tate. Young
Mr. X represents the school—not Ransom, Tate, or Blackmur."

What was to be called the New Criticism appears to have
been first practiced in America among the contributors to
The Fugitive (1922–25) at Nashville; and their leader, John
Crowe Ransom (1888–   ), has, appropriately enough,
come to be recognized as the leader of the New Critics. Both
at Vanderbilt (1914–37) and later at Kenyon, where he edited
the *Kenyon Review,* he was in a position to encourage

the younger poets and critics. His own poetry is witty, ironic, tightly woven in the best combination of Southern elegance and metaphysical technique. His critical works, *God Without Thunder* (1930), *The World's Body* (1938), and *The New Criticism* (1941), have become basic texts in the movement, and his concern with the texture and structure of poetry, with the unique knowledge of poetry, and with the essentially nondidactic nature of poetry has produced excellent results not only in his own work but in that of his friends and followers.

Closely associated with Ransom in the Fugitive group, as well as in the Southern Agrarian movement of the early thirties, Allen Tate (1899–   ) is a traditionalist ("Poetry does not dispense with tradition; it probes the deficiencies of a tradition"), a conservative, a stylist of great virtuosity, and a poet in his own right. Although he calls himself "a casual essayist of whom little consistency can be expected," Tate has shown more than a little consistency in the essays which make up such collections as *Reactionary Essays on Poetry and Ideas* (1936) and *The Man of Letters in the Modern World* (1955). The key word in most of his criticism of poetry is *tension*—by which he means both the unity of all the meanings of the poem, from denotative to connotative, from concrete to abstract, and the unity of the poem which arises from the operation of wit, irony, paradox, and other conflict-structures. In "Techniques of Fiction"—perhaps indicating a shift by the New Critics from understanding poetry to understanding fiction—Tate scrutinizes fiction as closely as he has been accustomed to do with poetry. In his examination of Emma Bovary's behavior at the window he gives an example of what Eliot called the objective correlative, and at the same time arouses in the reader's mind that sense of understanding the passage under consideration which is a mark of the best criticism. It is in such passages as these that Tate makes up for the acid air of superiority which sometimes mars his criticism.

Because of his insistence that the moral evaluation of literature is the central function of the critic, Yvor Winters (1900–   ) has frequently been regarded as a kind of maverick Humanist. But although he has been attacked by other

New Critics, notably Ransom, and although he acknowledges a debt to Babbitt, Winters' techniques have generally been those of the New Criticism. *In Defense of Reason* (1947), a revision of three earlier books, and *The Function of Criticism* (1957), a collection of his later essays, are evidence of his refusal to be forced from his chosen track. He has revised his opinions about numerous writers in the last thirty years, and his conclusions are often so far removed from those of his peers as to be eccentric, but his practice of that "final act of judgment, a unique act" which he describes in "Preliminary Problems" has had an integrity that demands admiration.

Although the New Critics in general have applied non-literary knowledge to the study of literature, Richard P. Blackmur (1904–   ) has been even more assiduous than the rest in his study of history, sociology, theology, and other fields in preparation for consideration of a particular work of art. Above all, he has been concerned with words, for "Words and their intimate arrangements must be the ultimate as well as the immediate source of every effect in the written or spoken arts." Throughout *The Double Agent* (1935), *The Expense of Greatness* (1940), and *The Lion and the Honeycomb* (1955) Blackmur's judgments are based on verbal and linguistic points and upon perhaps the closest reading of the actual text of any critic now practicing. In "Language as Gesture" he carries his technique a logical step forward, finding, with Kenneth Burke, "that the language of poetry may be regarded as symbolic action"; he goes beyond Burke, however, in his insistence that it is not enough to set up methods for analysis—the critic must also judge the results.

Cleanth Brooks (1906–   ) has been a thorough practitioner of the techniques of the New Criticism, one of its leading theoreticians, and probably its best propagandist: as much as any writer after Eliot he has influenced that re-evaluation of English poets which has elevated the metaphysicals at the expense of the romantics; his theories of irony and paradox have been starting points for other critics; and in highly successful textbooks—most notably his collaboration with Robert Penn Warren, *Understanding Poetry* (1938, 1950, 1960)—

he has helped to indoctrinate large numbers of college professors and college students who later became professors. *Modern Poetry and the Tradition* (1939) and *The Well Wrought Urn* (1947) are impressive investigations of poetry in English, using such standards as complexity of plot, irony, paradox, and symbolism, but always beginning "by making the closest possible examination of what the poem says as poem." As in his analysis, at first subtitled "Critique of the Myth," of *The Waste Land,* Brooks frequently applies—most successfully—nonliterary knowledge to his study of poetry.

One strong reaction against the New Criticism came from the so-called Chicago Critics—they dislike being called Neo-Aristotelian—whose monumental volume, *Critics and Criticism, Ancient and Modern* (1952), consists of a series of attacks against the New Critics, a proposed new approach to criticism, and a program for putting the proposal into effect. Under the leadership of Ronald S. Crane, literary historian turned critic, but with strong direction from Richard McKeon, Aristotelian scholar turned critic, the group had been publishing their views for some fifteen years, chiefly in *Modern Philology*. (The New Critics, it should be noted, had had the advantage of controlling, at one time or another, several periodicals of larger circulation: the *Southern, Sewanee, Kenyon,* and *Hudson* reviews, for example.) In essence, the Chicago attack, starting from the premise that criticism is only one of the four humanistic disciplines—the others are history, linguistics, and analysis of ideas—concentrated on what they regarded as the irresponsibility of the New Critics in relegation of criticism to mere commentary on language and in neglecting "distinctions of form and function as between different works." As Crane pointed out in his introduction, "criticism itself seems constantly to be making new starts but never, as a discipline, getting anywhere in particular."

Although shorter than most essays by the Chicago group, "A Symbolic Reading of the *Ancient Mariner*" is typical of the group's two-pronged attack against both theory and practice of their opponents, for here Elder Olson (1909–   ) objects to Warren's reading on the double grounds that Warren has first of all misread Coleridge's intention and second been too extravagant and not very effective in his own interpretation of the poem. Robert Penn Warren (1905–   ), a member of the innermost circle of the New Critics, as well as a major poet and novelist, has been amply defended against these charges in a number of counterattacks by his associates.

Perhaps the most pertinent objection to the Chicagoans has been that they devote too much effort to writing about what ought to be done and too little to doing it. "The Chicago critics are people who have a fine blueprint of an automobile and sit around complaining that Henry Ford got started on the wrong principles," said W. K. Wimsatt, and there is some truth in the observation. On the other hand, . . . ; their concern with problems of "imitation," with distinctions of genre, with large-scale matters of structure have been highly successful in such specific applications of theory as Crane's studies of *Tom Jones* and *Gulliver's Travels* and Norman Maclean's interpretation of *King Lear*. In these and in longer works . . . like Elder Olson's *The Poetry of Dylan Thomas* (1954) and Crane's *The Languages of Criticism and the Structures of Poetry* (1953), a sustained argument for the necessity of "as many different critical methods as there are distinguishable major aspects in the construction, appreciation and use of literary works," is the evidence that the Chicago group are capable, literate, and much-needed critics.

V

The latest important revision in American criticism has come by way of the so-called myth critics. Like those novelists who followed in the wake of Hemingway, Faulkner, and Fitzgerald, certain younger writers—anywhere from a half to a full generation younger than Tate, Blackmur, and Burke—have been almost forced, as a matter of self-preservation, to find a new way of seeing things. Their work actually follows from, but shows little affinity with, the kind of analysis that came out of England in Jessie Weston's *From Ritual to Romance* (1920) and Maud Bodkin's *Archetypal Patterns in Poetry*

(1934). Like Miss Bodkin, only in a much more lively fashion, they explore the hypothesis propounded by the psychoanalyst C. G. Jung—that certain kinds of literature stir within the reader's mind archetypal patterns that occur repeatedly through the "collective unconscious."

One branch of the myth critics—including Leslie Fiedler, Richard Chase, and Philip Young, whose essays have been chosen as representative here—can be identified by these characteristics: (1) the quest for myth; (2) the utilization of depth psychology, comparative anthropology, and folkloristic materials; (3) a shifted emphasis on image and symbol; (4) an acceptance of D. H. Lawrence's theory of duplicity in American literature; and (5) a revisionist attitude toward the New Criticism, which, they feel, gave too much of itself to "mere textual analysis." Perhaps—to use one of their own methods—the myth critics can best be identified by those terms which most often occur in their work: ritual, romance, myth, mythos, archetype, melodrama, gothic, love and death, light and dark, sacrificial king or artist, fable, folkloristic, Oedipal, Freudian, Jungian, subconscious, unconscious, duplicity, initiation, rebirth. . . .

Leslie Fiedler (1917–   ), who is probably the most productive of this school, may also be the most representative. His essay "Archetype and Signature: A Study of the Relationship between Biography and Poetry" (1952) provides the rationale for the psycho-mythic approach. In its own way, this piece (reprinted at the end of his last book, *No! In Thunder,* 1960) acts as an answer to, and tangential development of, Eliot's "Tradition and the Individual Talent"—the archetype (which no one has yet called the "super-id") being an appositive to tradition, and the signature appositive to individual talent. This essay also effectively argues against the restrictiveness of the New Criticism, particularly its anti-biographical attitude.

Perhaps the best known of Fiedler's essays is his controversial "Come Back to the Raft Ag'in, Huck Honey!" which, republished in *An End to Innocence* (1955), raised a national furor not often beheld in the sedately combative world of criticism. With its concept of homoerotic miscegenation, its tracing out of an escape pattern from the world of women and civilization, this piece indicated the shape of things to come from Fiedler's investigation of the underside of American literature; its insights have been accorded the entire scale of adjectives, pro and con. "Adolescence and Maturity in the American Novel," which is in the same collection as the Twain article, has been chosen for inclusion here because it deals with a number of twentieth-century novelists, and because it states the nub of a thesis which Fiedler made into his fullest book, *Love and Death in the American Novel* (1960). The essay also reveals that which characterizes Fiedler's work as much as the psychoanalytic and mythic qualities—namely, the iconoclastic urge, an urge made plain by title and introduction to *No! In Thunder.*

Although he has produced studies of several American worthies—Melville, Dickinson, and Whitman—Richard Chase (1914–   ) has become most widely known for *The American Novel and Its Tradition* (1957). In this book he attempts to illustrate how American fiction has distinguished itself by assimilating romance and melodrama into the substance of the novel, and has thus, more freely than its English ancestor, veered toward "mythic, allegorical, and symbolic forms." Here he deals with myths and archetypes in such works as *Moby Dick* and *The Deerslayer* (which contains "an initiation recapitulated in some ways by Mark Twain's Huckleberry Finn . . . Hemingway's Nick Adams . . . and Ike McCaslin in Faulkner's *The Bear . . .*"). In "The Stone and the Crucifixion: Faulkner's *Light in August,*" he illustrates the method of tracing clusters of images and metaphors to their mythic conclusions.

Peculiarly enough, with an appendix to *The American Novel and Its Tradition,* Chase disaffiliates himself from myth criticism, stating: "I am not myself a 'myth critic' although I have been interested in myth . . . and although my first book, *Quest for Myth,* was a historical study of the subject." This is a strange disavowal, until Chase's reasons are understood: myth critics, he declares, are principally interested in one thing, "namely, the death and rebirth of a god." Also, he feels, myth critics accept literature mainly as anthropological documents, paying little attention to literary and socially realistic elements. Fiedler, too, it should be remarked, has shown some uneasiness about settling into this critical mold: his introduction to *No! In Thunder* indicates he may be edging away from the area of mythic analysis, getting ready to jump the chasm to Existentialism.

Aside from a number of articles in literary journals, Philip Young (1918–   ), the third of the myth critics included, is highly regarded for an acute and accurate study, *Ernest Hemingway* (1952), in which he combines straight biography with Freudian and textual analysis. The last two chapters of this book indicate a beginning interest in "an American myth," mainly in terms of Huck Finn and the Hemingway Hero. With recent researches into such American myth-figures as Rip Van Winkle and Pocahontas—as well as American utilization of the Beatrice Cenci story—he is probably the most folkloristic, or perhaps "legendary," of the three critics mentioned in this group. Though not closely related to the work of Stith Thompson, or even Constance Rourke, Young's "Fallen from Time: The Mythic Rip Van Winkle" fuses folklore and literary concepts into a psycho-mythic pattern. Two of Young's characteristics that startle the reader in this field are his informally precise style and his addiction to sense.

Like Fiedler and Chase, Young also has shown signs of disenchantment—becoming aware of certain critical shortcomings that can result from an overcommitment to myth. Reviewing Daniel G. Hoffman's *Form and Fable in American Fiction* (1961), he writes: "In a couple of years I will bet (ambitious young critics please note?) that a lot of people are going to be ripe for a really good book on the realistic tradition in American fiction, which is in the process of being forgotten." (The parenthetical play on words is revealing, conscious or unconscious.)

VI

Literary history cannot be written in the form of linked footnotes; and any attempt to identify critics or schools of criticism on the basis of salient features inevitably tends to oversimplify. But even a cursory consideration of the authors outlined in this brief introduction will reveal that American literary criticism (while it is certainly not some timid Prufrockian creature) is largely a matter of shifting focus, contracting into special points of view, expanding into a comprehensive view that displays an awareness and sophistication indicative of maturity. Of late, even those writers who seem most committed to a single critical position are very much aware of the self-imposed limitations of literary sighting: "Ideally," Leslie Fiedler writes, "an object of critical attention should be set in all its relevant contexts; but this is the never-completed communal task of criticism as a continuing institution, and no one critic is able to do more than a small part of the whole job." Other writers have expressed the same wish for ideality with the same recognition of actuality. At the end of *The Armed Vision*, Stanley Edgar Hyman attempts an integration of critical views, and concludes: "This synthesis of critical method is not simple multiplicity or plurality or anarchy, but a genuine dialectic contest or *agon*. From it, too, truth will arise. We may get it within the individual critic, in an integrated method, or outside the individual critic, in the group symposium, but in some form or other we must get it. . . ."

Thus, in a sense, the search for the Great American Critic continues, just as the search for the Great American Novelist, or Poet, or Dramatist does. The eventual nominee will no doubt possess the strongly individualized vision of writers like H. L. Mencken, Yvor Winters, and Leslie Fiedler. But he will also possess that quality of mind shared by T. S. Eliot, Edmund Wilson, and Kenneth Burke, all three of whom, on different levels and in different ways, have achieved distinction through a shifting synthesis of vision, which contains (as Lionel Trilling once wrote of certain nineteenth-century American authors) "both the yes and the no of their culture . . . the very essence of the culture." In any event, this future paragon of critical perspicacity will have to discover the numerous clues—some of which are to be found in the following pages—that now lie in wait for the newest criticism.

BERNARD S. OLDSEY and ARTHUR O. LEWIS, JR.

University Park, Pa.
June, 1962

Visions and Revisions
in
Modern American Literary Criticism

The New Criticism

JOEL E. SPINGARN

"WHAT DROLL creatures these college professors are whenever they talk about art," wrote Flaubert in one of his letters, and voiced the world's opinion of academic criticism. For the world shares the view of the Italian poet that "monks and professors cannot write the lives of poets," and looks only to those rich in literary experience for its opinions on literature. But the poets themselves have had no special grudge against academic criticism that they have not felt equally for every other kind. For the most part, they have objected to all criticism, since what each mainly seeks in his own case is not criticism, but uncritical praise. "Kill the dog, he is a reviewer," cried the young Goethe; and in an age nearer our own William Morris expressed his contempt for those who earn a livelihood by writing their opinions of the works of others. Fortunately for Criticism, it does not live by the grace of poets, to whom it can be of small service at its best, but by the grace of others who have neither the poet's genius nor the critic's insight. I hope to persuade you this evening that the poets have been mistaken in their very conception of the critic's craft, which lives by a power that poets and critics share together. The secret of this power has come to men slowly, and the knowledge they have gained by it has transformed their idea of Criticism. What this secret is, and into what new paths Criticism is being led by it, is the subject of my lecture to-night.

I

At the end of the last century, France once more occupied the center of that stage whose auditors are the inheritors of

European civilization. Once more all the world listened while she talked and played, and some of the most brilliant of her talk was now on the question of the authority of Criticism. It is not my purpose to tell you (what you know already) with what sober and vigorous learning the official critics of the *Revue des deux Mondes* espoused the cause of old gods with the new weapons of science, and with what charm and tact, with what grace and suppleness of thought, Jules Lemaître and Anatole France, to mention no others, defended the free play of the appreciative mind. Some of the sparks that were beaten out on the anvil of controversy have become fixed stars, the classical utterances of Criticism, as when Anatole France described the critic not as a judge imposing sentence, but as a sensitive soul detailing his "adventures among masterpieces."

To have sensations in the presence of a work of art and to express them, that is the function of Criticism for the impressionistic critic. His attitude he would express somewhat in this fashion: "Here is a beautiful poem, let us say Shelley's *Prometheus Unbound*. To read it is for me to experience a thrill of pleasure. My delight in it is itself a judgment, and what better judgment is it possible for me to give? All that I can do is to tell how it affects me, what sensations it gives me. Other men will derive other sensations from it, and express them differently; they too have the same right as I. Each of us, if we are sensitive to impressions and express ourselves well, will produce a new work of art to replace the work which gave us our sensations. That is the art of Criticism, and beyond that Criticism cannot go."

We shall not begrudge this exquisite soul the pleasure of his sensations or his cult of them, nor would he be disconcerted if we were to point out that the interest has been shifted from the work of art to his own impressions. Let us suppose that you say to him: "We are not interested in you, but in *Prometheus Unbound*. To describe the state of your health is not to help us to understand or to enjoy the poem. Your criticism constantly tends to get away from the work of art, and to center attention on yourself and your feelings."

But his answer would not be difficult to find: "What you

say is true enough. My criticism tends to get farther and farther from the work of art and to cast a light upon myself; but all criticism tends to get away from the work of art and to substitute something in its place. The impressionist substitutes himself, but what other form of criticism gets closer to *Prometheus Unbound?* Historical criticism takes us away from it in a search of the environment, the age, the race, the poetic school of the artist; it tells us to read the history of the French Revolution, Godwin's *Political Justice,* the *Prometheus Bound* of Aeschylus, and Calderón's *Mágico Prodigioso.* Psychological criticism takes me away from the poem, and sets me to work on the biography of the poet; I wish to enjoy *Prometheus Unbound,* and instead I am asked to become acquainted with Shelley the man. Dogmatic criticism does not get any closer to the work of art by testing it according to rules and standards; it sends me to the Greek dramatists, to Shakespeare, to Aristotle's *Poetics,* possibly to Darwin's *Origin of Species,* in order that I may see how far Shelley has failed to give dramatic reality to his poem, or has failed to observe the rules of his *genre;* but that means the study of other works, and not of *Prometheus Unbound.* Aesthetics takes me still farther afield into speculations on art and beauty. And so it is with every form of Criticism. Do not deceive yourself. All criticism tends to shift the interest from the work of art to something else. The other critics give us history, politics, biography, erudition, metaphysics. As for me, I redream the poet's dream, and if I seem to write lightly, it is because I have awakened, and smile to think I have mistaken a dream for reality. I at least strive to replace one work of art by another, and art can only find its *alter ego* in art."

It would be idle to detail the arguments with which the advocates of the opposing forms of Criticism answered these questionings. Literary erudition and evolutionary science were the chief weapons used to fight this modern heresy, but the one is an unwieldy and the other a useless weapon in the field of aesthetic thought. On some sides, at least, the position of the impressionists was impregnable; but two points of attack were open to their opponents. They could combat the notion that taste is a substitute for learning, or learning a substitute for taste, since both are vital to Criticism; and they could maintain that the relativity of taste does not in any sense affect its authority. In this sense impressionistic Criticism erred only less grievously than the "judicial" Criticism which opposed it.

But these arguments are not my present concern; what I wish to point out is that the objective and dogmatic forms of Criticism were fighting no new battle against impressionistic Criticism in that decade of controversy. It was a battle as old as the earliest reflection on the subject of poetry, if not as old as the sensitiveness of poets. Modern literature begins with the same doubts, with the same quarrel. In the sixteenth century the Italians were formulating that classical code which imposed itself on Europe for two centuries, and which, even in our generation, Brunetière has merely disguised under the trappings of natural science. They evolved the dramatic unities, and all those rules which the poet Pope imagined to be "Nature still but Nature methodized." But at the very moment when their spokesman Scaliger was saying that "Aristotle is our emperor, the perpetual dictator of all the fine arts," another Italian, Pietro Aretino, was insisting that there is no rule except the whim of genius and no standard of judgment beyond individual taste.

The Italians passed on the torch to the French of the seventeenth century, and from that day to this the struggle between the two schools has never ceased to agitate the progress of Criticism in France. Boileau against Saint-Évremond, Classicists against Romanticists, dogmatists against impressionists, —the antinomy is deep in the French nature, indeed in the nature of Criticism itself. Listen to this: "It is not for the purpose of deciding on the merit of this noble poet [Virgil], nor of harming his reputation, that I have spoken so freely concerning him. The world will continue to think what it does of his beautiful verses; and as for me, I judge nothing, I only say what I think, and what effect each of these things produces on my heart and mind." Surely these words are from the lips of Lemaître himself! "I judge nothing; I only say what I feel."

But no, these are the utterances of the Chevalier de Méré, a wit of the age of Louis XIV, and he is writing to the secretary of that stronghold of authority, the French Academy. For some men, even in the age of Boileau, criticism was nothing but an "adventure among masterpieces."

No, it is no new battle; it is the perpetual conflict of Criticism. In every age Impressionism (or enjoyment) and dogmatism (or judgment) have grappled with one another. They are the two sexes of Criticism; and to say that they flourish in every age is to say that every age has its masculine as well as its feminine criticism,—the masculine criticism that may or may not force its own standards on literature, but that never at all events is dominated by the object of its studies; and the feminine criticism that responds to the lure of art with a kind of passive ecstasy. In the age of Boileau it was the masculine type which gave the tone to Criticism; in our own, outside of the universities, it has certainly been the feminine. But they continue to exist side by side, ever falling short of their highest powers, unless mystically mated,—judgment erecting its edicts into arbitrary standards and conventions, enjoyment lost in the mazes of its sensuous indecision.

Yet if we examine these opposing forms of Criticism in our own age, we shall find, I think, that they are not wholly without a common ground to meet on; that, in fact, they are united in at least one prepossession which they do not share with the varying forms of Criticism in any of the earlier periods of its history. The Greeks conceived of literature, not as an inevitable expression of creative power, but as a reasoned "imitation" or reshaping of the materials of life; for Aristotle, poetry is the result of man's imitative instinct, and differs from history and science in that it deals with the probable or possible rather than with the real. The Romans conceived of literature as a noble art, intended (though under the guise of pleasure) to inspire men with high ideals of life. The classicists of the sixteenth and seventeenth centuries accepted this view in the main; for them, literature was a kind of exercise, —a craft acquired by study of the classics, and guided in the interpretation of nature by the traditions of Greek and Roman art. For these men literature was as much a product of reason as science or history. The eighteenth century complicated the course of Criticism by the introduction of vague and novel criteria, such as "imagination," "sentiment," and "taste," yet it was only in part able to liberate itself from the older tradition.

But with the Romantic Movement there developed the new idea with coördinates all Criticism in the nineteenth century. Very early in the century, Mme de Staël and others formulated the idea that literature is an "expression of society." Victor Cousin founded the school of art for art's sake, enunciating "the fundamental rule, that expression is the supreme law of art." Later, Sainte-Beuve developed and illustrated his theory that literature is an expression of personality. Still later, under the influence of natural science, Taine took a hint from Hegel and elaborated the idea that literature is an expression of race, age, and environment. The extreme impressionists prefer to think of art as the exquisite expression of delicate and fluctuating sensations or impressions of life. But for all these critics and theorists, literature is an expression of something, of experience or emotion, of the external or internal, of the man himself or something outside the man; yet it is always conceived of as an art of expression.

The objective, the dogmatic, the impressionistic critics of our day may set for themselves very different tasks, but the idea of expression is implicit in all they write. They have, as it were, this bond of blood: they are not merely man and woman, but brother and sister; and their father, or grandfather, was Sainte-Beuve. The bitter but acute analysis of his talent which Nietzsche has given us in the *Twilight of the Idols* brings out very clearly this dual side of his seminal power, the feminine sensitiveness and the masculine detachment. For Nietzsche, he is "nothing of a man; he wanders about, delicate, curious, tired, pumping people, a female after all, with a woman's revengefulness and a woman's sensuousness, a critic without a standard, without firmness, and without backbone." Here it is the impressionist in Sainte-Beuve that arouses the German's wrath. But in the same breath we find Nietzsche blaming him for "holding up objectivity as a mask"; and it is on this objective side that Sainte-Beuve becomes the source of all those historical and psychological forms of critical study which have influenced the academic thought of our day, leading insensibly, but inevitably, from empirical investigation to empirical law. The pedigree of the two schools thereafter is not difficult to trace: on the one side, from Sainte-Beuve through *l'art pour l'art* to impressionism, and on the other, from Sainte-Beuve through Taine to Brunetière and his egregious kin.

French criticism has been leaning heavily on the idea of expression for a century or more, but no attempt has been made in France to understand its aesthetic content, except for a few vague echoes of German thought. For the first to give philosophic precision to the theory of expression, and to found a method of Criticism based upon it, were the Germans of the age that stretches from Herder to Hegel. All the forces of philosophical thought were focused on this central concept, while the critics enriched themselves from out this golden store. I suppose you all remember the famous passage in which Carlyle describes the achievement of German criticism in that age. "Criticism," says Carlyle, "has assumed a new form in Germany. It proceeds on other principles and proposes to itself a higher aim. The main question is not now a question concerning the qualities of diction, the coherence of metaphors, the fitness of sentiments, the general logical truth in a work of art, as it was some half century ago among most critics, neither is it a question mainly of a psychological sort to be answered by discovering and delineating the peculiar nature of the poet from his poetry, as is usual with the best of our own critics at present; but it is, not indeed exclusively, but inclusively, of its two other questions, properly and ultimately a question of the essence and peculiar life of the poetry itself. . . . The problem is not now to determine by what mechanism Addison composed sentences and struck out similitudes, but by what far finer and more mysterious mechanism Shakespeare organized his dramas and gave life and individuality to his Ariel and his Hamlet. Wherein lies that life; how have they attained that shape and individuality? Whence comes that

[margin annotation: CARLYLE DESCRIBES GERMAN CRITICISM W OF MODERN INVENTION] empyrean fire which irradiates their whole being, and pierces, at least in starry gleams, like a diviner thing, into all hearts? Are these dramas of his not veri-similar only, but true; nay, truer than reality itself, since the essence of unmixed reality is bodied forth in them under more expressive similes? What is this unity of pleasures; and can our deeper inspection discern it to be indivisible and existing by necessity because each work springs as it were from the general elements of thought and grows up therefrom into form and expansion by its own growth? Not only who was the poet and how did he compose, but what and how was the poem, and why was it a poem and not rhymed eloquence, creation and not figured passion? These are the questions for the critic. Criticism stands like an interpreter between the inspired and the uninspired; between the prophet and those who hear the melody of his words, and catch some glimpse of their material meaning, but understand not their deeper import."

I am afraid that no German critic wholly realized this ideal; but it was at least the achievement of the Germans that they enunciated the doctrine, even if they did not always adequately illustrate it in practice. It was they who first realized that art has performed its function when it has expressed itself; it was they who first conceived of Criticism as the study of expression. "There is a destructive and a creative or constructive criticism," said Goethe; the first measures and tests literature according to mechanical standards, the second answers the fundamental questions: "What has the writer proposed to himself to do? and how far has he succeeded in carrying out his own plan?" Carlyle, in his essay on Goethe, almost uses Goethe's own words, when he says that the critic's first and foremost duty is to make plain to himself "what the poet's aim really and truly was, how the task he had to do stood before his eye, and how far, with such materials as were afforded him, he has fulfilled it."

This has been the central problem, the guiding star, of all modern criticism. From Coleridge to Pater, from Sainte-Beuve to Lamaître, this is what critics have been striving for, even when they have not succeeded; yes, even when they have

been deceiving themselves into thinking that they were striving for something else. This was not the ideal of the critics of
Aristotle's day, who, like so many of their successors, censured
a work of art as "irrational, impossible, morally hurtful, self-
contradictory, or contrary to technical correctness." This was
not Boileau's standard when he blamed Tasso for the introduction of Christian rather than pagan mythology into epic poetry;
nor Addison's, when he tested *Paradise Lost* according to the
rules of Le Bossu; nor Dr. Johnson's, when he lamented the
absence of poetic justice in *King Lear,* or pronounced dog-
matically that the poet should not "number the streaks of the
tulip." What has the poet tried to do, and how has he fulfilled
his intention? What is he striving to express and how has he
expressed it? What impression does his work make on me,
and how can I best express this impression? These are the
questions that modern critics have been taught to ask when
face to face with the work of a poet. Only one *caveat* must be
borne in mind when attempting to answer them: the poet's intentions must be judged at the moment of the creative act, as
mirrored in the work of art itself, and not by the vague ambitions which he imagines to be his real intentions before or
after the creative act is achieved.

II

The theory of expression, the concept of literature as an art
of expression, is the common ground on which critics have
met for a century or more. Yet how many absurdities, how
many complicated systems, how many confusions have been
superimposed on this fundamental idea; and how slowly has
its full significance become the possession of critics! To accept
the naked principle is to play havoc with these confusions and
complications; and no one has seen this more clearly, or driven
home its inevitable consequences with more intelligence and
vigor, than an Italian thinker and critic of our own day, Benedetto Croce, who has been gaining ground in the English-
speaking world from the day when Mr. Balfour, seven or
eight years ago, gave him a kind of official introduction in his

Romanes Lecture. But I for one needed no introduction to his work; under his banner I enrolled myself long ago, and here re-enroll myself in what I now say. He has led aesthetic thought inevitably from the concept that art is expression to the conclusion that all expression is art. Time does not permit, nor reason ask, that we should follow this argument through all its *pros* and *cons*. If this theory of expression be once and for all accepted, as indeed it has been partly though confusedly accepted by all modern critics, the ground of Criticism is cleared of its dead lumber and its weeds. I propose now merely to point out this dead lumber and these weeds. In other words, we shall see to what conclusions the critical thought and practice of a century have been inevitably converging, and what elements of the old Criticism and the old literary history are disappearing from the new.

In the first place, we have done with all the old Rules. The very conception of "rules" harks back to an age of magic, and reminds the modern of those mysterious words which the heroes of the fairy-tales are without reason forbidden to utter; the rules are a survival of the savage *taboo*. We find few arbitrary rules in Aristotle, who limited himself to empirical inductions from the experience of literature; but they appear in the later Greek rhetoricians; and in the Romans, empirical induction has been hardened into dogma. Horace lays down the law to the prospective playwright in this manner: "You must never have more than three actors on the stage at any one time; you must never let your drama exceed five acts." It is unnecessary to trace the history of these rules, or to indicate how they increased in number, how they were arranged into a system by the classicists of the sixteenth and seventeenth centuries, and how they burdened the creative art of that period. They were never without their enemies. We have seen how Aretino was pitted against Scaliger, Saint-Évremond against Boileau; and in every age the poets have astounded the critics by transgressing rules without the sacrifice of beauty; but it was not until the end of the eighteenth century that the Romanticists banished them from the province of Criticism. The pedantry of our own day has borrowed "conventions" from history and "technique" from science as substitutes for the outworn formulae of the past; but these are merely new names for the old mechanical rules; and they too will go, when Criticism clearly recognizes in every work of art a spiritual creation governed by its own law.

We have done with the *genres* or literary kinds. Their history is inseparably bound up with that of the classical rules. Certain works of literature have a general resemblance and are loosely classed together (for the sake of convenience) as lyric, comedy, tragedy, epic, pastoral, and the like; the classicists made of each of these divisions a fixed norm governed by inviolable laws. The separation of the *genres* was a consequence of this law of classicism: comedy should not be mingled with tragedy, nor epic with lyric. But no sooner was the law enunciated than it was broken by an artist impatient or ignorant of its restraints, and the critics have been obliged to explain away these violations of their laws, or gradually to change the laws themselves. But if art is organic expression, and every work of art is to be interrogated with the question, "What has it expressed, and how completely?" there is no place for the question whether it has conformed to some convenient classification of critics or to some law derived from this classification. The lyric, the pastoral, the epic, are abstractions without concrete reality in the world of art. Poets do not really write epics, pastorals, lyrics, however much they may be deceived by these false abstractions; they express themselves, and this expression is their only form. There are not, therefore, only three, or ten, or a hundred literary kinds; there are as many kinds as there are individual poets. But it is in the field of literary history that this error is most obvious. Shakespeare wrote *King Lear, Venus and Adonis,* and a sequence of sonnets. What becomes of Shakespeare, the creative artist, when these three works are separated from one another by the historian of poetry; when they lose their connection with his single creative soul, and are classified with other works with which they have only a loose and vague relation? To slice up the history of English literature into compartments marked comedy, tragedy, lyric, and the like, is to be guilty of a complete misunderstanding of the meaning of Criticism; and literary history becomes a logical absurdity when its data are not organically related but cut up into sections, and placed in such compartments as these. Only in one sense has any of these terms any profound significance, and that is the use of the word "lyric" to represent the free expressiveness of art. All art is lyrical,—the *Divine Comedy, King Lear,* Rodin's "Thinker," the Parthenon, a Corot landscape, a Bach fugue, or Isadora Duncan's dancing, as much as the songs of Heine or Shelley.

We have done with the comic, the tragic, the sublime, and an army of vague abstractions of their kind. These have grown out of the generalizations of the Alexandrian critics, acquiring a new lease of life in the eighteenth century. Gray and his friend West corresponded with each other on the subject of the sublime; later, Schiller distinguished between the naïve and the sentimental; Jean Paul defined humor, and Hegel defined the tragic. If these terms represent the content of art, they may be relegated to the same category as joy, hate, sorrow, enthusiasm; and we should speak of the comic in the same general way in which we might speak of the expression of joy in a poem. If, on the other hand, these terms represent abstract classifications of poetry, their use in criticism sins against the very nature of art. Every poet re-expresses the universe in his own way, and every poem is a new and independent expression. The tragic does not exist for Criticism, but only Aeschylus and Calderón, Shakespeare and Racine. There is no objection to the use of the word tragic as a convenient label for somewhat similar poems, but to find laws for the tragic and to test creative artists by such laws as these is simply to give a more abstract form to the outworn classical conception of dramatic rules.

We have done with the theory of style, with metaphor, simile, and all the paraphernalia of Graeco-Roman rhetoric. These owe their existence to the assumption that style is separate from expression, that it is something which may be added or subtracted at will from the work of art, a flourish of the pen, an external embellishment, instead of the poet's individual vision of reality, "the music of his whole manner of being." But we know that art *is* expression, that it is complete in itself, that to alter it is to create another expression and therefore to create another work of art. If the poet, for example, says of springtime that " 'Tis now the blood runs gold," he has not employed a substitute for something else, such as "the blood tingles in our veins"; he has expressed his thought in its completeness, and there is no equivalent for his expression except itself.

> Each perfect in its place; and each content
> With that perfection which its being meant.

Such expressions are still called metaphors in the text-books; but metaphor, simile, and all the old terms of classical rhetoric are signs of the zodiac, magical incantations, astrological formulae, interesting only to antiquarian curiosity. To Montaigne they suggested "the prattle of chambermaids"; to me they suggest rather the drone and singsong of many schoolmistresses. We still hear talk of the "grand style," and essays on style continue to be written, like the old "arts of poetry" of two centuries ago. But the theory of styles has no longer a real place in modern thought; we have learned that it is no less impossible to study style as separate from the work of art than to study the comic as separate from the work of the comic artist.

We have done with all moral judgment of literature. Horace said that pleasure and profit are the end of art, and for many centuries the critics quarreled over the terms "pleasure" and "profit." Some said that poetry was meant to instruct; some, merely to please; some, to do both. Romantic criticism first enunciated the principle that art has no aim except expression; that its aim is complete when expression is complete; that "beauty is its own excuse for being." It is not the function of poetry to further any moral or social cause, any more than it is the function of bridge-building to further the cause of Esperanto. If the achievement of the poet be to express any material he may select, and to express it with a completeness that we recognize as perfection, obviously morals can play no part in the judgment which Criticism may form of his work. To say that poetry is moral or immoral is as meaningless as to say that an equilateral triangle is moral and an isosceles triangle immoral, or to speak of the immorality of a musical chord or a Gothic arch. It is only conceivable in a world in which dinner table conversation runs after this fashion: "This cauliflower would be good if it had only been prepared in accordance with international law." "Do you know why my cook's pastry is so good? Because he has never told a lie or seduced a woman." We do not concern ourselves with morals when we test the engineer's bridge or the scientist's researches; indeed we go farther, and say that it is the moral duty of the scientist to disregard any theory of morals in his search for truth. Beauty's world is remote from both these standards; she aims neither at morals nor at truth. Her imaginary creations, by definition, make no pretence to reality, and cannot be judged by reality's tests. The poet's only moral duty, as a poet, is to be true to his art, and to express his vision of reality as well as he can. If the ideals enunciated by poets are not those which we admire most, we must blame not the poets but ourselves: in the world where morals count we have failed to give them the proper material out of which to rear a nobler edifice. No critic of authority now tests literature by the standards of ethics.

We have done with the confusion between the drama and the theatre which has permeated dramatic criticism for over half a century. The theory that the drama is not a creative art, but a mere product of the physical exigencies of the theatre, is as old as the sixteenth century. An Italian scholar of that age was the first to maintain that plays are intended to be acted on a stage, under certain restricted physical conditions, and before a large and heterogeneous crowd; dramatic performance has developed out of these conditions, and the test of its excellence is therefore the pleasure it gives to the mixed audience that supports it. This idea was taken hold of by some of the German romanticists, for the purpose of justifying the Shakespearean drama in its apparent divergence from the classical "rules." Shakespeare cannot be judged by the

rules of the Greek theatre (so ran their argument), for the
drama is an inevitable product of theatrical conditions; these
conditions in Elizabethan England were not the same as those
of Periclean Athens; and it is therefore absurd to judge Shakespeare's practice by that of Sophocles. Here at least the idea
helped to bring Shakespeare home to many new hearts by
ridding the age of mistaken prejudices, and served a useful
purpose, as a specious argument may persuade men to contribute to a noble work, or a mad fanatic may rid the world
of a tyrant. But with this achievement its usefulness but not
its life was ended. It has been developed into a system, and
become a dogma of dramatic critics; it is our contemporary
equivalent for the "rules" of seventeenth-century pedantry.
As a matter of fact, the dramatic artist is to be judged by no
other standard than that applied to any other creative artist:
what has he tried to express, and how has he expressed it? It
is true that the theatre is not only an art but a business, and
the so-called "success" of a play is of vital interest to the
theatre in so far as it is a commercial undertaking. "The success may justify the playwright," said an old French critic,
"but it may not be so easy to justify the success." The test of
"success" is an economic test, and concerns not art or the
criticism of art, but political economy. Valuable contributions
to economic and social history have been made by students
who have investigated the changing conditions of the theatre
and the vicissitudes of taste on the part of theatrical audiences; but these have the same relation to Criticism, and to
the drama as an art, that a history of the publisher's trade and
its influence on the personal fortunes of poets would bear to
the history of poetry.

We have done with technique as separate from art. It has
been pointed out that style cannot be disassociated from art;
and the false air of science which the term "technique" seems
to possess should not blind us to the fact that it too involves
the same error. "Technique is really personality; that is the
reason why the artist cannot teach it, why the pupil cannot
learn it, and why the aesthetic critic can understand it," says
Oscar Wilde, in a dialogue on "The Critic as Artist," which,

amid much perversity and paradox, is illumined by many flashes of strange insight. The technique of poetry cannot be separated from its inner nature. Versification cannot be studied by itself, except loosely and for convenience; it remains always an inherent quality of the single poem. No two poets ever write in the same metre. Milton's line:—

These my sky-robes spun out of Iris' woof

is called an iambic pentameter; but it is not true that artistically it has something in common with every other line possessing the same succession of syllables and accents; in this sense it is not an iambic pentameter; it is only one thing: it is the line:—

These my sky-robes spun out of Iris' woof.

We have done with the history and criticism of poetic themes. It is possible to speak loosely of the handling of such a theme as Prometheus by Aeschylus and by Shelley, of the story of Francesca da Rimini, by Dante, Stephen Phillips, and D'Annunzio, or the story of King Arthur by Malory and Tennyson; but strictly speaking, they are not employing the same theme at all. Each artist is expressing a certain material and labeling it with an historic name. For Shelley Prometheus is only a label; he is expressing his artistic conception of life, not the history of a Greek Titan. It is the vital flame he has breathed into his work that makes it what it is, and with this vital flame (and not with labels) the critic should concern himself in the works of poets. The same answer must be given to those critics who insist on the use of contemporary material in poetry, and praise the poets whose subjects are drawn from the life of our own time. But even if it were possible for critics to determine in advance the subject-matter of poetry or to impose subjects on poets, how can a poet deal with anything but contemporary material? How can a twentieth-century poet, even when he imagines that he is concerned with Greek or Egyptian life, deal with any subject but the life of his own time, except in the most external and superficial detail? Cynics have said since the first outpourings of men's hearts, "There is nothing new in art; there are no new subjects." But the very reverse is true. There are no old subjects; every subject is new as soon as it has been transformed by the imagination of the poet.

We have done with the race, the time, the environment of a poet's work as an element in Criticism. To study these phases of a work of art is to treat it as an historic or social document, and the result is a contribution to the history of culture or civilization, with only a subsidiary interest for the history of art. "Granted the times, the environment, the race, the passions of the poet, what has he done with his materials, how has he converted poetry out of reality?" To answer this question of the Italian De Sanctis as it refers to each single work of art is to perform what is truly the critic's vital function; this is to interpret "expression" in its rightful sense, and to liberate aesthetic Criticism from the vassalage to *Kulturgeschichte* imposed on it by the school of Taine.

We have done with the "evolution" of literature. The concept of progress was first applied to literature in the seventeenth century, but at the very outset Pascal pointed out that a distinction must here be made between science and art; that science advances by accumulation of knowledge, while the changes of art cannot be reduced to any theory of progress. As a matter of fact, the theory involves the ranking of poets according to some arbitrary conception of their value; and the ranking of writers in order of merit has become obsolete, except in the "hundred best books" of the last decade and the "five-foot shelves" of yesterday. The later nineteenth century gave a new air of verisimilitude to this old theory by borrowing the term "evolution" from science; but this too involves a fundamental misconception of the free and original movement of art. A similar misconception is involved in the study of the "origins" of art; for art has no origin separate from man's life.

> In climes beyond the solar road,
> Where shaggy forms o'er ice-built mountains roam,
> The Muse has broke the twilight-gloom;

but though she wore savage raiment, she was no less the Muse.

Art is simple at times, complex at others, but it is always art. The simple art of early times may be studied with profit; but the researches of anthropology have no vital significance for Criticism, unless the anthropologist studies the simplest forms of art in the same spirit as its highest; that is, unless the anthropologist is an aesthetic critic.

Finally, we have done with the old rupture between genius and taste. When Criticism first propounded as its real concern the oft-repeated question: "What has the poet tried to express and how has he expressed it?" Criticism prescribed for itself the only possible method. How can the critic answer this question without becoming (if only for a moment of supreme power) at one with the creator? That is to say, taste must reproduce the work of art within itself in order to understand and judge it; and at that moment aesthetic judgment becomes nothing more nor less than creative art itself. The identity of genius and taste is the final achievement of modern thought on the subject of art, and it means that fundamentally, in their most significant moments, the creative and the critical instincts are one and the same. From Goethe to Carlyle, from Carlyle to Arnold, from Arnold to Symons, there has been much talk of the "creative function" of Criticism. For each of these men the phrase held a different content; for Arnold it meant merely that Criticism creates the intellectual atmosphere of the age,—a social function of high importance, perhaps, yet wholly independent of aesthetic significance. But the ultimate truth toward which these men were tending was more radical than that, and plays havoc with all the old platitudes about the sterility of taste. Criticism at last can free itself of its age-long self-contempt, now that it may realize that aesthetic judgment and artistic creation are instinct with the same vital life. This identity does not sum up the whole life of the complex and difficult art of Criticism, but without it, Criticism would really be impossible. "Genius is to aesthetics what the ego is to philosophy, the only supreme and absolute reality," said Schelling; and without subduing the mind to this transcendental system, it remains true that what must always be inexplicable to mere reflection is just what gives power to poetry;

that intellectual curiosity may amuse itself by asking its little questions of the silent sons of light, but they vouchsafe no answer to art's pale shadow, thought; the gods are kind if they give up their secret in another work of art, the art of Criticism, that serves as some sort of mirror to the art of literature, only because in their flashes of insight taste and genius are one.

Theodore Dreiser

H. L. MENCKEN

OUT OF THE DESERT of American fictioneering, so populous
and yet so dreary, Dreiser stands up—a phenomenon unescap-
ably visible, but disconcertingly hard to explain. What forces
combined to produce him in the first place, and how has he
managed to hold out so long against the prevailing blasts—
of disheartening misunderstanding and misrepresentation, of
Puritan suspicion and opposition, of artistic isolation, of commercial seduction? There is something downright heroic in
the way the man has held his narrow and perilous ground,
disdaining all compromise, unmoved by the cheap success
that lies so inviting around the corner. He has faced, in his
day, almost every form of attack that a serious artist can conceivably encounter, and yet all of them together have
scarcely budged him an inch. He still plods along in the laborious, cheerless way he first marked out for himself; he is quite
as undaunted by baited praise as by bludgeoning, malignant
abuse; his later novels are, if anything, more unyieldingly
Dreiserian than his earliest. As one who has long sought to
entice him in this direction or that, fatuously presuming to
instruct him in what would improve him and profit him, I
may well bear a reluctant and resigned sort of testimony to his
gigantic steadfastness. It is almost as if any change in his
manner, any concession to what is usual and esteemed, any
amelioration of his blind, relentless exercises of *force majeure,*
were a physical impossibility. One feels him at last to be au-
thentically no more than a helpless instrument (or victim) of
that inchoate flow of forces which he himself is so fond of
depicting as at once the answer to the riddle of life, and a
riddle ten times more vexing and accursed. . . .

Of the general ideas which lie at the bottom of all of
Dreiser's work it is impossible to be in ignorance, for he has

exposed them at length in *A Hoosier Holiday* and summarized them in *Life, Art and America*. In their main outlines they are not unlike the fundamental assumptions of Joseph Conrad. Both novelists see human existence as a seeking without a finding; both reject the prevailing interpretations of its meaning and mechanism; both take refuge in "I do not know." Put *A Hoosier Holiday* beside Conrad's *A Personal Record*, and you will come upon parallels from end to end. Or better still, put it beside Hugh Walpole's *Joseph Conrad*, in which the Conradean metaphysic is condensed from the novels even better than Conrad has done it himself: at once you will see how the two novelists, each a worker in the elemental emotions, each a rebel against the current assurance and superficiality, each an alien to his place and time, touch each other in a hundred ways.

"Conrad," says Walpole, "is of the firm and resolute conviction that life is too strong, too clever and too remorseless for the sons of men." And then, in amplification: "It is as though, from some high window, looking down, he were able to watch some shore, from whose security men were forever launching little cockleshell boats upon a limitless and angry sea. . . . From his height he can follow their fortunes, their brave struggles, their fortitude to the very end. He admires their courage, the simplicity of their faith, but his irony springs from his knowledge of the inevitable end." . . .

Substitute the name of Dreiser for that of Conrad, and you will have to change scarcely a word. Perhaps one, to wit, "clever." I suspect that Dreiser, writing so of his own creed, would be tempted to make it "stupid," or, at all events, "unintelligible." The struggle of man, as he sees it, is more than impotent; it is gratuitous and purposeless. There is, to his eye, no grand ingenuity, no skilful adaptation of means to end, no moral (or even dramatic) plan in the order of the universe. He can get out of it only a sense of profound and inexplicable *dis*order. The waves which batter the cockleshells change their direction at every instant. Their navigation is a vast adventure, but intolerably fortuitous and inept—a voyage without chart, compass, sun or stars. . . .

So at bottom. But to look into the blackness steadily, of course, is almost beyond the endurance of man. In the very moment that its impenetrability is grasped the imagination begins attacking it with pale beams of false light. All religions, I daresay, are thus projected from the questioning soul of man, and not only all religions, but also all great agnosticisms. Nietzsche, shrinking from the horror of that abyss of negation, revived the Pythagorean concept of *der ewigen Wiederkunft* —a vain and blood-curdling sort of comfort. To it, after a while, he added explanations almost Christian—a whole repertoire of whys and wherefores, aims and goals, aspirations and significances. The late Mark Twain, in an unpublished work, toyed with an equally daring idea: that men are to some unimaginably vast and incomprehensible Being what the unicellular organisms of his body are to man, and so on *ad infinitum*. Dreiser occasionally inclines to much the same hypothesis; he likens the endless reactions going on in the world we know, the myriadal creation, collision and destruction of entities, to the slow accumulation and organization of cells *in utero*. He would make us specks in the insentient embryo of some gigantic Presence whose form is still unimaginable and whose birth must wait for Eons and Eons. Again, he turns to something not easily distinguishable from philosophical idealism, whether out of Berkeley or Fichte it is hard to make out —that is, he would interpret the whole phenomenon of life as no more than an appearance, a nightmare of some unseen sleeper or of men themselves, an "uncanny blur of nothingness"—in Euripides' phrase, "a song sung by an idiot, dancing down the wind." Yet again, he talks vaguely of the intricate polyphony of a cosmic orchestra, cacophonous to our dull ears. Finally, he puts the observed into the ordered, reading a purpose in the displayed event: "life was intended to sting and hurt" . . . But these are only gropings, and not to be read too critically. From speculations and explanations he always returns, Conrad-like, to the bald fact: to "the spectacle and stress of life." All he can make out clearly is "a vast compulsion which has nothing to do with the individual desires or tastes or impulses of individuals." That compulsion springs "from the settling processes of forces which we do not in the least understand, over which we have no control, and in whose grip we are as grains of dust or sand, blown hither and thither, for what purpose we cannot even suspect."[1] Man is not only doomed to defeat, but denied any glimpse or understanding of his antagonist. Here we come upon an agnosticism that has almost got beyond curiosity. What good would it do us, asks Dreiser, to know? In our ignorance and helplessness, we may at least get a slave's consolation out of cursing the unknown gods. Suppose we saw them striving blindly, too, and pitied them? . . .

But, as I say, this scepticism is often tempered by guesses at a possibly hidden truth, and the confession that this truth may exist reveals the practical unworkableness of the unconditioned system, at least for Dreiser. Conrad is far more resolute, and it is easy to see why. He is, by birth and training, an aristocrat. He has the gift of emotional detachment. The lures of facile doctrine do not move him. In his irony there is a disdain which plays about even the ironist himself. Dreiser is a product of far different forces and traditions, and is capable of no such escapement. Struggle as he may, and fume and protest as he may, he can no more shake off the chains of his intellectual and cultural heritage than he can change the shape of his nose. What that heritage is you may find out in detail by reading *A Hoosier Holiday*, or in summary by glancing at the first few pages of *Life, Art and America*. Briefly described, it is the burden of a believing mind, a moral attitude, a lingering superstition. One-half of the man's brain, so to speak, wars with the other half. He is intelligent, he is thoughtful, he is a sound artist—but there come moments when a dead hand falls upon him, and he is once more the Indiana peasant, snuffing absurdly over imbecile sentimentalities, giving a grave ear to quackeries, snorting and eye-rolling with the best of them. One generation spans too short a time to free the soul of man. Nietzsche, to the end of his days, remained a Prussian pastor's son, and

[1] *Life, Art and America*, p. 5.

hence two-thirds a Puritan; he erected his war upon holiness, toward the end, into a sort of holy war. Kipling, the grandson of a Methodist preacher, reveals the tin-pot evangelist with increasing clarity as youth and its ribaldries pass away and he falls back upon his fundamentals. And that other English novelist who springs from the servants' hall—let us not be surprised or blame him if he sometimes writes like a bounder.

The truth about Dreiser is that he is still in the transition stage between Christian Endeavour and civilization, between Warsaw, Indiana and the Socratic grove, between being a good American and being a free man, and so he sometimes vacillates perilously between a moral sentimentalism and a somewhat extravagant revolt. *The "Genius,"* on the one hand, is almost a tract for rectitude, a Warning to the Young; its motto might be *Scheut die Dirnen!* And on the other hand, it is full of a laborious truculence that can only be explained by imagining the author as heroically determined to prove that he is a plain-spoken fellow and his own man, let the chips fall where they may. So, in spots, in *The Financier* and *The Titan,* both of them far better books. There is an almost moral frenzy to expose and riddle what passes for morality among the stupid. The isolation of irony is never reached; the man is still evangelical; his ideas are still novelties to him; he is as solemnly absurd in some of his floutings of the Code Américain as he is in his respect for Bouguereau, or in his flirtings with the New Thought, or in his naïve belief in the importance of novel-writing. Somewhere or other I have called all this the Greenwich Village complex. It is not genuine artists, serving beauty reverently and proudly, who herd in those cockroached cellars and bawl for art; it is a mob of half-educated yokels and cockneys to whom the very idea of art is still novel, and intoxicating—and more than a little bawdy.

Not that Dreiser actually belongs to this ragamuffin company. Far from it, indeed. There is in him, hidden deep-down, a great instinctive artist, and hence the makings of an aristocrat. In his muddled way, held back by the manacles of his race and time, and his steps made uncertain by a guiding theory which too often eludes his own comprehension, he yet manages to produce works of art of unquestionable beauty and authority, and to interpret life in a manner that is poignant and illuminating. There is vastly more intuition in him than intellectualism; his talent is essentially feminine, as Conrad's is masculine; his ideas always seem to be deduced from his feelings. The view of life that got into *Sister Carrie,* his first book, was not the product of a conscious thinking out of Carrie's problems. It simply got itself there by the force of the artistic passion behind it; its coherent statement had to wait for other and more reflective days. The thing began as a vision, not as a syllogism. Here the name of Franz Schubert inevitably comes up. Schubert was an ignoramus, even in music; he knew less about polyphony, which is the mother of harmony, which is the mother of music, than the average conservatory professor. But nevertheless he had such a vast instinctive sensitiveness to musical values, such a profound and accurate feeling for beauty in tone, that he not only arrived at the truth in tonal relations, but even went beyond what, in his day, was known to be the truth, and so led an advance. Likewise, Giorgione da Castelfranco and Masaccio come to mind: painters of the first rank, but untutored, unsophisticated, uncouth. Dreiser, within his limits, belongs to this cabot-shod company of the elect. One thinks of Conrad, not as artist first, but as savant. There is something of the icy aloofness of the laboratory in him, even when the images he conjures up pulsate with the very glow of life. He is almost as self-conscious as the Beethoven of the last quartets. In Dreiser the thing is more intimate, more disorderly, more a matter of pure feeling. He gets his effects, one might almost say, not by designing them, but by living them.

But whatever the process, the power of the image evoked is not to be gainsaid. It is not only brilliant on the surface, but mysterious and appealing in its depths. One swiftly forgets his intolerable writing, his mirthless, sedulous, repellent manner, in the face of the Athenian tragedy he instils into his seduced and soul-sick servant girls, his barbaric pirates of finances, his conquered and hamstrung supermen, his wives who sit and wait. He has, like Conrad, a sure talent for depicting the spirit in disintegration. Old Gerhardt, in *Jennie Gerhardt,* is alone worth all the *dramatis personae* of popular American fiction since the days of *Rob o' the Bowl;* Howells could no more have created him, in his Rodinesque impudence of outline, than he could have created Tartuffe or Gargantua. Such a novel as *Sister Carrie* stands quite outside the brief traffic of the customary stage. It leaves behind it an unescapable impression of bigness, of epic sweep and dignity. It is not a mere story, not a novel in the customary American meaning of the word; it is at once a psalm of life and a criticism of life—and that criticism loses nothing by the fact that its burden is despair. Here, precisely, is the point of Dreiser's departure from his fellows. He puts into his novels a touch of the eternal *Weltschmerz.* They get below the drama that is of the moment and reveal the greater drama that is without end. They arouse those deep and lasting emotions which grow out of the recognition of elemental and universal tragedy. His aim is not merely to tell a tale; his aim is to show the vast ebb and flow of forces which sway and condition human destiny. One cannot imagine him consenting to Conan Doyle's statement of the purpose of fiction, quoted with characteristic approval by the New York *Times:* "to amuse mankind, to help the sick and the dull and the weary." Nor is his purpose to instruct; if he is a pedagogue it is only incidentally and as a weakness. The thing he seeks to do is to stir, to awaken, to move. One does not arise from such a book as *Sister Carrie* with a smirk of satisfaction; one leaves it infinitely touched.

Sherwood Anderson

VAN WYCK BROOKS

SHERWOOD ANDERSON . . . with his deep feeling alike for the
natural and the human,—the perpetual student of life as it is
in all its variations . . . was also concerned with the unstudied,
the lifelike, in form. No one avoided more than he any suggestion of the artificial, and, having rejected O. Henry as a
model because he had "learned too many tricks," Anderson
shrank from everything that was meretricious. If he was
drawn to Gertrude Stein, it was mainly because she reminded
him of a countrywoman baking her own bread, and he was
determined that his stories were not to be like the factory-
made kind that is put up, with sawdust inside, in standard-
sized shapes. They were rather to be stories that "began nowhere and ended nowhere," as life itself seemed to begin and
end, and in their way not unlike the stories that Dr. Parcival
told his own George Willard. As for "good old human nature,"
this story-teller born had been absorbing it ever since he was
a boy, sitting on the curb of the main street of a small Ohio
town, listening to people, watching, wondering about them.
He had loitered in the late afternoons about the little frame
hotel when the travelling men gathered on the chairs and told
their stories, and he had spent hours with his back against the
barn wall when the men were talking within at the end of the
day. As a house-painter, a salesman, a soldier, an assembler
in a bicycle-factory, a worker in a Chicago warehouse rolling
kegs, and especially as a stable-boy following race-horses from
town to town, he had been all eyes and ears for "horses and
men." He had watched the loafers in livery-stables and the
flashmen and touts on the race-tracks, the old Mississippi
steamboat-gamblers of whom he was to write; and with what
intensity he had observed the drifting souls in the rooming-
houses in which as an advertising writer he had lived in

29

Chicago. They were mostly lonely office-workers who had come into the city from dreary little meaningless towns in the surrounding states. One of them, no doubt, was the Rosalind Westcott who seemed always to be trying to break through the wall that separated her from life and who went home to Willow Springs to tell her father and mother that she was in love with her middle-aged married employer. Then she walked away in the night,—"out of nowhere into nothing."

While Sherwood Anderson himself had broken with this small-town life, he was always returning to it both in fact and in fancy, in search of the little people he liked to write about, the "obscure" people who, as he put it, had given him life. Years later he would disappear at times and stop for weeks in one of these towns in some dingy hotel room or mountain shack, walking the deserted streets at night with a heart that went out, as he later said, to all the defeated people in the little wooden houses. He had wished to escape from them at first, hoping as a boy to get up in the world and even to be one of the Western captains of finance, for the story *Windy McPherson's Son* was largely his own story, although he had never been "one of the big men of Chicago." Like Sam, he had sold more newspapers than any other boy in town,—he had been one of the salesmen who sat in the chairs, in front of the country hotels, on Sunday mornings,—and, if he had not been the head of the great firearms trust, he had had his own advertising business and his own factory as well. Then, like Sam, like John Webster in *Many Marriages* and like Bruce Dudley in *Dark Laughter*, he had dropped everything suddenly at the peak of his success. The great Sam McPherson had become a wandering workingman in New York and Pennsylvania, "seeking the truth," and John Webster, the washing-machine manufacturer, who felt he was "walking in the bed of a river," had put on his hat and vanished without a word. Just so, Bruce Dudley, the Chicago newspaperman, left his wife, changed his name and ran away, floating down the Mississippi in an open boat, like Huckleberry Finn, who was always in Anderson's mind. Anderson himself, who walked away, woke up in the ward of a Cleveland hospital, for he had had a breakdown and his mind was a blank. He had been writing novels at night,—together with a long book, *Why I Am a Socialist,* which he presently destroyed,—and this was his way of rejecting the business in which he had ceased to believe, the "blind grappling for gain" and the slogans of prosperity and progress. He was washing himself "clean," like John Webster, from the "guilt" of his life, as his mind turned back to an earlier time before the factories came, bringing the "filth and disorder of modern civilization." He was to picture in *Poor White* the rising system of the machine that destroyed the old village life of handicraft in the days when the ne'er-do-well Windy McPherson, who was Anderson's own father,—the story-teller and actor,—was a kind of artist.

Anderson's characters were always "walking off,"—they felt "walled in" and "choked" in the life they were leading; and Anderson's new life was a sort of return to the wandering life of his father, a caricature in advance as it were of his own. For a long time he roamed the country writing in the back rooms of saloons, in railway-stations,—anywhere,—in Alabama, in Detroit, in little Indiana, Iowa, Illinois towns, as year after year his Hugh McVey drifted eastward from Mudcat Landing till he finally became an inventor in Bidwell, Ohio. Anderson's mind was possessed with his childhood, the village and especially the father whom he himself resembled in certain ways, for he too was an actor half-consciously,—a showman, as he said,—who did not repudiate the name of a champion liar. He liked to relate that his secretary accused him of playing the innocent, feigning that he was naïve when he was really foxy, while he combined the air of an actor and a labourer, a race-horse owner, a gambler and a man of business. He enjoyed romancing about his life as his war-touched father had also done,—the blustering old man who pretended to think that not Lincoln nor Grant but he himself had thrown the winning die in the war between the states. What touching tales the old man told about the imaginary sister in the homestead in North Carolina, in Georgia, in Kentucky,—the homestead that would have given his sons a proud Southern ancestry if the war had not unhappily blown it away. Wandering

stricken and forlorn through life, weeping over the injustice
of fate, which had made him an obscure house-painter in a
little farming village, amazed and helpless before facts, this
veteran talker, boasting on the streets, was a master of excuses,
bluff and histrionics. In the rustic vaudeville in the village
schoolhouse he could play the comic Irishman or German or
farmer, he sang and he danced and tooted the cornet in the
band, but whenever there was work to be done he complained
of his wounds. When the rent fell due, when there was a
shortage of food in the house, he was always looking for work
somewhere else.

This father, who appeared in so many of his books, was
Anderson's greatest creation, side by side with the mother of
the family who saved the household by desperate ruses like
those to which Dreiser's mother had also been driven. Who
could forget how she obtained the winter's supply of cabbages
tucked safely away under the snow? Anderson's own chosen
world was mostly made up of the obscure, or what he called
the "starved side of small-town life,"—for there was a side that
was not starved, the side of the up-and-coming people, the
gregarious church-going people of William Allen White.[1]
Anderson was drawn to the misfits, the half-wits, the sex-mad,
like Mike McCarthy who was finally sent to the asylum, to
Belle Carpenter, the milliner's assistant, Wing Biddlebaum of
the fluttering hands and the strange shapeless man who lived
at Tom Willard's hotel. He was interested in Alice, the girl
who was left behind and who realized that she was becoming
old and queer, and the quiet old farm-hand who ran out
across the fields at night shouting his protests against everything that made life ugly. Around them one felt and saw the
small frame houses with decayed piazzas, the alleyways run-

---

[1] Some of White's characters, on the other hand, in *A Certain
Rich Man* and *In Our Town*, had much in common with types that
Anderson loved, among them Watts McHurdie, the old harness-
maker who had also a local fame as a newspaper poet. Then Anderson would have shared White's feeling for the old "jour" printers
who roamed the country, sometimes competent writers and re-
citers of Shakespeare who might have been grotesques from
Dickens or the drawings of Cruikshank.

ning behind the stores on Main Street, the disorderly hotel with its ragged carpets and Biff Carter's lunch-room, Tom Willy's saloon and the doctor with his jaded white horse.

What was new in Anderson's tales of solitary souls and village grotesques was the sense of a buried life they gave the reader, the hidden depths that lay behind the mechanical gestures and banal remarks that expressed the surface-existence of all these people. Anderson had begun to write his stories, which he likened to the "twisted little apples that grow in the orchards of Winesburg," before he had read, before he had heard of, Freud, Chekhov or D. H. Lawrence; and his inarticulate people with their strange turns of mind seemed curiously emblematic of American life. They were types of a post-pioneer world in which countless individuals felt they were astray or somehow lost, while their lives went on like the prairie, an infinity of flat lands, people who were aware of something that had been killed in themselves or perhaps of a secret something that was striving to grow. Yet Anderson found a certain poetry in this old Ohio village life in the days when every man was a craftsman or a farmer, when class-divisions were scarcely known and the future seemed "in every mind," as he said in *Poor White*, "bright with promise." In the rich black soil about the village the corn grew like forest trees, as he remembered in his poems *Mid-American Chants*, and the broad leaves in the vast cabbage-fields were riotous with colour, a thousand shades of green, purple, blue and red.

What Anderson especially loved to remember was the handicraft of that earlier time before money began to "count big," as people said, before the old patterns of life broke up when all the men worked in the fields or at carpentry, horse-shoeing, wagon-building and what not. There were thousands of little shops in which people fashioned things with their hands directly from the raw materials furnished by nature, with a feeling for surfaces, a sensuous pleasure in the wood or the iron they worked with and a pride that accompanied their love of craftsmanship. It pleased Anderson to note the sure quiet touch with which these older workers handled their tools, as he liked to dwell on the barber, for instance, who made violins in *Marching Men* and found a way to increase their beauty of tone. With what pride Sponge in *Dark Laughter*, despising his present factory-work, looked back on his former skill as a carriage-painter at a time when the wheelwright's trade, with carriage-building and harness-making, bore witness to the all-essential and ever-present horse.[2] For that was the day of the horse and his full glory, when trotting and pacing and racing were the talk of every town and country tradesmen owned famous mares and stallions. Anderson, who had worked with horses at many a race-meeting and county fair, delighted in the beautiful, temperamental creatures, their flying legs and distended nostrils, the whistle of the wind from their great lungs, the play of the muscles over their powerful chests. They and their world of the sporting fraternity inspired the best of all his tales, *I Want to Know Why*, for instance, and *I'm a Fool*.

[2] Anderson's father was a harness-maker for a while, and the hero of Brand Whitlock's best novel, *J. Hardin and Son*, was a maker of fine wagons and buggies. This was a better novel than any that Anderson wrote, for he was good only in shorter forms, but Anderson himself might have conceived its theme,—the rise of the new monopolies that drove the old craftsmen to the wall and produced cheap inferior wagons by factory methods.

Victorian Realism

VERNON L. PARRINGTON

IT WAS NOT till the eighties that the movement of realism in fiction began to excite wide interest, and then began a brisk and often acrimonious discussion of the merits and shortcomings of the new technique that filled the pages of the literary magazines. The prejudices against it were many and robust. To most Victorians realism meant Zola, sex, and the exploitation of the animal, and all the pruderies of the Age of Innocence rose up in protest against defiling letters with such themes. The judgment of Aldrich's on realism—"A miasmatic breath blown from the slums"—was a characteristic Yankee echo of Tennyson's condemnation, "wallowing in the slough of Zolaism." All the high priests of the genteel rallied to combat such a desecration of literature, and when it knocked at the door of a respectable magazine in the person of Stephen Crane's *Maggie* the editor could do nothing else than turn it into the street. In the late nineties, when *Jude the Obscure* appeared in one of the family magazines, even the great reputation of Hardy was reckoned a poor excuse for such an offense to morality.

American taste was still romantic, and from his villa at Florence, F. Marion Crawford regularly sent forth heavy romances that were regarded as contributions to our literature. In defense of his wares he threw into the discussion of realism a compact little volume, *The Novel; What It Is,* in which he defined the novel as a pocket drama, the chief interest of which lies in the plot—a retort courteous to Howells's contention that plot is childish and a story ends well that ends faithfully; wedding bells at the end are of no interest to grown men and women, but rather what life brings after the wedding bells. To the aid of Crawford came the brilliant Scot, Robert Louis Stevenson, the literary idol of America in the nineties, whose brave tales were on every center-table. A confirmed romantic, Stevenson could not resist breaking a lance in the cause, and his *Humble Remonstrance* was a persuasive defense of the perennial appeal of romance.

But in spite of protests the spirit of realism spread quietly through the lesser works of fiction and the high-flown romantic was laid away in the grave of John Esten Cooke. The new realism was a native growth, sprung from the soil, unconcerned with European technique. In its earlier expression it inclined to a romantic or idyllic coloring, but as it developed it came to rely more and more on the beauty of truth. This primitive realism issued chiefly from the local color school of the short story, but it was supplemented by the sociological school. The influence of Lowell and the *Atlantic Monthly* on the development of the realistic short story had been encouraging, and in the next decade that development was to go forward swiftly. With the exploitation of local materials came a sharp division on sectional lines, and as Howells pointed out, America was soon parceled out geographically into local groups. Edward Eggleston in southern Indiana, George Washington Cable in New Orleans, Charles Egbert Craddock in eastern Tennessee, James Lane Allen in Kentucky, Octave Thanet in Arkansas, Sarah Orne Jewett and Mary Wilkins Freeman in New England, were representative of the new concern for local truth in fiction that was to tell against the romantic. In fixing attention on narrow and homely fields they were turning towards realism, for the charm of their work lay in fidelity to the *milieu,* the exact portrayal of character and setting. With the spread of an interest in the local the vogue of the strange and the remote declined and a quiet sobriety of tone displaced the romantic. The way was being prepared for a more adequate realism. "Nothing could testify with more force," said H. H. Boyesen in 1894, "to the fact that we have outgrown romanticism than this almost unanimous desire, on the part of our authors, to chronicle the widely divergent phases of our American civilization."[1]

---

[1] *Literary and Social Silhouettes,* p. 73.

But that waited upon profound changes in the American outlook on life. In the seventies and eighties conditions were not ripe for it and the naturalism that in France, Russia, Germany, and Scandinavia was carrying everything before it, was still alien to the American temper. It was not so much that it offended our innate Puritanism as that it seemed to us belied by the open facts of American life. The psychology of the dispersion still marked us. Although we were feverishly building great cities we were still emotionally a country people, far from urban-minded. We still thought in terms of the slack earlier freedoms, uncritical of our ways, untroubled about the future. For the American born before the Civil War, naturalism was impossible; his mind had not been shaped by the industrial city or come under the dominion of science. The traditional outlook on life was unchanged; he still clung to the old moralities, the old verities, the old faith in the goodness of life in America. The intellectual revolution must be gone through with before naturalism should be at home in America, a native expression of native conditions; and it would then be a vehicle only for writers born and bred in the new city environment. In the meanwhile—in the genial years when the earlier optimisms still veiled the harsher realities of science and industrialism—the movement of realism got under way in the work of two distinguished craftsmen who, bred up in Victorian culture, interpreted life in terms of the middle and upper classes.*

II

HENRY JAMES AND
THE NOSTALGIA OF CULTURE

There is a suggestion of irony in the fact that one of our earliest realists, who was independent enough to break with

---

* The first subsection of this chapter in the Contents is entitled "William James and Pragmatism." None of this appears in the manuscript, and it seems likely that Professor Parrington planned to transfer the subject to a later part of the book. The numbering is, however, left as it is given in the Contents.—*Publisher.*

the romantic tradition, should have fled from the reality that his art presumably would gird itself up to deal with. Like his fellow spirit Whistler, Henry James was a lifelong pilgrim to other shrines than those of his native land, who dedicated his gifts to ends that his fellow Americans were indifferent to. Life, with him, was largely a matter of nerves. In this world of sprawling energy it was impossible to barricade himself securely against the intrusion of the unpleasant. His organism was too sensitive, his discriminations too fine, to subject them to the vulgarities of the Gilded Age, and he fled from it all. He early convinced himself that the American atmosphere was uncongenial to the artist.[2] The grotesqueries of the frontier irruption, the crude turmoil released by the new freedoms, were no materials to appeal to one in search of subtleties, to one who was a lover of nocturnes in gray. And so, like Whistler, he sought other lands, there to refine a meticulous technique, and draw out ever thinner the substance of his art.

The explanation of the curious career of Henry James, seeking a habitation between worlds and finding a spiritual home nowhere, is that he was never a realist. Rather he was a self-deceived romantic, the last subtle expression of the genteel, who fell in love with culture and never realized how poor a thing he worshiped. It was the first mistake of Henry James that he romanticized Europe, not for its fragments of the medieval picturesque, but for a fine and gracious culture that he professed to discover there. With the naïveté of the Age of Innocence he assumed that an aristocratic society—shall we say that of Mayfair or the Quartier Saint Germain?—is a complex of subtle imponderables that one comes to understand and embody only through heritage; and it was an assumption even more romantic that these imponderables were so subtly elusive as to escape any but the subtlest art. Like Edith Wharton he erected this suppositious culture into an abstract

[2] "Civilization at its highest pitch was the master passion of his mind, and his preoccupation with the international aspects of character and custom issued from the conviction that the rawness and rudeness of a young country were not incapable of cure by contact with more developed forms." Pelham Edgar, *Henry James, Man, Author*, pp. 40–41.

tertium quid, something apart from social convention or physical environment, something embodied in the choicer spirits of a class that for generations presumably had cherished them. Born of an unconscious inferiority complex in presence of a long-established social order to which he was alien, this romanticization of European culture worked to his undoing, for it constrained the artist to a lifelong pursuit of intangible realities that existed only in his imagination. The gracious culture that James persistently attributed to certain choice circles in Europe was only a figment of his romantic fancy—a fact that after long rambling on the Continent and nearly forty years' unbroken residence in England, he came finally to recognize. It was this failure to find the substance of his dream that imparted to his work a note of wistfulness. He had quitted the land of his birth to seek his spiritual home elsewhere, yet increasingly he came to question the wisdom of his act. He suffered the common fate of the *déraciné;* wandering between worlds, he found a home nowhere. It is not well for the artist to turn cosmopolitan, for the flavor of the fruit comes from the soil and sunshine of its native fields.

The spirit of Henry James marks the last refinement of the genteel tradition, the completest embodiment of its vague cultural aspirations. All his life he dwelt wistfully on the outside of the realm he wished to be a free citizen of. Did any other professed realist ever remain so persistently aloof from the homely realities of life? From the external world of action he withdrew to the inner world of questioning and probing; yet even in his subtle psychological inquiries he remained shut up within his own skull-pan. His characters are only projections of his brooding fancy, externalizations of hypothetical subtleties. He was concerned only with *nuances*. He lived in a world of fine gradations and imperceptible shades. Like modern scholarship he came to deal more and more with less and less. It is this absorption in the stream of psychical experience that justifies one in calling Henry James a forerunner of modern expressionism. Yet how unlike he is to Sherwood Anderson, an authentic product of the American consciousness!

III

From such nostalgia, that left a note of wistfulness in his pages, William Dean Howells was saved by his frank and undivided loyalties. Intellectually and emotionally he was native to the American soil, and however widely he might range he remained always a conscious American. He had no wish to Europeanize his mind; he felt no secret hankerings for the ways of Mayfair or the culture of the Quartier Saint Germain. The homely American reality satisfied the needs of his art, and he accepted it with the finality of Walt Whitman. If he failed to depict it in all its sprawling veracity, if much of its crude robustness never got into his pages, the lack was due to no self-imposed alienation, but to the temperament of the artist and the refined discretions of his environment.

The current school of realism is inclined to deal harshly with Howells. His quiet reticences, his obtrusive morality, his genial optimism, his dislike of looking ugly facts in the face, are too old-fashioned today to please the professional purveyors of our current disgusts. They find his writings as tedious as the gossip of old ladies. To their coarser palates his respectable commonplace is as flavorless as biscuit and tea. Yet it must not be forgotten that for years he was reckoned new-fashioned. Whatever may be one's final judgment on his work it is certain that for twenty years he was a prophet of realism to his generation, the leader of a movement to turn American literature from the path of romanticism and bring it face to face with the real and actual. It was not his fault that the ways of one generation are not those of another, and it is well to remember that if his realism seems wanting to a generation bred up on Theodore Dreiser, it seemed a debasement of the fine art of literature to a generation bred up on Thomas Bailey Aldrich. Realism like dress changes its modes.

The Howells we know best was not a simple child of the frontier, like Mark Twain, whom all could laugh with and love because the sallies of his wit awakened a native response. He did not remain completely native to the older folk-ways. He was rather a composite of the ideals reckoned excellent by the post-war generation—an American Victorian, kindly, urbane, tolerant, democratic, accepting America as a land that God's smile rests on, and convinced that here, wedded to a generous democracy, culture must eventually produce offspring finer than the world has hitherto known. Bred up in the mystical Swedenborgian faith, he shrank from all fleshliness and loved purity with the devotion of a Galahad. A child of the Ohio frontier, he retained to the last the western feeling of democratic equality. An adopted son of Brahmin Cambridge, he immersed himself in culture—Italian, English, Yankee— and served the ideal of excellence with a lifelong devotion; a reverent pilgrim to the shrine of truth, he followed such paths as his generation knew to lay his art at the high altar. In all these things—in his ample culture, his kindly democracy, his high standards of workmanship—as well as in the instinctive reverences of a clean and sweet nature, he was an embodiment of the best in American life, a child of Jacksonian democracy who made use of his freedoms to serve the excellent cause of culture.

But he was much more than that, and if the critics who are wont to damn his Victorian squeamishness would penetrate to the inner core of Howells they would discover an intellectual, alert and sensitive to changing currents of thought, seeing with his own eyes, pursuing his own ends, who wrought out for himself a culture that was individual and native. If he was not, like Henry Adams, plagued with an itch of curiosity, he traveled widely in the realm of the mind. Culture meant to him open-mindedness, familiarity with diverse schools of thought, a willingness to venture upon the unorthodox and to defend the unpopular. He was never a child of the Gilded Age. He was unsoiled by its vulgarity, unconcerned with its sordid ambitions. Neither at heart was he a child of Brahmin culture. He loved Lowell and Norton and Godkin and Aldrich, and he wanted to be approved by them; but he ranged far more widely than they, into places they thought indiscreet.

The mature Howells came to stand apart from Brahminism, dissatisfied with a literary Toryism, convinced that a sterile genteel tradition could not suffice the needs of American literature. His very drift toward realism was a negation of the Brahmin influence. On the whole it was unfortunate that he lived so long in the Cambridge atmosphere. The New England influence may not have been a factor in shaping his too leisurely technique, but certainly it postponed the day of his intellectual release. If he had removed to New York a decade earlier, before his literary method hardened into rigidity, his technique might have changed with his more radical intellectual outlook and become the vehicle of a more adequate realism than he ever achieved.

But the significant thing is that the mind of Howells refused to imprison itself in Brahmin orthodoxies, but set forth on perilous expeditions while Lowell and Norton were discreetly evading the intellectual heresies raging outside their libraries. While Henry James was moving towards aristocratic Mayfair, Howells was journeying towards the proletarian East Side. The scientific revolution seems early to have washed in upon him, undermining the theological cosmos of his youth and turning him into a liberal freethinker. His scientific views very likely came to him second-hand, through the medium of literature; but with his wide reading in Continental fields—Spanish, French, German, Scandinavian—he could not fail to become saturated with the evolutionary view then permeating all current letters. In this he was only following with John Fiske and Henry Holt and Henry Adams the path of a new orthodoxy; nevertheless in applying the scientific spirit to fiction and espousing an objective realism, he quite definitely broke with Brahmin tradition. And when, under the guise of fiction, he turned to social questions, and wove into the placid texture of his work the vexing problem of social justice, he ventured on perilous ground where his Brahmin friends would not follow. To espouse the teachings of Herbert Spencer was one thing, to espouse the teachings of Karl Marx was quite another.

Howells came late to an interest in sociology, held back by the strong literary and aesthetic cast of his mind. But in the eighties, when he had reached middle life, he was no longer able to ignore or evade the economic maladjustments of the Gilded Age. The social unrest that was coming to bloody issue in strikes and lockouts gave him acute concern, and slowly under pressure of a sensitive social conscience there began a quiet intellectual revolution that was to transform the detached observer of the American scene into a Marxian socialist. A democrat, a lover of his kind, a just soul endowed with a tender conscience, an idealist who dreamed of a brotherhood of free men who should create in America a civilization adequate to human needs, what else could he do? He loved peace but war was all about him. And so in the mid-afternoon of life he turned to the work of spreading the gospel of social democracy in the America of the Gilded Age. He had no private or personal causes to serve. He had not, like Godkin and Dana, given hostages to fortune in the shape of a newspaper or magazine; he had no call to be partisan to his own interests. He was free to plead the cause of justice in his own way and at his own time. It is easy for the later radical to sneer at him as a parlor socialist who talked well but carefully refrained from disturbing the capitalistic machine from which he drew his income; but that is to ignore the courage of the artist in confronting a hostile world. He stood stoutly for the rights of workingmen that the passions of the times swept rudely away. When the Haymarket Riot in Chicago brought its shameful hysteria, and all respectable America was crying for blood, Howells was one of the few intellectuals who spoke for justice, one of the few who held aloof from the mob spirit, thereby bringing on his head a wave of criticism. It was a brave thing in 1886 to speak for the "Chicago anarchists."

But it was not till his removal to New York, where he found himself at the center of the great revolution, that he set about seriously studying the ways of plutocracy. For the student of Cambridge society it involved a mental upheaval. The urbanity of his literary manner conceals for most readers the intensity of emotion that underlies his quiet style; yet it is clear enough that having examined the ways of private capitalism and considered its works, he rejected it. Thenceforth to the end of his life he hated the thing and quietly preached against it. His affections went back fondly to the earlier agricultural order that had shaped his youth, and in the character of Dryfoos, in *A Hazard of New Fortunes,* he suggests the moral degeneration that he believed followed in the train of the substitution of a speculative capitalist economy for the wholesomer agrarian economy. But though, remembering his frontier youth, he might prefer the older ways, he was realist enough to understand that capitalism was the order of his generation, and he turned eagerly to explore the new proletarian philosophies that came out of Germany. Howells was the first distinguished American man of letters to espouse Marxian socialism. For a cultivated American in the Gilded Age to sympathize with proletarian theory and to proclaim himself a socialist, was enough to excite amazement in his fellows. In the eighties American social thought was still naïve and provincial. Old-world theories were as alien as old-world institutions, and in spite of the wide interest aroused by *Looking Backward* the intelligent American in 1890 knew as little about Marxianism as he knows today about Bolshevism.

The doubts and hesitations that troubled Howells during these years of changing outlook, are skillfully dramatized in *A Hazard of New Fortunes.* The story of the removal of the Marshes from New England to New York, told with more than usual leisureliness, is the story of the transition from the peacefulness of his earlier literary life to the anxieties of his later thought. Slowly into a story of the familiar Howells commonplace comes the note of social dissension. Antagonistic social philosophies meet and clash, and the movement draws inevitably to the great climax of the strike that brings tragedy into the scene. Of the mood that grew upon him as he wrote he afterwards said:

It became, to my thinking, the most vital of my fictions; through my quickened interest in the life about me, at a moment of great psychological import. We had passed through a period of strong emotioning in the direction of humaner economics, . . . the rich seemed not so much to despise the poor, and the poor did not so hopelessly repine. That shedding of blood which is for the remission of sins had been symbolized by the bombs and scaffolds of Chicago, and the hearts of those who felt this bound up with our rights, the slavery implicated in our liberty, were thrilling with griefs and hopes hitherto strange to the average American breast. Opportunely for me there was a great street-car strike in New York, and the story began to find its way to issues nobler and larger than those of the love-affairs common to fiction.[3]

The years of unrest marked by the great agrarian revolt were years of great intellectual activity for Howells, during which his thought ripened and mellowed. His own liberal spirit drew to him the liberal spirits of the younger generation, and he became the counselor and friend of many of the young rebels of the day. His sympathy went out to all who were concerned at the injustice of the world. He questioned the right of none to uphold his creed, nor sought to impose his own beliefs upon others. As he watched the great struggle of the times his heart was always on the side of the weak and exploited. Very likely he knew little about the economics of money and finance, over which rival partisans were quarreling savagely, but he understood the human side of the farmers' problem and it was always the balance in the human ledger that weighed with him.

He was a friend of Hamlin Garland and rejoiced when *Main-Travelled Roads* was given to the world, writing for it an introduction warmly and tenderly sympathetic. As an artist he grew concerned lest under the stimulus of B. O. Flower the zeal of the propagandist should submerge the art of the story-teller; but he had no quarrel with the "causes" that were fermenting in the mind of the young Populist, and would not lessen one whit the ardor of his social faith. Throughout the passionate campaign of 1896, that brought most of his friends to a blind and scurrilous partisanship of the gold standard, his

[3] Quoted in "The Social Consciousness of William Dean Howells," *New Republic*, Vol. 26, p. 193.

heart kept his mind just and his sympathy for the unrequited producers served as counterbalance to the shrill vituperation of his friend Godkin. He had thought too long and too honestly to be moved by the *claque* of the press.

It was in the black days of the panic of '93 that he seems to have brooded most thoughtfully over the ways of capitalistic America, and in the following year he published *The Traveller from Altruria,* the first of his two Utopian romances in which he subjected the system of capitalism to critical analysis. It is a clever book that quite disarms the reader. Howells delivers no broadside attack on the capitalistic system, and he suggests its mean and selfish exploitation with such genial urbanity, such sly satire, as to arouse no sleeping lions. The concern in his heart is belied by the twinkle in his eye. He hints that the Altrurian critic is only the figment of a dream, and he smilingly suggests the sources of the Altrurian commonwealth in the long line of Utopian dreamers from Plato and Sir Thomas More to Bellamy and William Morris. But the urbanity is only a mask. Protected by it Howells delivers many a shrewd thrust at the ways of capitalism. American democracy does not show to advantage under his analysis. The Altrurian comes upon the canker of social injustice in every chink and cranny of life—a canker that is slowly destroying democratic America; and Howells takes a sly pleasure in contrasting our democratic professions with our plutocratic practice. There is a delightful irony in his attack on the professional classes—the professor, the minister, the writer—for their quick defense of the exploiting classes. What may we expect of the science of economics, he suggests, when our academic economists are only apologists for the existing order?

The Traveller from Altruria is a shrewd analysis of American life set against a Marxian background, and in forecasting the future Howells follows the Marxian law of concentration. The Age of Accumulation, with its gigantic monopolies gathered in ever fewer hands, prepared the way for a new order when industrialism, grown overbig, falls into the control of the state as naturally as the harvest is gathered into the granary. There was no need of a class war. When the times were ripe political means sufficed, for the democracy retained the effective weapon of the vote. Thirteen years later Howells completed his Utopian venture with *Through the Eye of the Needle,* in which he sketches in fuller detail the order of life in Altruria. It was not till men learned that coöperation is a better social cement than competition, altruism than egoism, that the new order was possible; and in this later work he depicts the kindly, rational society that emerged when men left off fighting each other and turned to working together instead. On every page the influence of William Morris is revealed—not only in the rejection of an urban society founded on the machine and a return to a decentralized anarchistic order, but in the emphasis on the psychology of work and the satisfactions that spring from free creative labor. *Through the Eye of the Needle* is curiously reminiscent of *News from Nowhere* and suggests how sympathetically Howells followed English social thought in its reaction against industrialism.

It was while he was thus engaged that he put into compact form his speculations on the theory of realism. For more than a decade he had been the most distinguished advocate of realism in America, and for longer still his successive novels had revealed to a critical world what substance and form he believed the realistic novel should possess. The immediate sources of his theory are obscure, though it is clear enough that the work of Jane Austen was a creative influence. From the school of French and Russian naturalism, then at the height of its vigor, he drew back in repulsion, and it was not till after his technique was matured that Tolstoi became an influence in his intellectual life. It is reasonable to assume that his realism was a native growth, the result of temperament unfolding through quiet years of reading in the English classics. A quizzical observer with the gift of humor is not likely to run into romanticism, and a youthful passion for Pope and Heine is not the best preparation for it. His intense dislike of the romantic, that led him to an inadequate and partial conception of it, seems to have sprung from certain instinctive feelings and convictions that strengthened with the years: a deep and sincere love of truth, a native sympathy with the simple homely phases of life, a quiet loyalty to American fact, and a sharp distrust of the aristocratic spirit. Endowed with such feelings he came to ascribe his own partisanships to literary methods; the romantic became for him the aristocratic, and the realistic became the democratic. As an American he was content to take the common stuff of life, as he found it in America, and depict it in unpretentious sincerity. Plain American life was not only worthy of literature, he was convinced, but the only material worthy of American literature. The path to the universal runs as directly through the commonplace American parlor as through the hall of the medieval baron or the drawing-room of Mayfair.

In *Criticism and Fiction* (1894), Howells ascribes the rise of modern realism to the twin sources of science and democracy. From science it derives its passion for truth, for "realism," he asserts, "is nothing more and nothing less than the truthful treatment of material." "We must ask ourselves before we ask anything else, Is it true?—true to the motives, the impulses, the principles, that shape the life of actual men and women." The question, what is essential truth, that has been the apple of discord amongst the realists, Howells answers in democratic fashion by appealing to the average. The "foolish man," he says, "wonders at the unusual, but the wise man at the usual." The realist, therefore, will deal objectively with the usual and common rather than with the unusual or strange, and in so doing he draws closer to the common heart of humanity, and learns the respect for simple human nature that is the source and wellspring of democracy. In delineating truthfully the prosaic lives of common people realism reveals the essential dignity and worth of all life. The romantic, on the other hand, is aristocratic. "It seeks to withdraw itself, to stand aloof; to be distinguished and not to be identified." "The pride of caste has become the pride of taste," and romance is the last refuge of the aristocratic spirit that, defeated elsewhere, has taken refuge in culture. Not aloofness, but comradeship, is the need of the world; not distinction, but identity. Realism is the child of democracy because the realist is one who "feels in every nerve the equality of things and the unity of men," and the great artist is one with a talent "robust enough to front the everyday world and catch the charm of its work-worn, care-worn, brave, kindly face."

To this characteristic conception that realism is democratic Howells adds certain other dicta that to his own generation seemed as true as to ours they seem doubtful: that art must serve morality, that it must teach rather than amuse, and that truthfulness to American life requires a note of cheerfulness. Art cannot flout the "eternal amenities," Howells asserted, for "morality penetrates all things, it is the soul of all things." Nor can it stand aloof, disdaining the office of teacher, for unless it "tends to make the world better and kinder" it is empty and futile; and it can do this only "from and through the truth." But the truth that will uplift society does not dwell in the kennel and pigsty; it will not be come upon by exploring the animal in man, or in wrapping the shroud of pessimism about life. In America at least, realism must concern itself with the "large cheerful average of health and success and happy life," for after all "the more smiling aspects of life" are "the more American." From such postulates Howells developed his familiar technique, which in minimizing plot, rejecting the unusual and strange and heroic, reduced his stories to the drab level that bores so many of his readers, and evokes the criticism that in elaboration of the commonplace he evades the deeper and more tragic realities that reach to the heart of life.

The criticism is just. More than any other thing this concern for the usual weakens Howells's work and renders it trivial. He does not probe the depths of emotional experience. Neither the life of the spirit nor the passions of the flesh is the stuff from which he weaves his stories. The lack—and allowing for all his solid excellence it remains grave—sprang in part from his own timid nature that recoiled from the gross and the unpleasant, and in part from the environment in which he perfected his technique. For years he lived in an atmosphere of complacent convention, a society dominated by women, culture, and conscience. Cambridge and Boston in the seventies and eighties were still in the Age of Innocence greatly concerned with erecting defenses against the intrusion of the unpleasant, reverencing the genteel in life and letters, soberly moral and making much of the eternal verities. In such a world of refined manners and narrow outlook what should the realist do but report faithfully of what he saw and heard? And so Howells, perforce, became a specialist in women's nerves, an analyst of the tenuous New England conscience, a master of Boston small-talk. It was such materials that shaped his leisurely technique until it falls about his theme with the amplitude of crinoline.

Through these chronicles of the Age of Innocence runs a persistent note of the neurotic. There are more scruples to a page of Howells than in any other writer except Henry James —for the most part filmy cobwebs invisible to the coarser vision of a later generation. The action percolates through the sand of small-talk, welling up from the tiniest springs and stopped by the smallest obstruction. Like Franklin's two-headed snake his characters are in danger of dying from thirst because of much argument over the right path to water. It is hard to weave a substantial fabric from such gossamer threads, and when in *The Rise of Silas Lapham* endless pages are devoted to the ethical subtleties of a woman's accepting the hand of a man who the family had believed was in love with her sister, or when in *April Hopes* the fantastic scruples of a neurotic girl are elaborated with a refinement of art worthy of a Fra Angelico Madonna, the stuff is too filmy to wear well. Commonplace men and neurotic women are poor materials from which to fashion an adequate realism, and with the passing of the Age of Innocence the scruples of Howells went out of fashion.

The fault, in part at least, must be traced to the artist's deep reverence for New England. From his youth he had cherished an exalted notion of the sufficiency of New England culture, and had accepted its parochialisms as ultimate standards. To a bookish lad, inclined to be too consciously literary, such loyalty to a declining school could only accentuate his native aloofness from life. His four years at Venice had been given over to an ardent pursuit of culture, as culture was understood by Lowell and Norton. It was the natural impulse of a sensitive mind, conscious of its limitations, reveling for the first time in the wealth that had been denied his frontier boyhood. His poetic *Venetian Days* was an infallible passport to Boston favor, and when after his return he was taken up by the *Atlantic* group he carried with him to Boston an unconscious inferiority complex that did his genius an evil turn. It was natural for the self-taught western youth to be reverent in presence of the great of earth; but it is not well for the artist to be humble in the presence of his masters. Unless he is something of a rebel, given to questioning the dogmas of the schools, he will never ripen into creative originality.

An inferiority complex is a common mark of the frontier mind that finds itself diffident in presence of the old and established, and Howells suffered from it greatly. For years his keen eyes lacked their usual shrewdness in judging Boston ways, and to the end of his life he overestimated the greatness of the men to whom his youthful loyalty had gone out. Not only did he accept Lowell and Holmes and Longfellow at the Boston rating, but he regarded the lesser group of cultivated Boston gentlemen with partial eyes. It would have been far better for his art if like Hamlin Garland he had never been received within the charmed circle; if he had had to make his way alone. To justify his acceptance Howells felt that he must prove himself as completely Bostonian as the best, and in consequence he sloughed off his western heritage, perverted his genius, and shaped his realism to the slender materials discovered in Back Bay drawing-rooms. The genteel tradition was in the way of strangling his realism.

Subjected to such refinements his realism in the end became little more than technique—a meticulous transcription of New England conventions, the casual action submerging itself in an endless stream of talk. No doubt Howells was true to what he saw; certainly no one has ever fixed more exactly the thin substance of the Age of Innocence. Nevertheless the fidelity of his observation, the refinement of his prose style, and the subtlety of his humor that plays lambently about the edges of his words, do not compensate for the slightness of his materials. The record he has left is not that of a great soul brooding over the meaning of life, puzzled, uncertain, yet tender toward the victims that fate has seized and crushed. He was restrained by too many inhibitions to deal frankly with natural human passions. He felt deeply and tenderly, but he was too diffident to let himself go. It is likely that Howells never realized the inadequacy of his temperament and the futility of his method to any serious realism. Even in his acutest study *A Hazard of New Fortunes,* which comes upon brutal economic reality, the story is entangled in a mass of minute detail and never quite breaks through. The indecisions, the repetitions, the whimsical descriptions, the drifting talk, are all true to life, but they are not essential or vital truth. The real issue toward which the story moves—the problem of social justice and the contrasting systems of wage-slavery, bond-slavery, and social democracy—is obscured in a welter of asides and never quite reaches the front of the stage. He is more effective in such works as *Indian Summer,* when he deals with characters on vacation who play whimsically with love, and in *April Hopes,* when he dwells fondly on the infinitely eloquent trivialities of young love-making. In such studies the minute fidelity to word and gesture, the humorous playing with invisible scruple, is a pleasant substitute for solider material.

Howells had real gifts, of which he made the most. Refinement, humor, sympathy—fidelity to external manner and rare skill in catching the changing expression of life—a passion for truth and a jealous regard for his art: he had all these qualities, yet they were not enough to make him a great realist. He belonged to the Age of Innocence and with its passing his works have been laid away. He has had no followers to keep his method alive. If one may hazard an explanation of the lot that has befallen him, it would be this. Howells the artist mistook his calling. He was not by temperament a novelist. He lacked the sense of drama, a grasp of the rough fabric of life, the power to deal imaginatively with the great and tragic realities. His genius was rather that of a whimsical essayist, a humorous observer of the illogical ways of men. He was an eighteenth-century spirit—a subtler Goldsmith—set down in another age and an uncongenial world. In his later years he

must have come to realize this, for more and more he turned
to the essay form. There his quiet humor and shrewd observation fitted his sinuous prose style to a nicety. In such sketchy
autobiography as *My Literary Passions*, and more whimsically
in such genial travel essays as *Certain Delightful English
Towns*, his refined art arrived at its most perfect expression.
Not an original genius like Mark Twain, far from a turbulent
soul like Herman Melville, Howells was the reporter of his
generation—the greatest literary figure of a drab negative age
when the older literary impulse was slackening, and the new
was slowly displacing it. He marks the transition between the
earlier idealism and the later naturalism. A humane and lov-
able soul, he was the embodiment of all that was kindly and
generous in an America that was not wholly given over to the
ways of the Gilded Age—an America that loved beauty and
served culture even amidst the turmoil of revolution.

Modern Currents in American Literature[1]

PAUL ELMER MORE

IT IS A DISABILITY inherent in my theme that it leaves no place to speak of the work of our most accomplished novelist, Edith Wharton, or of our eminent poets, Edwin Arlington Robinson and Robert Frost. The dignified standing of these writers has long been recognized; but they are not modern or American, perhaps I should say they are not at once both modern and American, in the sense of those who have signed the new Declaration of Independence in letters. For somewhat similar reasons I pass over the host of prolific penmen, extending from the fairly distinguished output of Booth Tarkington, through the respectable mediocrity of Hamlin Garland and Meredith Nicholson and their kind, down to that nadir of popular success, Harold Bell Wright, whose very name to all reputable critics—unless I dare to except myself, who have a kind of sneaking admiration for the rascal—is a byword of infamy.

There is in fact not very much to say about these purveyors to the market, from Mrs. Wharton to Mr. Wright, save that they are turning out books of more or less honest craftsmanship, in better or worse English, with this or that smear of local colour. We read them for entertainment, but do not talk about them a great deal. The writers who belong to the modern movement as a conscious school are fewer in number but more clamorous for notice; and if at any time we forget to take them seriously, one of the clan, sacrificing himself for the good of his fellows, publishes a book so audacious, or so salacious, that the frightened authorities try to suppress its circulation, and then we begin to talk again. For their artistic principles these rebels to tradition are in the main, of course, trailing

[1] The following essay was written some time ago at the request of the *Revue de Paris* and was intended primarily for French readers.

after a similar movement in England, as their British models in turn have taken their cue from France or perhaps from Russia. And, generally speaking, it would not be much of an exaggeration to say that in such matters London follows what was the mode in Paris twenty or thirty years earlier, while New York toils after London at about an equal interval of time. But in one article of their creed the Americans stand by themselves: without exception they are animated by a wholehearted contempt for New England Puritanism and all it means. The young bloods of London may speak disdainfully of their Victorian, especially their mid-Victorian, predecessors, in some cases on the good old ground, *pereant qui ante nos nostra dixerunt;* but their antipathy is mild beside the red rage which suffuses the brain of a "modern" on this side of the water at the mere suggestion that any allegiance or even respect should be accorded to the literary prigs who used to utter their platitudes from Boston. Now there is no other bond of union so strong as a common hate, and if our new men disagree widely in what they like, they agree wonderfully in what they dislike. And though there are, as we shall see, other forces of a more positive sort at work among them, it is this community of revolt that binds them all together into the semblance of a school; while it is chiefly the Americanism of the object of their revolt that marks them off as American from similar schools in Europe. They know, as we all know, that the most characteristic production of these States to the present day is just the output of these Puritan New Englanders,—Emerson, Longfellow, Lowell, Whittier, Hawthorne, Thoreau; and some of us, while recognizing the limitations of this literature in comparison with the masterpieces of Europe, yet esteem it for its originality, and cherish it as something in its way very fine and precious. But not so the children of the rebellion; they anathematize it for its very virtues. So far as they acknowledge any ancestors in this land, it is to Whitman and Poe and, among the more recent writers, Stephen Crane they pay homage.

There are many causes that contribute to this repudiation of New England's primacy. For one thing mere local jealousy plays its part here as in politics; and the citizens of Oshkosh or Kalamazoo in the broad lands of the West are convinced that their birthplace is, or shall be, as truly a centre of light for the world as was the metropolis of the Puritans. You will see these gentlemen of Oshkosh and Kalamazoo, even of Chicago, flocking to New York as soon as they have found their literary legs, for New York is any man's, or no man's, city, a place where millions congregate to do business and to eat and die, where Yiddish or Italian and occasionally a kind of English is spoken, but where no one was ever born—to Boston you will see them migrating, never!

And then there is the larger jealousy of patriotism. It is rumoured that the Brahmins of Boston, as they used to be called, got their culture from abroad and wrote a language slavishly like that of London, whereas our new men are determined at any cost to be themselves, to employ a dialect which they fondly call "good United States," and to create a literature the like of which has not been known hitherto in the world. Of course they are wrong; for as a matter of fact, however the poets and essayists of New England's golden age may have clung to the traditional laws of grammar and the established forms of art, they were in the deeper things of the spirit more distinctly national, as the nation then was, than are the present advocates of independence. Certainly, if there be anything common to the writing folk of the earth today and not peculiarly American, it is the creed of the modernist, that what has been shall be no more, and that quite suddenly we have been liberated from the old laws and conventions and fears, from the ancient gods and their precepts of morality.

Above all the gods and their morality. The Puritans of the early and middle decades of the last century may have "come out," as we say, from all the traditional dogmas and rites of religion—Emerson gave up his pulpit because the very mild and defecated formalities of Unitarian worship "ceased to interest" him—but Emerson and all his tribe were frightfully moral; their works are as stuffed with the stale moralities of religion as were the tragedies and epics of ancient Athens. There are naturally various stages in this revolt, an advance

guard and a rear guard. To some immorality and irreligion are
an avowed and joyous creed; for the object of their attack they
have coined the contemptuous words "moralism" and "religionism," and wherever the infamous thing raises its head,
whether in life or art, they pursue it with inquisitorial fury.
Others are not so consistent. They will admit, if pressed, that
morality and even religion may have a useful function in the
actual affairs of life, but insist that they have nothing to do
with the canons of art. Whatever may be the law of life, art
exists for its own blessed sake.

These then are the animosities that unite the otherwise
centrifugal champions of liberty into a brotherhood: hatred of
Puritanism, rejection of "moralism" and "religionism," eman-
cipation of art from the responsibilities of life. They have
learned a lesson from the despised Pilgrims of New England,
and have really "come out."

In a broad way our moderns[2] may be divided into two different and often antagonistic schools, the æsthetic and the
realistic. Of the æsthetic school, until her recent death, Amy
Lowell was perhaps the leading spirit, as she was undoubtedly
the most finished artist. For the most part she was content to
adopt the instruments forged by more daring hands. In the
fashion of the day she threw off the trammels of rhyme and
metre for the supposed enlargement of free verse, borrowing
her form, as a good American, from Whitman, and then, as a
true cosmopolite, shaping it after Parisian models; and her
practice of "imagism" was admittedly French. But a modern
æsthete must be original, and so Miss Lowell added to her
repertory what she called "polyphonic prose." The idea of
such an invention she found, indeed, in the writing of Paul
Fort, but instead of basing her rhythm on the Alexandrine
verse, as did M. Fort, she chose "the long, flowing cadence of
oratorical prose," and so created a new *genre*, or at least a
new name. Polyphonic prose then, as Miss Lowell defines it,

[2] As a matter of fact the principal writers here criticised are no
longer young, nor would they be recognized as typically "modern"
by some of the advanced aesthetes. But the younger group has
not yet caught the ear of the public.

is "an orchestral form; its tone is not merely single and melodic as is that of *vers libre,* for instance, but contrapuntal and various." The programme is large and made some stir in the more recondite poetical circles when first issued; but the results, it must be admitted, have been meagre. Whatever reputation Miss Lowell retains will depend, I am sure, less on her polyphonic prose than on her more regular verse. Here her vein of genuine talent cannot be questioned, and some of her pieces have a beauty of hard incisive imagery of no common order. No one can say what she might have accomplished, had she not been hampered in her gait by a kind of æsthetical scholasticism; I think of her sometimes as a genius hag-ridden by theory. She enjoyed a *succès d'estime* during her life, and the merry legend of her eccentricities still adds to the gayety of at least one nation, but her literary influence is small and, I suspect, already waning. In fact the mere liberty of form in verse no longer satisfies the advance guard of the insurrection; I have heard a college sophomore, whose aspiration towards free morals in literature led to his rustication,—I have heard him speak of Carl Sandburg, the chanter of Chicago's "smoke and steel" in very free verse, as simply "dead."

Of the living æsthetes James Branch Cabell, a somewhat enigmatical figure, is unquestionably the most talked of. He was, if truth be told, resting in peaceful obscurity not many years ago, when suddenly he was made famous by the activity of the Federal authorities who took alarm at the free ethics of his *Jurgen* and forbade its transmission through the Post. Forthwith his fame was established as a martyr of high art; for the American intelligentsia is rather naïvely convinced that whatever is illicit is artistic. As for the book itself I confess some uncertainty of judgment. You will hear men of wide reading and presumably of trained taste pronounce it an immortal masterpiece and its author our most consummate craftsman; others, the majority of the sober, will tell you the book is a bore, and smile at the writer as a pretentious "four-flusher." So far as I can discover the most radical of our youth do not take the work seriously; but then they do not take anything seriously—except perhaps the portentous *Ulysses* of James Joyce, and he is not American. . . .

The æsthetes in America today are a small band. Indeed, besides Mr. Cabell himself it would be hard to name any living writer who has gained real distinction in this *genre*—unless by chance one wished to include Joseph Hergesheimer in that family. Now Mr. Hergesheimer possesses a kind of cleverness that removes him from the ranks of ordinary realism, but his style is so uncertain, so riddled with affectations and obscurities and glaring solecisms, that one hesitates to place him on the other side with the artists. Bad English may be the proper badge of the realist, but it disqualifies an æsthete. And certainly it cannot be said that Mr. Hergesheimer even tries to follow the rule so constantly in the mouth of Mr. Cabell: "to write perfectly of beautiful happenings."[3]

It is a fact of some significance that both our leading æsthetes spring from prominent families long established in the two most conservative of our Eastern States, and that they are educated. Miss Lowell was a kinswoman of James Russell Lowell and a sister of President Lowell of Harvard, belonging by inheritance to the Brahmin circles of Massachusetts. Mr. Cabell's people are well known in Virginia, and he himself once taught Greek in the William and Mary College of which he is an alumnus—and Greek is not exactly a common adjunct of our writing folk.

As a contrast the realists who throng the left wing of the modern school come almost without exception from small towns sprinkled along the Mid-Western States from Ohio to Kansas, where for the most part they have grown up quite innocent of education in any such sense as would be recognized in Paris or London. It would not be easy to exaggerate the importance of the fact that in letters they are self-made men with no inherited background of culture. One of them, indeed, Sinclair Lewis, coming out of Sauk Center, Minnesota, has a degree from Yale University; but intellectually he is perhaps

[3] Mr. Thornton Wilder's *Bridge of San Luis Rey*, published since the writing of this essay, contains promise of better things.

the crudest member of the group, cruder, for instance, than Theodore Dreiser who got most of his education in the streets of Chicago and from the free libraries of this and that town, or than Sherwood Anderson who apparently owes his acquaintance with the alphabet to the grace of God. Another of the group, John Dos Passos, was born in Chicago, is a graduate of Harvard, and has been influenced, one guesses, by certain French Writers and by the Spaniard Ibáñez; his work is too knowing to be called crude intellectually or perhaps even artistically, but as a reflection of life it is about the lowest we have yet produced. His much-bruited novel *Manhattan Transfer*, with its unrelated scenes selected to portray the more sordid aspect of New York, and with its spattered filth, might be described in a phrase as an explosion in a cesspool.

I give these biographical facts not in a spirit of snobbishness, nor in any contempt for the Mid-West (to which indeed I myself belong), but because they have stamped the whole school, giving it a certain unity of character and marking it off from the contemporary realism of England, not to mention France. Of all the group Mr. Dreiser is pretty generally recognized as the most powerful and, with the possible exception of Mr. Anderson, the most typical, and it will not be out of place to look a little more closely into his career. Fortunately for our purpose Mr. Dreiser, like his compeers, is tremendously occupied with his personal importance and unimportance in the universe, to such an extent that his own character peeps in and out through all his fiction, while, again like his fellows, he has thought it necessary, or profitable, to give the world his autobiography. One may smile at the conceit of an author who, at the age of fifty and with no fixed tenure on fame, spreads out the small doings of his youth and early manhood over five hundred pages octavo; and one may shrink from the immodesty—or shall we say frankness?—of a man who regrets in print that he did not seduce an innocent and trusting girl while his passion for her was strong instead of waiting to marry her after his lust had cooled down. There are some things which even a realist need not tell. But the book is a document of the highest value.

Theodore Dreiser was born in Terre Haute in 1871. His father, a German, was by the son's account a poor feckless creature, a "religionist" of the maudlin sentimental sort, who passed his later days going the round of the Roman Catholic churches of Chicago, whither he had taken his family. At an early age the boy Theodore was travelling the streets of Chicago selling shabby goods for an "easy-payment instalment house," from which occupation he broke away after stealing twenty-five dollars. The fear of detection and punishment, he says, made him "very cautious." In his twenty-second year he got a small job on a struggling newspaper, owned and controlled by a ward politician. In 1892 he moved to St. Louis, where for a while he had the advantage of reporting under "Little Mac," an editor of outstanding ability and in those days of almost incredible repute throughout the South-Western States. Here I am able to check up Mr. Dreiser's narrative in part, for he came to the city of my birth just when I was leaving it, and I can testify to his account of its streets and institutions, and to his characterization of some of its well-known citizens, as truthful and extraordinarily vivid. From St. Louis he soon drifted eastward, and ended in New York, the Mecca of all our writing men, to whom Chicago is a kind of halfway house. Lean years still lay before him; but his stories began to attract attention, and his *American Tragedy,* a novel spun out through two long volumes, has captured the heedless reading mob and has been acclaimed a masterpiece by reputable reviewers here and abroad.

For my own part I regard his autobiography, despite or possibly because of its shameless "exhibitionism," as more significant than any of his novels, as perhaps, with Sherwood Anderson's similar *Story Teller's Story,* the most significant thing that has come out of our school of realism. I may be prejudiced in its favour by the fact that the autobiography, though the events of Mr. Dreiser's life were different enough from my own, recalls so vividly the intellectual and sentimental atmosphere of the America in which my youth was passed, and which is rapidly disappearing. But, apart from such accidental reasons, it is notable that the *Book About My-*

self has the telling straightforward style and method natural to a trained reporter, whereas the English of Mr. Dreiser, when, as sometimes in his novels, he tries to be literary, is of the mongrel sort to be expected from a miscegenation of the gutter and the psychological laboratory. Certainly for those interested in such matters the springs of American realism are laid bare in these autobiographical records with startling frankness. Take a boy of humble origin in a Mid-Western town some forty years ago. The only breath of immaterial things to reach him would be through religion, in the case of Mr. Dreiser a perfectly uncritical catholicism, but with most of the others a thin poverty-stricken Protestantism from which all ritual and symbolism had dropped and every appeal to the imagination had exuded. Art and letters would be about as remote from him as from the Bushmen of Africa. Intellectually and æsthetically and emotionally he is starved. Suppose then that such a lad, with no schooling to speak of or with a degree from some lonely hungry "college," is carried to the bustling conceited Chicago of those days, and, aspiring to write, gets a job on a sensation-mongering newspaper. Of knowledge of life in its larger aspects he has brought nothing, and in the new school of experience he is pretty well confined to the police courts, the morgue, scenes of crime and calamity, sodden streets where unsavoury news may be picked up, homes which scandal has made public property. We need not guess at the colours the world would assume in the eyes of such a youth, for Mr. Dreiser has described his own reactions with sufficient energy. He began his work "still sniffing about the Sermon on the Mount and the Beatitudes, expecting ordinary human flesh and blood to do and be those things"; he discovered that most of the people among whom he was now thrown "looked upon life as a fierce, grim struggle in which no quarter was either given or taken, and in which all men laid traps, lied, squandered, erred through illusion," or, more succinctly in the words of one of his admired and imitated friends, "life is a God-damned stinking, treacherous game."

Meanwhile our young aspirant to fame and wealth, being

endowed with no ordinary brain, begins to read. Translations of Balzac and Zola fall into his hands, and he learns that the society of Paris, the *ville lumière*, is playing a game very much like that which he sees about him, only on a more magnificent scale and with vastly greater opportunities. And he learns, or thinks he learns, that the high art of letters is to develop the sort of realism he is acquiring as a reporter. Later he dips into the works of Huxley and Tyndall and Spencer, and finds his "gravest fears as to the unsolvable disorder and brutality of life eternally verified" by authorities who were then supposed by the uneducated or the scientifically educated to have uttered the last word on the mysteries of the universe, the last word *eternally verified*. "Up to this time," he observes rather innocently, "there had been in me a blazing and unchecked desire to get on and the feeling that in doing so we did get somewhere; now in its place was the definite conviction that spiritually one got nowhere, that there was no hereafter, that one lived and had his being because one had to, and that it was of no importance. Of one's ideals, struggles, deprivations, sorrows and joys, it could only be said that they were chemic compulsions, something which for some inexplicable but unimportant reason responded to and resulted from the hope of pleasure and the fear of pain. Man was a mechanism, undevised and uncreated, and a badly and carelessly driven one at that."

Add to this education a spark of genius, an eye to note and record the panorama of the streets, a nervous system highly sensitive to the moods of those about him, and you have the realism of which *An American Tragedy* is the most notable achievement. In his drawing of characters from the lower strata of life and from the gilded haunts of Broadway Mr. Dreiser shows an easy competence. In particular the hero of this tale, from his suppressed childhood in the home of ignorant wandering evangelists, through his career as bell-boy in a hotel, and employee in a factory, ending in trial and conviction for the murder of his mistress, is portrayed with a masterly understanding of the devious ways of a weak untutored nature. But when the author passes to the doings of conventional society, even to the account of a game of tennis, he displays a ludicrous ignorance and awkwardness. The same sort of contrast is seen in other fields. At one moment the tone of comment is callous and cynical, befitting his acquired theory of life's unsolvable disorder and brutality; and then there will break through the native note of sentimentality that pervaded the atmosphere he breathed in the rural Mid-West of his childhood. Just as he himself remains, as he says, "a poetic melancholic, crossed with a vivid materialistic lust of life." In one place religion is only "religionism," a contemptible yet hated deception; and then again the spell laid on his early years reasserts itself, and at the end of the story you might suppose that his deepest sympathy was with the self-sacrificing minister of the Gospel who befriends the condemned murderer, and with the poor mother on whose face was written the "fighting faith in the wisdom and mercy of the definite overruling and watchful and merciful power" of God.

I lay down Mr. Dreiser's novel with a feeling that it is an American tragedy in a sense never intended by him when he chose that title. If only he knew the finer aspects of life as he knows its shabby underside; if only his imagination had been trained in the larger tradition of literature instead of getting its bent from the police court and the dregs of science; if only religion had appeared to him in other garb than the travesty of superstition and faded fanaticism; if only he had had a chance, he might possibly have produced that fabulous thing, the great American novel. As it is he has brought forth a *monstrum informe cui lumen ademptum.*

Though the work of Mr. Dreiser is the conspicuous phenomenon of the noisy realism that has invaded our literature, the honour of starting the school, if honour it may be called, belongs rather to Edgar Lee Masters, whose *Spoon River Anthology* first stripped the veils of decency from existence in a Mid-Western town. The book was in its way a notable achievement; but the unfailing dullness of Mr. Masters' subsequent productions shows that the *Anthology* was at best only a malodorous flash in the pan. Then came the *Main Street* of Sinclair Lewis, which, so to speak, wove a long novel out

of the lives of the mean people whose virulent epitaphs Mr.
Masters had composed. If popularity were the test, *Main
Street* might dispute with *An American Tragedy* the place of
pre-eminence in the school; at least I found two years ago that
it had penetrated England and that about every man I met
there was curious to know whether it gave a true picture of
our democracy. But I suspect that *Main Street* owed its vogue
in part to its title, which is a veritable stroke of genius, and
in part to its flattery of those who like to believe that, whatever their sins, they are better folk than the dull hypocrites
who grovel and boast in so typical a community as Gopher
Prairie (*alias* Sauk Center or any other town in which one of
our realists may have been born). Otherwise it is hard to account for the success of so monotonous a tale written in so
drab and drizzling a style. One might feel there was something wholesome in this satirical treatment of the very sources
of realism, were it only possible to discover anywhere in the
pages of Mr. Lewis—or in those of Mr. Masters for that matter—an indication that the author himself had risen more than
an inch above the æsthetic and ethical level of the people he
insults.

If Mr. Dreiser has any rival to the throne, it is Sherwood
Anderson, a realist also after a fashion, but one in whose brain
the solid facts of life have an odd way of dissolving before
your very eye into the clouds of dreamland. And here again
the author's most significant work seems to me to be in the
autobiographical record of his own childhood and youth (told
with a good deal of *Dichtung* interspersed), and in his tales of
Winesburg, Ohio, which reproduce the atmosphere of a town
like one of those in which he grew up. Again we are brought
close to the cradle of our realistic movement. As for the quality of these books, particularly of *A Story Teller's Story,* I
think Gertrude Stein, that adventuress into the lunar mad-
nesses of literary cubism, might have had them in mind when
she described her own method of composition: "In these two
books there was elaboration of the complexities of using everything and of a continuous present and of beginning again and
again and again." Some of Miss Stein's reviewers have laughed

at her notion of a continuous present, but they might see it exemplified well enough in Mr. Anderson. Certainly he has the trick of beginning again and again and again, and of mixing the past and the present into a kind of unprogressive circulation. He starts to narrate some incident, and forthwith a host of memories from the past are conjured up; what he is describing we behold as a fixed object seen at intervals through floating masses of mist. One gets the impression of a physiological cause at work; as if the writing had been done in that state between waking and sleeping induced by a low fever, when the mind goes round and round in a kind of timeless suspense, and we do not know whether we are living in the past or the present. Something of the same sort may be said of the sex-obsession in Mr. Anderson's novels which offends so many readers not otherwise squeamish. At the core I should say there was something wholesome and clean in the author's attitude towards these matters, expressed, as he puts it rather bluntly, in the desire of a man to have "his woman," his own mate to go with him through the lonely adventures of life; but the idea is lost, and seen, and lost again in a drift of morbid fancies and unclean images that float up unsummoned, and unrestrained, from the submerged depths of his nature. To peruse Mr. Anderson is to be reminded of Plato's account of the appetites that sometimes awake in a man when he falls asleep, and the wild beast within him, freed from the control of reason, goes forth to commit him to all kinds of follies and shameful deeds from which in his waking moments he would shrink in abhorrence. It is not such a sleep that sets loose in Mr. Anderson's mind these prurient fancies that the normal man holds in abeyance, but a kind of low vitality, a sickly feverishness of the imagination. In his healthier moments he shows a vein of genuine and idyllic poetry which might have been developed to almost any extent; he is not without wise notions of living; he has a hearty distaste for the shiftlessness and disorder and dirt which plagued his own steps; he knows that "it is the impotent man who is vile"; he sees that the problem for the worker today is "to reach down through all the broken surface distractions of modern life to the old love of craft out of which culture springs." There was the stuff of a good artist in Mr. Anderson; the pity of it is that, through indulgence encouraged by evil communications, there has come about an almost complete impotence to check the flood of animal suggestions from his subconscious-self; some of his later books are a painful illustration of what "the stream of consciousness" means when it is allowed to grow putrid.

In the end an unprejudiced critic of these men is likely to be divided between indignation at so much perversity and a feeling of pity that so much talent and earnestness should be expended upon the making of books, no one of which, despite their present fame, is likely to be remembered twenty years from now, or in fact has any claim to be called literature at all. There are, as I have tried to show, various causes contributing to this failure, among them sheer ignorance; but the deepest and most universal cause of all is that strange theory which, after many wanderings to and fro, has just reached these western shores, the theory that there are no moral laws governing life, or that, if such laws are, they have no jurisdiction in the artistic representation of life. For it really is an extraordinary theory if you consider its implications, and, when held with the childlike simplicity of the newly enlightened, leads to about as distorting results in literature as would befall a scientist who set out to experiment under the belief that there were no physical laws. For the moral law of character Mr. Cabell undertakes to substitute an æsthetic philosophy of beauty; but so far as I can fathom his ambiguities, he has only one thesis serviceable to art, viz., that the pursuit of perfect beauty leads in the end to inevitable disillusion and disappointment,—not a very original thesis nor capable of a very wide application. Meanwhile his human actors have about as much depth as the dolls which children cut out of paper and bedeck with fantastic names. How could it be otherwise when he has denied the validity of the laws that shape our destiny and control the deeper sources of emotion? On the other side Mr. Dreiser, so far at least as his creative instinct does not break through his parochial theory of art, simply reproduces the surface of life as he has seen it, with no attempt to reorganize it artistically or to interpret its larger significance. He does not create characters, he does not create anything; he merely extends the front page of the newspaper to the volume of a book, rarely venturing to go beyond the training he received as a reporter. And he reaps his reward; for he gives the great mob of readers—shop girls and tired clerks and thoughtless boys riding back and forth to business —exactly what they want and can understand, not literature which requires for its appreciation an intellectual readjustment, but a sensational dressing up of the world they know.

So much for what would commonly be regarded as the modern and really vital current in American literature today. It makes rather a sad story in the telling, and, taken alone, would give a hopeless notion of the intellectual state of the country. Fortunately it is not the whole story. Besides the poets and novelists, competent craftsmen some of them, who are pursuing the more beaten track, and whom for that reason I have passed by in this article, there are a few writers who, while not modern in the popular sense of the word, are doing altogether the most original and aggressive work we can show to the world,—a work more noteworthy, I make bold to say, than anything of its kind now done in England and equal to anything produced in France. I refer to the little group of critics of life and letters scattered over the land, who have set their faces against the all-invading currents of irresponsible half-thinking, and, with full knowledge of what has been thought and done in the past, are trying to lay the foundations of a new humanism for the present. Of these the outstanding figure is Irving Babbitt, of Harvard, perhaps our most powerful intellect, as he is certainly the most virile personality, in the whole realm of criticism and scholarship. He is also one of the few Americans who have made themselves felt in France, and quite recently was elected a corresponding member of the Institut. Others who are contributing to the same salutary end, and whom I can only name, are F. J. Mather, of Princeton, primarily an authority in the history of painting but an incorruptible champion of good taste in other fields as well; P. H. Frye, of the University of Nebraska, author among other books of a volume of essays on *Romance and Tragedy* which contains the most penetrating study of the ethical basis of Greek drama known to me in any language; S. B. Gass, also of Nebraska, whose *Lover of the Chair* is replete with mellow wisdom on the central problems of education and life and art; and, among the younger men, Robert Shafer, of Cincinnati, whose *Christianity and Naturalism* is in itself a considerable achievement in philosophic criticism, and holds the promise of better things to come.

It will be observed that all these writers—and I could name three or four others of the same class—hold academic positions. The only exception to this rule would be W. C. Brownell, the honoured doyen of our letters, a thoroughbred New Yorker, who is affiliated with no college and proves, against all presumption to the contrary, that something intellectually fine can come out of our Babylon on the Hudson. For one who believes, as I do, that the difficulties now confronting civilization, if solution there be, must be solved by education, it is encouraging to run down this list of college men who are at once successful teachers and sound thinkers and forcible writers. The discouraging aspect of the situation is that the universities as institutions are doing so little to help. If these scholars were publishing in any European country they would be widely read and discussed, and would have weight as forming a united phalanx arrayed against the forces of disorganization. Here they are dispersed over thousands of miles of area, isolated in depressing loneliness, and barely heard amid the hubbub of the pedants on the one side and the illiterates on the other side. One of them produces a book which ought to bring him recognition as a leader of public opinion, and what is the result? In most cases there is no result; nothing happens; voices calling in the desert. Ask the first scholar or supposedly cultured reader what he thinks, let us say, of Professor Frye's *Romance and Tragedy* or Professor Gass's *Lover of the Chair*, and the probable answer will be that he has never so much as heard the name of either of them. This lamentable condition is owing in part to the very size of the country and to its lack of any recognized centre of culture, of any true capital such as London or Paris. But it is just here that our institutions of learning are failing us. I think of the possible consequences if any one of our major universities had the foresight and courage to gather into its faculty such a group of men as I have mentioned. Each would be fortified and comforted by the others, and together they would make such a push as would be felt from the Atlantic to the Pacific. Nor is this a counsel of perfection; within measure it might easily be effected.

The sad truth is that the English departments of our colleges, from whom such an impulse of organization ought to proceed, are not only irresponsive to their opportunity, but are unsympathetic, too often even antipathetic, to the kind of discipline that would produce and hold such men. They want experts in Anglo-Saxon and Mediæval French and Chaucerian bibliography, or in the name of literature they admit a makeshift of romantic æstheticism; while in the path of any student who turns aside from the narrow line prescribed for the doctor of philosophy to acquire a broad education and a sound understanding of life they place almost insurmountable obstacles. Thus the field at large is left open to the unleavened impudence of noise, and the critical ideas of the immature and ignorant are formed by brawling vulgarians like H. L. Mencken.

Yet withal there are wholesome signs of rebellion among the younger students, indications that the benumbing reign of pedantry may be broken, and that in the next generation our colleges may awaken to their duty of providing what above all else American literature needs,—the discipline of a classical humanism, which will train the imagination in loyalty to the great traditions, while cherishing the liberty to think and the power to create without succumbing to the seductions of the market-place or the gutter.

Tradition and the Individual Talent

T. S. ELIOT

I

IN ENGLISH WRITING we seldom speak of tradition, though we occasionally apply its name in deploring its absence. We cannot refer to "the tradition" or to "a tradition"; at most, we employ the adjective in saying that the poetry of So-and-so is "traditional" or even "too traditional." Seldom, perhaps, does the word appear except in a phrase of censure. If otherwise, it is vaguely approbative, with the implication, as to the work approved, of some pleasing archaeological reconstruction. You can hardly make the word agreeable to English ears without this comfortable reference to the reassuring science of archaeology.

Certainly the word is not likely to appear in our appreciations of living or dead writers. Every nation, every race, has not only its own creative, but its own critical turn of mind; and is even more oblivious of the shortcomings and limitations of its critical habits than of those of its creative genius. We know, or think we know, from the enormous mass of critical writing that has appeared in the French language the critical method or habit of the French; we only conclude (we are such unconscious people) that the French are "more critical" than we, and sometimes even plume ourselves a little with the fact, as if the French were the less spontaneous. Perhaps they are; but we might remind ourselves that criticism is as inevitable as breathing, and that we should be none the worse for articulating what passes in our minds when we read a book and feel an emotion about it, for criticizing our own minds in their work of criticism. One of the facts that might come to light in this process is our tendency to insist, when we praise a poet, upon those aspects of his work in which he least resembles anyone else.

In these aspects or parts of his work we pretend to find what is individual, what is the peculiar essence of the man. We dwell with satisfaction upon the poet's difference from his predecessors, especially his immediate predecessors; we endeavour to find something that can be isolated in order to to be enjoyed. Whereas if we approach a poet without his prejudice we shall often find that not only the best, but the most individual parts of his work may be those in which the dead poets, his ancestors, assert their immortality most vigorously. And I do not mean the impressionable period of adolescence, but the period of full maturity.

Yet if the only form of tradition, of handing down, con- sisted in following the ways of the immediate generation before us in a blind or timid adherence to its successes, "tradition" should positively be discouraged. We have seen many such simple currents soon lost in the sand; and novelty is better than repetition. Tradition is a matter of much wider significance. It cannot be inherited, and if you want it you must obtain it by great labour. It involves, in the first place, the historical sense, which we may call nearly indispensable to anyone who would continue to be a poet beyond his twenty-fifth year; and the historical sense involves a percep- tion, not only of the pastness of the past, but of its presence; the historical sense compels a man to write not merely with his own generation in his bones, but with a feeling that the whole of the literature of Europe from Homer and within it the whole of the literature of his own country has a simultaneous existence and composes a simultaneous order. This historical sense, which is a sense of the timeless as well as of the temporal and of the timeless and of the temporal together, is what makes a writer traditional. And it is at the same time what makes a writer most acutely conscious of his place in time, of his contemporaneity.

No poet, no artist of any art, has his complete meaning alone. His significance, his appreciation is the appreciation of his relation to the dead poets and artists. You cannot value him alone; you must set him, for contrast and comparison, among the dead. I mean this as a principle of aesthetic, not merely historical, criticism. The necessity that he shall conform, that he shall cohere, is not one-sided; what happens when a new work of art is created is something that happens simultaneously to all the works of art which preceded it. The existing monuments form an ideal order among themselves, which is modified by the introduction of the new (the really new) work of art among them. The existing order is complete before the new work arrives; for order to persist after the supervention of novelty, the *whole* existing order must be, if ever so slightly, altered; and so the relations, proportions, values of each work of art toward the whole are readjusted; and this is conformity between the old and the new. Whoever has approved this idea of order, of the form of European, of English literature, will not find it preposterous that the past should be altered by the present as much as the present is directed by the past. And the poet who is aware of this will be aware of great difficulties and responsibilities.

In a peculiar sense he will be aware also that he must inevitably be judged by the standards of the past. I say judged, not amputated, by them; not judged to be as good as, or worse or better than, the dead; and certainly not judged by the canons of dead critics. It is a judgment, a comparison, in which two things are measured by each other. To conform merely would be for the new work not really to conform at all; it would not be new, and would therefore not be a work of art. And we do not quite say that the new is more valuable because it fits in; but its fitting in is a test of its value—a test, it is true, which can only be slowly and cautiously applied, for we are none of us infallible judges of conformity. We say: it appears to conform, and is perhaps individual, or it appears individual, and may conform; but we are hardly likely to find that it is one and not the other.

To proceed to a more intelligible exposition of the relation of the poet to the past: he can neither take the past as a lump, an indiscriminate bolus, nor can he form himself wholly on one or two private admirations, nor can he form himself wholly upon one preferred period. The first course is inadmissible, the second is an important experience of youth, and the third is a pleasant and highly desirable supplement. The poet must be very conscious of the main current, which does not at all flow invariably through the most distinguished reputations. He must be quite aware of the obvious fact that art never improves, but that the material of art is never quite the same. He must be aware that the mind of Europe—the mind of his own country—a mind which he learns in time to be much more important than his own private mind—is a mind which changes, and that this change is a development which abandons nothing *en route*, which does not superannuate either Shakespeare, or Homer, or the rock drawing of the Magdalenian draughtsmen. That this development, refinement perhaps, complication certainly, is not, from the point of view of the artist, any improvement. Perhaps not even an improvement from the point of view of the psychologist or not to the extent which we imagine; perhaps only in the end based upon a complication in economics and machinery. But the difference between the present and the past is that the conscious present is an awareness of the past in a way and to an extent which the past's awareness of itself cannot show.

Some one said: "The dead writers are remote from us because we *know* so much more than they did." Precisely, and they are that which we know.

I am alive to a usual objection to what is clearly part of my programme for the *métier* of poetry. The objection is that the doctrine requires a ridiculous amount of erudition (pedantry), a claim which can be rejected by appeal to the lives of poets in any pantheon. It will even be affirmed that much learning deadens or perverts poetic sensibility. While, however, we persist in believing that a poet ought to know as much as will not encroach upon his necessary receptivity and necessary laziness, it is not desirable to confine knowledge to whatever can be put into a useful shape for examinations,

drawing-rooms, or the still more pretentious modes of pub-
licity. Some can absorb knowledge, the more tardy must
sweat for it. Shakespeare acquired more essential history from
Plutarch than most men could from the whole British Museum. What is to be insisted upon is that the poet must develop or procure the consciousness of the past and that he
should continue to develop this consciousness throughout his
career.

What happens is a continual surrender of himself as he is
at the moment to something which is more valuable. The
progress of an artist is a continual self-sacrifice, a continual
extinction of personality.

There remains to define this process of depersonalization
and its relation to the sense of tradition. It is in this depersonalization that art may be said to approach the condition of
science. I shall, therefore, invite you to consider, as a sug-
gestive analogy, the action which takes place when a bit of
finely filiated platinum is introduced into a chamber containing oxygen and sulphur dioxide.

II

Honest criticism and sensitive appreciation is directed not
upon the poet but upon the poetry. If we attend to the confused cries of the newspaper critics and the susurrus of popular repetition that follows, we shall hear the names of poets
in great numbers; if we seek not Blue-book knowledge but
the enjoyment of poetry, and ask for a poem, we shall seldom
find it. In the last article I tried to point out the importance
of the relation of the poem to other poems by other authors,
and suggested the conception of poetry as a living whole of
all the poetry that has ever been written. The other aspect of
this Impersonal theory of poetry is the relation of the poem
to its author. And I hinted, by an analogy, that the mind of
the mature poet differs from that of the immature one not precisely in any valuation of "personality," not being necessarily
more interesting, or having "more to say," but rather by being

a more finely perfected medium in which special, or very varied, feelings are at liberty to enter into new combinations.

The analogy was that of the catalyst. When the two gases previously mentioned are mixed in the presence of a filament of platinum, they form sulphurous acid. This combination takes place only if the platinum is present; nevertheless the newly formed acid contains no trace of platinum, and the platinum itself is apparently unaffected; has remained inert, neutral, and unchanged. The mind of the poet is the shred of platinum. It may partly or exclusively operate upon the experience of the man himself; but, the more perfect the artist, the more completely separate in him will be the man who suffers and the mind which creates; the more perfectly will the mind digest and transmute the passions which are its material.

The experience, you will notice, the elements which enter the presence of the transforming catalyst, are of two kinds: emotions and feelings. The effect of a work of art upon the person who enjoys it is an experience different in kind from any experience not of art. It may be formed out of one emotion, or may be a combination of several; and various feelings, inhering for the writer in particular words or phrases or images, may be added to compose the final result. Or great poetry may be made without the direct use of any emotion whatever: composed out of feelings solely. Canto xv of the *Inferno* (Brunetto Latini) is a working up of the emotion evident in the situation; but the effect, though single as that of any work of art, is obtained by considerable complexity of detail. The last quatrain gives an image, a feeling attaching to an image, which "came," which did not develop simply out of what precedes, but which was probably in suspension in the poet's mind until the proper combination arrived for it to add itself to. The poet's mind is in fact a receptacle for seizing and storing up numberless feelings, phrases, images, which remain there until all the particles which can unite to form a new compound are present together.

If you compare several representative passages of the greatest poetry you see how great is the variety of types of combination, and also how completely any semi-ethical criterion of "sublimity" misses the mark. For it is not the "greatness," the intensity, of the emotions, the components, but the intensity of the artistic process, the pressure, so to speak, under which the fusion takes place, that counts. The episode of Paolo and Francesca employs a definite emotion, but the intensity of the poetry is something quite different from whatever intensity in the supposed experience it may give the impression of. It is no more intense, furthermore, than Canto XXVI, the voyage of Ulysses, which has not the direct dependence upon an emotion. Great variety is possible in the process of transmutation of emotion: the murder of Agamemnon, or the agony of Othello, gives an artistic effect apparently closer to a possible original than the scenes from Dante. In the *Agamemnon,* the artistic emotion approximates to the emotion of an actual spectator; in *Othello* to the emotion of the protagonist himself. But the difference between art and the event is always absolute; the combination which is the murder of Agamemnon is probably as complex as that which is the voyage of Ulysses. In either case there has been a fusion of elements. The ode of Keats contains a number of feelings which have nothing particular to do with the nightingale, but which the nightingale, partly, perhaps, because of its attractive name, and partly because of its reputation, served to bring together.

The point of view which I am struggling to attack is perhaps related to the metaphysical theory of the substantial unity of the soul: for my meaning is, that the poet has, not a "personality" to express, but a particular medium, which is only a medium and not a personality, in which impressions and experiences combine in peculiar and unexpected ways. Impressions and experiences which are important for the man may take no place in the poetry, and those which become important in the poetry may play quite a negligible part in the man, the personality.

I will quote a passage which is unfamiliar enough to be regarded with fresh attention in the light—or darkness—of these observations:

> And now methinks I could e'en chide myself
> For doating on her beauty, though her death
> Shall be revenged after no common action.
> Does the silkworm expend her yellow labours
> For thee? For thee does she undo herself?
> Are lordships sold to maintain ladyships
> For the poor benefit of a bewildering minute?
> Why does yon fellow falsify highways,
> And put his life between the judge's lips,
> To refine such a thing—keeps horse and men
> To beat their valours for her? . . .

In this passage (as is evident if it is taken in its context) there is a combination of positive and negative emotions: an intensely strong attraction toward beauty and an equally intense fascination by the ugliness which is contrasted with it and which destroys it. This balance of contrasted emotion is in the dramatic situation to which the speech is pertinent, but that situation alone is inadequate to it. This is, so to speak, the structural emotion, provided by the drama. But the whole effect, the dominant tone, is due to the fact that a number of floating feelings, having an affinity to this emotion by no means superficially evident, have combined with it to give us a new art emotion.

It is not in his personal emotions, the emotions provoked by particular events in his life, that the poet is in any way remarkable or interesting. His particular emotions may be simple, or crude, or flat. The emotion in his poetry will be a very complex thing, but not with the complexity of the emotions of people who have very complex or unusual emotions in life. One error, in fact, of eccentricity in poetry is to seek for new human emotions to express; and in this search for novelty in the wrong place it discovers the perverse. The business of the poet is not to find new emotions, but to use the ordinary ones and, in working them up into poetry, to express feelings which are not in actual emotions at all. And emotions which he has never experienced will serve his turn as well as those familiar to him. Consequently, we must believe that "emotion recollected in tranquillity" is an inexact formula. For it is neither emotion, nor recollection, nor, without distortion of meaning, tranquillity. It is a concentration, and a new thing resulting from the concentration, of a very great number of experiences which to the practical and active person would not seem to be experiences at all; it is a concentration which does not happen consciously or of deliberation. These experiences are not "recollected," and they finally unite in an atmosphere which is "tranquil" only in that it is a passive attending upon the event. Of course this is not quite the whole story. There is a great deal, in the writing of poetry, which must be conscious and deliberate. In fact, the bad poet is usually unconscious where he ought to be conscious, and conscious where he ought to be unconscious. Both errors tend to make him "personal." Poetry is not a turning loose of emotion, but an escape from emotion; it is not the expression of personality, but an escape from personality. But, of course, only those who have personality and emotions know what it means to want to escape from these things.

III

ὁ δὲ νοῦ, ἴσω, θειότερόν τι χαὶ ἀπαθές ἐστιν

This essay proposes to halt at the frontier of metaphysics or mysticism, and confine itself to such practical conclusions as can be applied by the responsible person interested in poetry. To divert interest from the poet to the poetry is a laudable aim: for it would conduce to a juster estimation of actual poetry, good and bad. There are many people who appreciate the expression of sincere emotion in verse, and there is a smaller number of people who can appreciate technical excellence. But very few know when there is expression of *significant* emotion, emotion which has its life in the poem and not in the history of the poet. The emotion of art is impersonal. And the poet cannot reach this impersonality without surrendering himself wholly to the work to be done. And he is not likely to know what is to be done unless he lives in what is not merely the present, but the present moment of the past, unless he is conscious, not of what is dead, but of what is already living.

Techniques of Fiction

ALLEN TATE

THERE MUST BE many techniques of fiction, but how many?
I suppose a great many more than there are techniques of
poetry. Why this should be so, if it is, nobody quite knows,
and if we knew, I do not know what use the knowledge would
have. For the great disadvantage of all literary criticism is its
practical ignorance, which in the very nature of its aims must
be incurable. Even the aims of criticism are unknown, beyond
very short views; for example, in the criticism of the novel,
Mr. Percy Lubbock tells us that the secret of the art is the
strategy of "point of view"; Mr. E. M. Forster that the novelist
must simply give us "life," or the illusion of "bouncing" us
through it—which looks like a broader view than Mr. Lubbock's, until we pause to examine it, when it turns out to be
worse than narrow, since to look at everything is to see nothing; or again Mr. Edwin Muir holds that "structure" is the key
to the novelist's success or failure. There is no need here to
explain what these critics mean by "point of view," or "life,"
or "structure"; but they all mean something useful—in a short
view, beyond which (I repeat) critics seem to know little or
nothing.

What the novelists know may be another thing altogether,
and it is that knowledge which ought to be our deepest concern. You will have to allow me the paradox of presuming to
know what the novelists know—or some of them at any rate—
while as a critic I profess to know nothing. The presumption
might encourage us to predict from the very nature of the
critic's ignorance the nature and quality of the knowledge
possible to good writers of fiction. The novelist keeps before
him constantly the structure and substance of his fiction as a
whole, to a degree to which the critic can never apprehend it.
For the first cause of critical ignorance is, of course, the limita-

tions of our minds, about which we can do little, work at them as we will. It is the special ignorance by which we, as critics, are limited in the act of reading any extended work of the imagination. The imaginative work must always differ to such a great degree as almost to differ in kind from philosophical works, which our minds apprehend and retain almost as wholes through the logical and deductive structures which powerfully aid the memory. Who can remember, well enough to pronounce upon it critically, all of *War and Peace,* or *The Wings of the Dove,* or even *Death in Venice,* the small enclosed world of which ought at least to do something to aid our memories? I have reread all three of these books in the past year; yet for the life of me I could not pretend to know them as wholes, and without that knowledge I lack the materials of criticism.

Because Mr. Lubbock seems to know more than anybody else about this necessary ignorance of the critic, and for other important reasons, I believe him to be the best critic who has ever written about the novel. His book, *The Craft of Fiction,* is very nearly a model of critical procedure. Even in so fine a study as Albert Thibaudet's *Gustave Flaubert* there is nothing like the actual, as opposed to the merely professed, critical modesty of numerous statements like this by Lubbock: "Our critical faculty may be admirable; we may be thoroughly capable of judging a book justly, if only we could watch it at ease. But fine taste and keen perception are of no use to us if we cannot retain the image of the book; and the image escapes and evades us like a cloud." Where, then, does Lubbock get the material of his criticism? He gets as much of it as any critic ever gets by means of a bias which he constantly pushes in the direction of extreme simplification of the novel in terms of "form," or "point of view" (after James's more famous phrase, the "post of observation"), or more generally in terms of the controlling intelligence which determines the range and quality of the scene and the action. It is the only book on fiction which has earned unanimous dislike among other critics (I do not know three novelists who have read it), and the reason, I think, is that it is, in its limited terms, wholly successful; or, if that is too great praise, it is successful in the same sense, and to no less degree than the famous lecture notes on the Greek drama taken down by an anonymous student at the Lyceum in the fourth century B.C. The lecture notes and *The Craft of Fiction* are studies of their respective arts in terms of form; and I think that Lubbock had incomparably the more difficult job to do. The novel has at no time enjoyed anything like the number and the intensity of objective conventions which the drama, even in its comparatively formless periods, has offered to the critic. The number of techniques possible in the novel are probably as many as its conventions are few.

Having said so much in praise of Mr. Lubbock, I shall not, I hope, seem to take it back if I say that even his intense awareness of what the novelist knows fails somehow, or perhaps inevitably, to get into his criticism. Anybody who has just read his account of *Madame Bovary* comes away with a sense of loss, which is the more intense if he has also just read that novel; though what the loss is he no more than Mr. Lubbock will be able to say. Yet no critic has ever turned so many different lights, from so many different directions, upon any other novel (except perhaps the lights that are called today the social and the historical); and yet what we get is not properly a revelation of the techniques of *Madame Bovary* but rather what I should call a marvelously astute chart of the operations of the central intelligence which binds all the pieces of drama together into the pictorial biography of a silly, sad, and hysterical little woman, Emma Bovary. It is this single interest, this undeviating pursuit of one great clue, this sticking to the "short view" till the last horn blows and night settles upon the hunting field, which largely explains both the greatness of Mr. Lubbock's book and the necessary and radical, except in so far as knowledge of the world, of ideas, and of man generally is broadening; but then that knowledge has nothing to do specifically with the critical job; it only keeps it from being inhuman. That is something; but it is not criticism. To be critical is to be narrow in the crucial act or process of judgment.

But after we gather up all the short views of good critics, and have set the limits to their various ignorances, we are confronted with what is left out or, if you will, left over: I have a strong suspicion that this residue of the novel or the story is what the author knew as he wrote it. It is what makes the little scenes, or even the big ones, "come off." And while we no doubt learn a great deal about them when, with Mr. Muir, we study the general structure, or the relation of scenes, or, with Mr. Lubbock, follow the godlike control of the mind of Flaubert or of James through all the scenes to the climax— while this knowledge is indispensable, I should, myself, like to know more about the making of the single scene, and all the techniques that contribute to it; and I suspect that I am not asking the impossible, for this kind of knowledge is very likely the only kind that is actually within our range. It alone can be got at, definitely and at particular moments, even after we have failed, with Mr. Lubbock (honorable failure indeed), to "retain the image of the book."

It sounds very simple, as no doubt it is essentially a simple task to take a scene from a novel apart, and to see what makes it tick; but how to do it must baffle our best intentions. Suppose you want to understand by what arts Tolstoy, near the beginning of *War and Peace*, before the ground is laid, brings Peter, the bastard son of old Count Bezuhov, into the old Count's dying presence, and makes, of the atmosphere of the house and of the young man and the old man, both hitherto unknown to us, one of the great scenes of fiction: you would scarcely know better than I where to take hold of it, and I have only the merest clue. Suppose you feel, as I do, that after Rawdon Crawley comes home (I believe from jail—it is hard to remember Thackeray) and finds Becky supping alone with Lord Steyne—suppose you feel that Thackeray should not have rung down the curtain the very moment Becky's exposure was achieved, but should have faced up to the tougher job of showing us Becky and Rawdon alone after Lord Steyne had departed: Is this a failure in a great novelist? If it is, why? The negative question, addressed to ourselves as persons interested in the techniques of an art, may also lead us to what the novelists know, or to much the same thing, what they should have known. And, to come nearer home, what is the matter with Ty Ty Walden's philosophical meditations, towards the end of *God's Little Acre,* which freezes up our credulity and provokes our fiercest denial? It is surely not that Ty Ty is merely expressing as well as he can the doctrine of the innate goodness of man in the midst of depravity. That doctrine will do as well as any other in the mouth of a fictional character provided his scene and his experience within the scene entitle him to utter it; but before we can believe that Ty Ty is actually thinking anything whatever, we have got in the first place to believe that Ty Ty is a man—which is precisely what Mr. Caldwell evidently did not think it important to make us do.

How shall we learn what to say about particular effects of the story, without which the great over-all structure and movement of the human experience which is the entire novel cannot be made credible to us? The professional critics pause only at intervals to descend to these minor effects which are of course the problems without which the other, more portentous problems which engage criticism could not exist. The fine artists of fiction, I repeat, because they produce these effects must understand them. And having produced them, they are silent about the ways they took to produce them, or paradoxical and mysterious like Flaubert, who told Maupassant to go to the station and look at the cab-drivers until he understood the typical cab-driver, and then to find the language to distinguish one cab-driver from all others in the world. It is the sort of *obiter dicta* which can found schools and movements, and the schools and movements often come to some good, even though the slogan, like this one, means little.

I suppose only the better novelists, like Defoe, Madame de La Fayette, Turgenev, Dickens, Flaubert, many others as great as these, some greater, like Tolstoy and Dostoevsky, knew the special secrets which I am trying, outside criticism, so to speak, to bring before you. There is almost a masonic tradition in the rise of any major art, from its undifferentiated social beginnings to the conscious aptitude which is the sign of a developed art form. Doubtless I ought to repeat once more that for some reason the moment the secrets of this aptitude come within the *provenance* of formal criticism, they vanish. They survive in the works themselves, and in the living confraternity of men of letters, who pass on by personal instruction to their successors the "tricks of the trade." The only man I have known in some twenty years of literary experience who was at once a great novelist and a great teacher, in this special sense, was the late Ford Madox Ford. His influence was immense, even upon writers who did not know him, even upon other writers, today, who have not read him. For it was through him more than any other man writing in English in our time that the great traditions of the novel came down to us. Joyce, a greater writer than Ford, represents by comparison a more restricted practice of the same literary tradition, a tradition that goes back to Stendhal in France, and to Jane Austen in England, coming down to us through Flaubert, James, Conrad, Joyce, Virginia Woolf and Ernest Hemingway.

It is a tradition which has its own secrets to offer; yet in saying that I am not claiming for it greater novelists than some other school can produce or novelists greater than those who just happen. There is Meredith (for those who, like Ramon Fernandez, can read him); there is Thomas Hardy, there is even the early H. G. Wells. But there is not Arnold Bennett; there is not John Galsworthy; not Hugh Walpole nor Frank Swinnerton. This is prejudice, not criticism. And these are all Britons, not Americans. I have no desire to play 'possum on the American question. Yet I am convinced that among American novelists who have had large publics since the last war, only Dreiser, Faulkner, and Hemingway are of major importance. There are "good" popular novelists who have done much to make us at home physically in our own country; they have given us our scenes, our people, and above all our history; and these were necessary to the preliminary knowledge of ourselves which we have been a little late in getting and which must be got and assimilated if we are going to be a mature people. Possibly the American novel had to

accomplish the task that in Europe had been done by primitive chronicle, mémoire, ballad, strolling player. The American novel has had to find a new experience, and only in our
time has it been able to pause for the difficult task of finding
out how to get itself written. That is an old story with us, yet
beneath it lies a complexity of feeling that from Hawthorne
down to our time has baffled our best understanding. The illustration is infinite in its variety. At this moment I think of my
two favorite historians, Herodotus and Joinville, and I am
embarrassed from time to time because Herodotus, the pagan,
seems nearer to my experience than Joinville, the Christian
chronicler of St. Louis. It is perhaps easier for us to feel comfortable with the remote and relatively neutral elements of
our culture. Those experiences of Europe which just precede
or overlap the American experience bemuse us, and introduce
a sort of chemical ambivalence into our judgment. Joinville is
both nearer to me than Herodotus, and less immediate. What
American could not be brought to confess a similar paradox?
To our European friends who are now beginning to know us,
and who in all innocence may subscribe to the popular convention of The Simple American Mind, I would say, if it is
not too impolite: Beware.

But the American novel is not my present subject, nor,
thank heaven, the American mind. My subject is merely the
technique of fiction which now at last I feel that I am ready
to talk about, not critically, you understand, but as a member
of a guild. Ford used to say that he wrote his novels in the
tone of one English gentleman whispering into the ear of
another English gentleman: how much irony he intended I
never knew; I hope a great deal. I intend none at all when I
say that these remarks are set down by an artisan for other
artisans.

Gustave Flaubert created the modern novel. Gustave Flaubert created the modern short story. He created both because
he created modern fiction. I am not prepared to say that he
created all our fictional forms and structures, the phases of
the art of fiction that interest Mr. Lubbock and Mr. Muir. He
did not originate all those features of the short story which

interest historians and anthologists. These are other matters
altogether. And I do not like to think that Flaubert created
modern fiction because I do not like Flaubert. It was the
fashion in France, I believe, until the Fall, to put Stendhal
above Flaubert. I am not sure but I suspect that a very tired
generation felt more at ease with a great writer whose typical
heroes are persons of mere energy and whose books achieve
whatever clarity and form that they do achieve as an accident
of the moral ferocity of the author. But without *Le Rouge et
Le Noir*, or without what it put into circulation in French
literary *milieu* after 1830, Flaubert could not have written
Madame Bovary. I do not like to think that Stendhal did this
because I do not like Stendhal. Both Stendhal and Flaubert
had the single dedication to art which makes the disagreeable
man. Doubtless it would be pleasanter if the great literary discoveries could be made by gentlemen like Henry James, who
did make his share, and who, of course, was a greater novelist
than either of these Frenchmen; or by English squires; but we
have got to take them, as Henry James would not do in the
instance of Flaubert, as they come, and they often come a
little rough.

A moment ago I introduced certain aspersions upon a few
English novelists of the recent past, but it was with a purpose,
for their limitations, sharply perceived by the late Virginia
Woolf in her famous essay *Mr. Bennett and Mrs. Brown*, will
make quite clear the difference between the novelist who,
with Mr. Forster, merely bounces us along and the novelist
who tries to do the whole job, the job that Flaubert first taught
him to do. Mrs. Woolf is discussing Hilda Lessways, Arnold
Bennett's heroine, and she says:

> But we cannot hear her mother's voice, or Hilda's voice;
> we can only hear Mr. Bennett's voice telling us facts about
> rents and freeholds and copyholds and fines. What can Mr.
> Bennett be about? I have formed my own opinion of what
> Mr. Bennett is about—he is trying to make us imagine for
> him. . . .

"Trying to make us imagine for him"—the phrase erects a

Chinese wall between all that is easy, pleasant, and perhaps merely socially useful in modern fiction, and all that is rigorous, sober, and self-contained. Mrs. Woolf, again, in speaking of the novels of Galsworthy, Bennett and Wells, says: "Yet what odd books they are! Sometimes I wonder if we are right to call them books at all. For they leave one with a strange feeling of incompleteness and dissatisfaction. In order to complete them it seems necessary to do something—to join a society, or, more desperately, to write a cheque."

That is very nearly the whole story: the novelist who tries to make us imagine for him is perhaps trying to make us write a check—a very good thing to do, and I am not sure that even the socially unconscious Flaubert was deeply opposed to it, though I shall not attempt to speak to him on the question of joining societies. Let us see this matter as reasonably as we can. All literature has a social or moral or religious purpose: the writer has something that he has got to say to the largest public possible. In spite of Flaubert's belief that he wrote only for himself, this is as true of *Madame Bovary* as of *Uncle Tom's Cabin*. Is there a real difference between these books that might justify us in setting apart two orders of literature? Perhaps; for the difference is very great between getting it all inside the book and leaving some of it irresponsibly outside. For even though the check be written in a good cause it is the result of an irresponsible demand upon the part of the novelist. But the distinction is not, I think, absolute, nor should it be. And I am sure that Sainte-Beuve was right when he wrote in his review of *Madame Bovary* that not all young married women in Normandy were like Emma: was there not the case of the childless young matron of central France who, instead of taking lovers and then taking arsenic, "adopted children about her . . . and instructed them in moral culture"? Very good; for it is obvious that persons who join societies and write checks for moral culture are proper characters of fiction, as indeed all human beings of all degrees of charity or misanthropy are. But that is not the point at issue.

That point is quite simply that Flaubert, for the first time consciously and systematically, but not for the first time in the history of fiction, and not certainly of poetry—Flaubert taught us how to put this overworked and allegorical check *into* the novel, into its complex texture of scene, character and action: which, of course, is one way of saying that he did the complete imaginative job himself, and did not merely point to what was going on, leaving the imaginative specification to our good will or to our intellectual vanity. (I pause here to remark the existence of a perpetual type of critic who prefers inferior literature, because it permits him to complete it. Flaubert understood the critics who, committed to the public function of teacher, resent being taught.) This completeness of presentation in the art of fiction was not, I repeat, something new, but I gather that it had previously appeared only here and there, by the sheer accident of genius: I think of Petronius; a few incidents in Boccaccio; half a dozen scenes by the Duke of Saint-Simon (the memorialists shade imperceptibly into the novelists); the great scene in which the Prince de Clèves tells his wife that he has refrained from expressing his love for her because he wished to avoid conduct improper to a husband; Emma Woodhouse with Mr. Knightly at the parlor table looking at the picture-album; countless other moments in early prose literature; but most of all that great forerunner, *Moll Flanders,* which is so much all of a . piece in the Flaubertian canon that sometimes I think that Flaubert wrote it; or that nobody wrote either Defoe or Flaubert. For when literature reaches this stage of maturity, it is anonymous, and it matters little who writes it.

This is extravagant language. Or is it? It is no more than we are accustomed to when we talk about poetry, or music, or most of all the classical drama. The fourth-century lecture notes, to which I have already referred, some time ago licensed the most pretentious claims for the stage, and for poetry generally. I am only saying that fiction can be, has been, and *is* an art, as the various poetries are arts. Is this an extravagant claim? Only, I am convinced, in the minds of the more relaxed practitioners of this art, who excuse something less than the utmost talent and effort, and in the minds of critics who find the critical task more exacting than historical reporting, which reduces the novel to a news supplement. Was, as a matter of fact, Emma typical of young Norman womanhood? Are the Okies and Arkies just as Steinbeck represents them? What a triumph for the historians when it was found that there had actually been a young man whose end was like Julien Sorel's! And is it true what Mr. Faulkner says about Dixie? If it is, is what Mr. Stark Young says also true? This, I submit, is the temper of American criticism of fiction, with rare exceptions of little influence.

It is time now, towards the end of this *causerie*, to produce an image, an *exemplum*, something out of the art of fiction that underlies all the major problems of "picture and drama," symmetry, foreshortening, narrative pattern, pace and language—all those complexities of the novelist's art which Henry James, alone of the great fictionists, tried to explain (how much he coyly evaded!) in his famous Prefaces: problems that laid the ground for Mr. Lubbock's beautiful study. I am looking for something very simple and, in its direct impact, conclusive; a scene or an incident that achieves fullness of realization in terms of what it gives us to see and to hear. It must offer us fullness of rendition, not mere direction or statement. Don't state, says James, time and again—render! Don't tell us what is happening, let it happen! So I would translate James. For our purposes here it cannot be too great a scene, if we would see all round it: it must be a scene that will give us the most elementary instruction in that branch of the art of which the critics tell us little. What shall it be? Shall it be Prince André lying wounded under the wide heavens? Shall it be Moll Flanders peeping out of the upstairs window of the inn at her vanishing fourth (or is it fifth?) and undivorced husband, slyly avoiding him because she is in the room with her fifth or is it sixth? I could find perfect *exempla* in James himself. What could be better than Milly Theale's last soirée before she becomes too ill to appear again? Then there are James's fine "sitting-room scenes," the man and the woman talking out the destiny of one or both of them: Lambert Strether and Maria Gostrey, John Marcher and May Bartram, Merton Densher and Milly Theale. Or there is Strether looking down upon the boat in which Chad Newsome and Madame de Vionnet, unaware of Strether's scrutiny, betray that air of intimacy which discloses them for the first time to Strether as lovers.

Yet about these excellent scenes there is something outside our purpose, a clue that would sidetrack us into the terms of form and structure which I have virtually promised to neglect. Let us select an easy and perhaps even quite vulgar scene, a stock scene, in fact, that we should expect to find in a common romantic novel, or even in a Gothic story provided the setting were reduced to the bourgeois scale. Let the situation be something like this: A pretty young married woman, bored with her husband, a small-town doctor, has had an affair of sentiment with a young man, who has by this time left town. Growing more desperate, she permits herself to be seduced by a neighboring landowner, a coarse Lothario, who soon tires of her. Our scene opens with the receipt of his letter of desertion. He is going away and will not see her again. The young woman receives the letter with agitation and runs upstairs to the attic, where having read the letter she gives way to hysteria. She looks out the window down into the street, and decides to jump and end it all. But she grows dizzy and recoils. After a moment she hears her husband's voice; the servant touches her arm; she comes to and recovers.

It is distinctly unpromising: James would not have touched it; Balzac, going the whole hog, might have let her jump, or perhaps left her poised for the jump while he resumed the adventures of Vautrin. But in any case there she stands, and as I have reported the scene you have got to take my word for it that she is there at all: you do not see her, you do not hear the rapid breathing and the beating heart, and you have, again, only my word for it that she is dizzy. What I have done here, in fact, is precisely what Mrs. Woolf accused the Georgian novelists of doing: I am trying to make you imagine for me, perhaps even covertly trying to make you write a check for the Society for the Improvement of Provincial Culture, or the Society for the Relief of Small Town Boredom, or for a subscription to the Book-of-the-Month Club which would no doubt keep the young woman at improving her mind, and her mind off undesirable lovers. I hope that we shall do all these good things. But you must bear in mind that the Book-of-the-Month Club would probably send her the kind of literature that I have just written for you, so that she too might take to writing checks. Is there any guarantee that they would be good checks? The question brings us up short against certain permanent disabilities of human nature, which we should do well to see as objectively as possible, in the language of a greater artist; which is just what we shall now proceed to do:

Charles was there; she saw him; he spoke to her; she heard nothing, and she went on quickly up the stairs, breathless, distraught, dumb, and ever holding this horrible piece of paper, that crackled between her fingers like a plate of sheet-iron. On the second floor she stopped before the attic-door, that was closed.

Then she tried to calm herself; she recalled the letter; she must finish it; she did not dare to. And where? How? She would be seen! "Ah, no! here," she thought, "I shall be all right."

Emma pushed open the door and went in.

The slates threw straight down a heavy heat that gripped her temples, stifled her; she dragged herself to the closed garret-window. She drew back the bolt, and the dazzling light burst in with a leap.

Opposite, beyond the roofs, stretched the open country till it was lost to sight. Down below, underneath her, the village square was empty; the stones of the pavement glittered, the weathercocks on the houses were motionless. At the corner of the street from a lower story, rose a kind of humming with strident modulations. It was Binet turning.

She leant against the embrasure of the window, and re-read the letter with angry sneers. But the more she fixed her attention upon it, the more confused were her ideas. She saw him again, heard him, encircled him with her arms, and the throbs of her heart, that beat against her breast like blows of a sledge-hammer, grew faster and faster, with uneven intervals. She looked about her with the wish that

the earth might crumble into pieces. Why not end it all?
What restrained her? She was free. She advanced, looked at
the paving-stones, saying to herself, "Come! Come!"

The luminous ray that came straight up from below
drew the weight of her body towards the abyss. It seemed
to her that the floor dipped on end like a tossing boat. She
was right at the edge, almost hanging, surrounded by vast
space. The blue of the heavens suffused her, the air was
whirling in her hollow head; she had but to yield, to let herself be taken; and the humming of the lathe never ceased,
like an angry voice calling her.

"Emma! Emma!" cried Charles.

She stopped.

"Wherever are you? Come!"

The thought that she had just escaped from death made
her faint with terror. She closed her eyes; then she shivered
at the touch of a hand on her sleeve; it was Félicité.

"Master is waiting for you, madame; the soup is on the
table."

And she had to go down to sit at table.

The English translation is not good; its failure to convey
the very slight elevation of tone is a fundamental failure. It is
not a rhetorical elevation, but rather one of perfect formality
and sobriety. We are not looking at this scene through Emma's eyes. We occupy a position slightly above and to one
side, where we see her against the full setting; yet observe
that at the same time we see nothing that she does not see,
hear nothing that she does not hear. It is one of the amazing
paradoxes of the modern novel, whose great subject is a man
alone in society or even against society, almost never with
society, that out of this view of man isolated we see developed
to the highest possible point of virtuosity and power a technique of putting man wholly into his physical setting. The
action is not stated from the point of view of the author; it is
rendered in terms of situation and scene. To have made this
the viable property of the art of fiction was to have virtually
made the art of fiction. And that, I think, is our debt to
Flaubert.

But we should linger over this scene if only to try our hands at what I shall now, for the first time, call sub-criticism, or the animal tact which permits us occasionally to see connections and correspondences which our rational powers, unaided, cannot detect. What capital feature of the scene seems (if it does) to render the actuality more than any other? The great fact, I think, is the actuality, and your sense of it is all that is necessary. Yet I like to linger over the whirring lathe of old Binet, a lay figure or "flat character" who has done little in the novel and will never do much, and whose lathe we merely noted from the beginning as a common feature of a small town like Yonville. I should like to know when Flaubert gave him the lathe, whether just to tag him for us; whether, writing the present scene, he went back and gave it to him as a "plant" for use here later; or whether, having given him the lathe, he decided it would be useful in this scene.

What is its use? James said that the work of fiction must be "a direct impression of life," a very general requirement; but in the perspective of nearly ninety years since the publication of *Madame Bovary* and the rise of the Impressionist novel through Henry James, James Joyce, and Virginia Woolf, the phrase takes on a more specific sense. Mind you the phrase is not "direct representation," which only the stage can give us. But here, using this mechanic's tool, Flaubert gives us a direct *impression* of Emma's sensation at a particular moment (which not even the drama could accomplish), and thus by rendering audible to us what Emma alone could hear he charged the entire scene with actuality. As Emma goes to the window she merely notes that Binet's lathe is turning—*C'était Binet qui tournait*. Then she looks down at the street which seems to rise towards her—*Allons! Allons!* she whispers, because she cannot find the will to jump. We have had rendered to us visually the shock of violent suicide. Now comes the subtle fusion of the reaction and of the pull toward self-destruction, which is the humming in her head: how can Flaubert *render* it for us? Shall we not have to take his word for it? Shall we not have to imagine for him? No: *l'air circulait dans sa tête creuse*, he says; and then: *le ronflement du tour ne discontinuait pas, comme une voix furieuse qui l'appelait*

—"the whirring of the lathe never stopped like a voice of fury calling her." The humming vertigo that draws the street towards her is rendered audible to us by the correlative sound of the lathe.

That is all, or nearly all, there is to it; but I think it is enough to set up our image, our *exemplum*. I leave to you, as I constantly reserve for myself, the inexhaustible pleasure of tracing out the infinite strands of interconnection in this and other novels, complexities as deep as life itself but ordered, fixed, and dramatized into arrested action. If I have made too much of Flaubert, or too much of too little of Flaubert, I can only say that I have not willfully ignored men as great or greater. It is proper to honor France, and to honor the *trouvère,* the discoverer; for it has been through Flaubert that the novel has at last caught up with poetry.

The Waste Land:
Critique of the Myth

CLEANTH BROOKS

To VENTURE to write anything further on *The Waste Land*, particularly after the work of F. R. Leavis and F. O. Matthiessen, may call for some explanation and even apology. I am obviously indebted to both critics. The justification for such a commentary as this must be made primarily in terms of a difference of intention. Leavis is interested predominantly in Eliot's method of organization. One or two passages in the poem are treated in detail and are highly valuable for a knowledge of the "meaning" of the poem, but the bulk of the poem does not receive this kind of examination. Moreover, I believe, Leavis makes some positive errors. Matthiessen examines more of the poem in detail, and, as far as it goes, his account is excellent. But the plan of his *Achievement of T. S. Eliot* does not allow for a consecutive examination either. He puts his finger on the basic theme, death-in-life, but I do not think that he has given it all the salience which it deserves.

I prefer not to raise here the question of how important it is for the reader of the poem to have an explicit intellectual account of the various symbols, and a logical account of their relationships. It may well be that such rationalization is no more than a scaffolding to be got out of the way before we contemplate the poem itself as a poem. But many readers (including myself) find the erection of such a scaffolding valuable—if not absolutely necessary—and if some readers will be tempted to lay more stress on the scaffolding than they properly should, there are perhaps still more readers who will be prevented from getting at the poem at all without the help of such a scaffolding. Furthermore, an interest attaches to Mr. Eliot's own mental processes, and whereas Mr. Matthiessen has quite properly warned us that Eliot's poetry cannot be read as autobiography, many of the symbols and ideas which occur in *The Waste Land* are ideas which are definitely central to Eliot's general intellectual position.

The basic symbol used, that of the waste land, is taken, of course, from Miss Jessie Weston's *From Ritual to Romance*. In the legends which she treats there, the land has been blighted by a curse. The crops do not grow, and the animals cannot reproduce. The plight of the land is summed up by, and connected with, the plight of the lord of the land, the Fisher King, who has been rendered impotent by maiming or sickness. The curse can only be removed by the appearance of a knight who will ask the meanings of the various symbols which are displayed to him in the castle. The shift in meaning from physical to spiritual sterility is easily made, and was, as a matter of fact, made in certain of the legends. A knowledge of this symbolism is, as Eliot has already pointed out, essential for an understanding of the poem.

Of hardly less importance to the reader, however, is a knowledge of Eliot's basic method. *The Waste Land* is built on a major contrast—a device which is a favorite of Eliot's and to be found in many of his poems, particularly his later poems. The contrast is between two kinds of life and two kinds of death. Life devoid of meaning is death; sacrifice, even the sacrificial death, may be life-giving, an awakening to life. The poem occupies itself to a great extent with this paradox, and with a number of variations on it.

Eliot has stated the matter quite explicitly himself in one of his essays. In his "Baudelaire" he says:

> One aphorism which has been especially noticed is the following: *la volupté unique et suprême de l' amour gît dans la certitude de faire le mal*. This means, I think, that Baudelaire has perceived that what distinguishes the relations of man and woman from the copulation of beasts is the knowledge of Good and Evil (of *moral* Good and Evil which are not natural Good and Bad or puritan Right and Wrong). Having an imperfect, vague romantic conception of Good, he was at least able to understand that the sexual act as evil is more dignified, less boring than as the natural, "life-giving," cheery automatism of the modern world. . . .

So far as we are human, what we do must be either evil or good; so far as we do evil or good, we are human; and it is better, in a paradoxical way, to do evil than to do nothing: at least, *we exist* [italics mine].

The last statement is highly important for an understanding of *The Waste Land.* The fact that men have lost the knowledge of good and evil keeps them from being alive, and is the justification for viewing the modern waste land as a realm in which people do not even exist.

This theme is stated in the quotation which prefaces the poem. The Sybil says: "I wish to die." Her statement has several possible interpretations. For one thing, she is saying what the people who inhabit the waste land are saying. But she also may be saying what the speaker says in *The Journey of the Magi,* . . . "this Birth was/Hard and bitter agony for us, like Death, our death/ . . . I should be glad of another death."

I

The first section of "The Burial of the Dead" develops the theme of the attractiveness of death, or of the difficulty in rousing oneself from the death in life in which the people of the waste land live. Men are afraid to live in reality. April, the month of rebirth, is not the most joyful season but the cruellest. Winter at least kept us warm in forgetful snow. The idea is one which Eliot has stressed elsewhere. Earlier in *Gerontion* he had written

> In the juvescence of the year
> Came Christ the tiger
>
> .   .   .   .   .   .
>
> The tiger springs in the new year. Us he devours.

More lately, in *Murder in the Cathedral,* he has the chorus say

> We do not wish anything to happen.
> Seven years we have lived quietly,
> Succeeded in avoiding notice,
> Living and partly living.

And in another passage: "Now I fear disturbance of the quiet seasons." Men dislike to be aroused from their death-in-life.

The first part of "The Burial of the Dead" introduces this theme through a sort of reverie on the part of the protagonist —a reverie in which speculation on life glides off into memory of an actual conversation in the Hofgarten and back into speculation again. The function of the conversation is to establish to some extent the class and character of the protagonist. The reverie is resumed with line 19.

> What are the roots that clutch, what branches grow
> Out of this stony rubbish?

The protagonist answers for himself:

>   Son of man,
> You cannot say, or guess, for you know only
> A heap of broken images, where the sun beats,
> And the dead tree gives no shelter, the cricket no relief,
> And the dry stone no sound of water.

In this passage there are references to Ezekiel and to Ecclesiastes, and these references indicate what it is that men no longer know: the passage referred to in Ezekiel ii pictures a world thoroughly secularized:

> 1. And he said unto me, Son of man, stand upon thy feet, and I will speak unto thee. 2. And the spirit entered into me when he spake unto me, and set me upon my feet, that I heard him that spake unto me. 3. And he said unto me, Son of man, I send thee to the children of Israel, to a rebellious nation that hath rebelled against me: they and their fathers have transgressed against me, even unto this very day.

The following passage from Ecclesiastes xii is not only referred to in this passage; a reference to it also is evidently made in the nightmare vision of Section V of the poem:

> 1. Remember now thy Creator in the days of thy youth, while the evil days come not, nor the years draw nigh, when thou shalt say, I have no pleasure in them; 2. While the sun, or the light, or the moon, or the stars, be not darkened, nor the clouds return after the rain: 3. In the day when the

keepers of the house shall tremble, and the strong men shall bow themselves, and the grinders cease because they are few, and those that look out of the windows be darkened, 4. And the doors shall be shut in the streets, when the sound of the grinding is low, and he shall rise up at the voice of the bird, and all the daughters of musick shall be brought low; 5. Also when they shall be afraid of that which is high, and fears shall be in the way, and the almond tree shall flourish, and the grasshopper shall be a burden, *and desire shall fail* [italics mine]: because man goeth to his long home, and the mourners go about the streets: 6. Or ever the silver cord be loosed, or the golden bowl be broken, or the pitcher be broken at the fountain, or the wheel broken at the cistern. 7. Then shall the dust return to the earth as it was: and the spirit shall return unto God who gave it. 8. Vanity of vanities, saith the preacher; all is vanity.

The next section which begins with the scrap of song quoted from Wagner (perhaps another item in the reverie of the pro-tagonist) states the opposite half of the paradox which under-lies the poem: namely, that life at its highest moments of meaning and intensity resembles death. The song from Act I of Wagner's *Tristan und Isolde*, "*Frisch weht der Wind,*" is sung in the opera by a young sailor aboard the ship which is bringing Isolde to Cornwall. The "*Irisch Kind*" of the song does not properly apply to Isolde at all. The song is merely one of happy and naïve love. It brings to the mind of the protagonist an experience of love—the vision of the hyacinth girl as she came back from the hyacinth garden. The poet says

> . . . my eyes failed, I was neither
> Living nor dead, and I knew nothing,
> Looking into the heart of light, the silence.

The line which immediately follows this passage, "*Oed' und leer das Meer,*" seems at first to be simply an extension of the last figure: that is, "Empty and wide the sea [of silence]." The line, however, as a matter of fact, makes an ironic con-trast; for the line as it occurs in Act III of the opera is the reply of the watcher who reports to the wounded Tristan that Isolde's ship is nowhere in sight; the sea is empty. And,

though the *"Irisch Kind"* of the first quotation is not Isolde, the
reader familiar with the opera will apply it to Isolde when he
comes to the line *"Oed' und leer das Meer."* For the question
in the song is in essence Tristan's question in Act III: "My
Irish child, where dwellest thou?" The two quotations from
the opera which frame the ecstasy-of-love passage thus take
on a new meaning in the altered context. In the first, love is
happy: the boat rushes on with a fair wind behind it. In the
second, love is absent; the sea is wide and empty. And the
last quotation reminds us that even love cannot exist in the
waste land.

The next passage, that in which Madame Sosostris figures,
calls for further reference to Miss Weston's book. As Miss
Weston has shown, the Tarot cards were originally used to
determine the event of the highest importance to the people,
the rising of the waters. Madame Sosostris has fallen a long
way from the high function of her predecessors. She is engaged merely in vulgar fortune-telling—is merely one item in
a generally vulgar civilization. But the symbols of the Tarot
pack are still unchanged. The various characters are still in-
scribed on the cards, and she is reading in reality, though she
does not know it, the fortune of the protagonist. She finds
that his card is that of the drowned Phoenician Sailor, and so
she warns him against death by water, not realizing any more
than do the other inhabitants of the modern waste land that
the way into life may be by death itself. The drowned Phoenician Sailor is a type of the fertility god whose image was
thrown into the sea annually as a symbol of the death of summer. As for the other figures in the pack: Belladonna, the
Lady of the Rocks, is woman in the waste land. The man with
three staves, Eliot says he associates rather arbitrarily with
the Fisher King. The term "arbitrarily" indicates that we are
not to attempt to find a logical connection here.

The Hanged Man, who represents the hanged god of
Frazer (including the Christ), Eliot states in a note, is associated with the hooded figure who appears in "What the
Thunder Said." That he is hooded accounts for Madame Sosostris' inability to see him; or rather, here again the palaver

of the modern fortune-teller is turned to new and important account by the poet's shifting the matter into a new and serious context. The Wheel and the one-eyed merchant will be discussed later.

After the Madame Sosostris passage, Eliot proceeds to complicate his symbols for the sterility and unreality of the modern waste land by associating it with Baudelaire's *fourmillante cité* and with Dante's Limbo. The passages already quoted from Eliot's essay on Baudelaire will indicate one of the reasons why Baudelaire's lines are evoked here. In Baudelaire's city, dream and reality seem to mix, and it is interesting that Eliot in *The Hollow Men* refers to this same realm of death-in-life as "death's dream kingdom" in contradistinction to "death's other kingdom."

The references to Dante are most important. The line, "I had not thought death had undone so many," is taken from the Third Canto of the *Inferno;* the line, "Sighs, short and infrequent, were exhaled," from the Fourth Canto. Mr. Matthiessen has already pointed out that the Third Canto deals with Dante's Limbo which is occupied by those who on earth had "lived without praise or blame." They share this abode with the angels, "Who were not rebels, nor were faithful to God, but were for themselves." They exemplify almost perfectly the secular attitude which dominates the modern world. Their grief, according to Dante, arises from the fact that they "have no hope of death; and their blind life is so debased, that they are envious of every other lot." But though they may not hope for death, Dante calls them "these wretches who never were alive." The people who are treated in the Fourth Canto are those who lived virtuously but who died before the proclamation of the Gospel—they are the unbaptized. This completes the categories of people who inhabit the modern waste land: those who are secularized and those who have no knowledge of the faith. Without a faith their life is in reality a death. To repeat the sentence from Eliot previously quoted: "So far as we do evil or good, we are human; and it is better, in a paradoxical way, to do evil than to do nothing: at least, we exist."

The Dante and Baudelaire references, then, come to the

same thing as the allusion to the waste land of the medieval legends; and these various allusions drawn from widely differing sources enrich the comment on the modern city so that it becomes "unreal" on a number of levels: as seen through "the brown fog of a winter dawn"; as the medieval waste land and Dante's Limbo and Baudelaire's Paris are unreal.

The reference to Stetson stresses again the connection between the modern London of the poem and Dante's hell. After the statement, "I could never have believed death had undone so many," follow the words "After I had distinguished some among them, I saw and knew the shade of him who made, through cowardice, the great refusal." The protagonist, like Dante, sees among the inhabitants of the contemporary waste land one whom he recognizes. (The name "Stetson" I take to have no ulterior significance. It is merely an ordinary name such as might be borne by the friend one might see in a crowd in a great city.) Mylae, as Mr. Matthiessen has pointed out to us, is the name of a battle between the Romans and the Carthaginians in the Punic War. The Punic War was a trade war—might be considered a rather close parallel to the war of 1914-18. At any rate, it is plain that Eliot in having the protagonist address the friend in a London street as one who was with him in the Punic War rather than as one who was with him in the World War is making the point that all the wars are one war; all experience, one experience. As Eliot put the idea in *Murder in the Cathedral:*

> We do not know very much of the future
> Except that from generation to generation
> The same things happen again and again.

I am not sure that Leavis and Matthiessen are correct in inferring that the line, "That corpse you planted last year in your garden," refers to the attempt to bury a memory. But whether or not this is true, the line certainly refers also to the buried god of the old fertility rites. It also is to be linked with the earlier passage—"What are the roots that clutch, what branches grow," etc. This allusion to the buried god will account for the ironical, almost taunting tone of the passage.

The burial of the dead is now a sterile planting—without hope. But the advice to "keep the Dog far hence," in spite of the tone, is, I believe, well taken and serious. The passage in Webster goes as follows

> O keep the wolf far hence, that's foe to men,
> Or with his nails he'll dig it up again.

Why does Eliot turn the wolf into a dog? And why does he reverse the point of importance from the animal's normal hostility to men to its friendliness? If, as some critics have suggested, he is merely interested in making a reference to Webster's darkest play, why alter the line? I am inclined to take the Dog (the capital letter is Eliot's) as Humanitarianism and the related philosophies which in their concern for man extirpate the supernatural—dig up the corpse of the buried god and thus prevent the rebirth of life. For the general idea, see Eliot's essay, "The Humanism of Irving Babbitt."

The last line of "The Burial of the Dead"—"You! hypocrite lecteur!—mon semblable,—mon frère!"—the quotation from Baudelaire, completes the universalization of Stetson begun by the reference to Mylae. Stetson is every man, including the reader and Mr. Eliot himself.

II

If "The Burial of the Dead" gives the general abstract statement on the situation, the second part of *The Waste Land,* "A Game of Chess," gives a more concrete illustration. The easiest contrast in this section—and one which may easily blind the casual reader to a continued emphasis on the contrast between the two kinds of life, or the two kinds of death, already commented on—is the contrast between life in a rich and magnificent setting, and life in the low and vulgar setting of a London pub. But both scenes, however antithetical they may appear superficially, are scenes taken from the contemporary waste land. In both of them life has lost its meaning.

I am particularly indebted to Mr. Allen Tate's brilliant comment on the first part of this section. To quote from him, "the woman . . . is, I believe, the symbol of man at the present time. He is surrounded by the grandeurs of the past, but he does not participate in them; they don't sustain him." And to quote from another section of his commentary: "The rich experience of the great tradition depicted in the room receives a violent shock in contrast with a game that symbolizes the inhuman abstraction of the modern mind." Life has no meaning; history has no meaning; there is no answer to the question: "What shall we ever do?" The only thing that has meaning is the abstract game which they are to play, a game in which the meaning is assigned and arbitrary, meaning by convention only—in short, a game of chess.

This interpretation will account in part for the pointed reference to Cleopatra in the first lines of the section. But there is, I believe, a further reason for the poet's having compared the lady to Cleopatra. The queen in Shakespeare's drama—"Age cannot wither her, nor custom stale/Her infinite variety"— is perhaps the extreme exponent of love for love's sake—the feminine member of the pair of lovers who threw away an empire for love. But the infinite variety of the life of the woman in "A Game of Chess" *has* been staled. There is indeed no variety at all, and love simply does not exist. The function of the sudden change in the description of the carvings and paintings in the room from the heroic and magnificent to the characterization of the rest of them as "other withered stumps of time" is obvious. But the reference to Philomela is particularly important, for Philomela, it seems to me, is one of the major symbols of the poem.

Miss Weston points out that a section of one of the Grail manuscripts, which is apparently intended as a gloss of the Grail story, tells how the court of the rich Fisher King was withdrawn from the knowledge of men when certain of the maidens who frequented the shrine were raped and had their golden cups taken from them. The curse on the land follows from this act. Miss Weston conjectures that this may be a statement, in the form of parable, of the violation of the older mysteries which were probably once celebrated openly, but were later forced underground into secrecy. Whether or not Mr. Eliot intends a reference to this passage, the violation of a woman makes a very good symbol of the process of secularization. John Crowe Ransom makes the point very neatly for us in his *God Without Thunder*. Love is the aesthetic of sex; lust is the science. Love implies a deferring of the satisfaction of the desire; it implies even a certain asceticism and a ritual. Lust drives forward urgently and scientifically to the immediate extirpation of the desire. Our contemporary waste land is in a large part the result of our scientific attitude—of our complete secularization. Needless to say, lust defeats its own ends. The portrayal of "The change of Philomel, by the barbarous king" is a fitting commentary on the scene which it ornaments. The waste land of the legend came in this way— the modern waste land has come in this way.

That this view is not mere fine-spun ingenuity is borne out somewhat by the change of tense which Eliot employs here and which Mr. Edmund Wilson has commented upon: "And still she cried, and still the world pursues." Apparently the "world" partakes in the barbarous king's action, and still partakes in that action.

To "dirty ears" the nightingale's song is not that which filled all the desert with inviolable voice—it is "jug, jug." Edmund Wilson has pointed out that the rendition of the bird's song here represents not merely the Elizabethan neutral notation of the bird's song, but carries associations of the ugly and coarse. The passage is therefore one of many instances of Eliot's device of using something which in one context is innocent but in another context becomes loaded with a special meaning.

The Philomela passage has another importance, however. If it is a commentary on how the waste land became waste, it also repeats the theme of the death which is the door to life —the theme of the dying god. The raped woman becomes transformed through suffering into the nightingale; through the violation comes the "inviolable voice." The thesis that suffering is action, and that out of suffering comes poetry is a favorite one of Eliot's. For example, "Shakespeare, too, was occupied with the struggle—which alone constitutes life for a poet—to transmute his personal and private agonies into something rich and strange, something universal and impersonal." Consider also his statement with reference to Baudelaire: "Indeed, in his way of suffering is already a kind of presence of the supernatural and of the superhuman. He rejects always the purely natural and the purely human; in other words, he is neither 'naturalist' nor 'humanist.' " The theme of the life which is death is stated specifically in the conversation between the man and the woman. She asks the question "Are you alive, or not?" and this time we are sufficiently prepared by the Dante references in "The Burial of the Dead" for the statement here to bear a special meaning. (She also asks "Is there nothing in your head?" He is one of the Hollow Men—"headpiece stuffed with straw.") These people, as people in the waste land, know nothing, see nothing, do not even live.

But the protagonist, after this reflection that in the waste land of modern life even death is sterile—"I think we are in rats' alley/Where the dead men lost their bones"—remembers a death which was not sterile, remembers a death that was transformed into something rich and strange, the death described in the song from *The Tempest*—"Those are pearls that were his eyes."

The reference to this section of *The Tempest* is, like the Philomela reference, one of Eliot's major symbols. We are to meet it twice more, in later sections of the poem. Some more general comment on it is therefore appropriate here. The song, one remembers, was sung by Ariel in luring Ferdinand, Prince of Naples, on to meet Miranda, and thus to find love, and through this love, to effect the regeneration and deliverance of all the people on the island. Ferdinand says of the song.

> The ditty doth remember my drowned father.
> This is no mortal business, nor no sound
> That the earth owes. . . .

The allusion is an extremely interesting example of the device of Eliot's already commented upon, that of taking an item from one context and shifting it into another in which it assumes a new and powerful meaning. This description of a death which is a portal into a realm of the rich and strange—a death which becomes a sort of birth—assumes in the mind of the protagonist an association with that of the drowned god whose effigy was thrown into the water as a symbol of the death of the fruitful powers of nature but which was taken out of the water as a symbol of the revivified god. (See *From Ritual to Romance*.) The passage therefore represents the perfect antithesis to the passage in "The Burial of the Dead": "That corpse you planted last year in your garden," etc. It also, as we have already pointed out, finds its antithesis in the sterile and unfruitful death "in rats' alley" just commented upon. (We shall find that this contrast between the death in rats' alley and the death in *The Tempest* is made again in "The Fire Sermon.")

We have yet to treat the relation of the title of the section, "A Game of Chess," to Middleton's play, *Women Beware Women*, from which the game of chess is taken. In the play, the game is used as a device to keep the widow occupied while her daughter-in-law is being seduced. The seduction amounts almost to a rape, and in a *double entendre* the rape is actually described in terms of the game. We have one more connection with the Philomela symbol therefore. The abstract game is being used in the contemporary waste land, as in the play, to cover up a rape and is a description of the rape itself.

In the second part of "A Game of Chess" we are given a picture of spiritual emptiness, but this time, at the other end of the social scale, as reflected in the talk between two cockney women in a London pub. The account here is straightforward enough and the only matter which calls for comment is the line spoken by Ophelia in *Hamlet* which ends the passage. Ophelia, too, was very much concerned about love, the theme of conversation of the two ladies. As a matter of fact, she was in very much the same position as that of the woman who has been the topic of conversation between the two good ladies we have just heard. She had remarked too once that

> Young men will do't, if they come to't!
> By cock, they are to blame.

And her poetry (including the line quoted from her here), like Philomela's, had come out of suffering. I think that we are probably to look for the relevance of the allusion to her in some such matter as this rather than in an easy satiric contrast between Elizabethan glories and modern sordidness. After all (in spite of the Marxists) Eliot's objection to the present world is not merely the sentimental one that this happens to be the twentieth century after Christ and not the seventeenth.

III

"The Fire Sermon" makes much use of several of the symbols already developed. The fire is the sterile burning of lust, and the section is a sermon, although a sermon by example only. This section of the poem also contains some of the most easily apprehended uses of literary allusion. The poem opens on a vision of the modern river. In Spenser's *Prothalamion* the scene described is also a river scene at London, and it is dominated by nymphs and their paramours, and the nymphs are preparing for a bridal. The contrast between Spenser's scene and its twentieth-century equivalent is jarring. The paramours are now "the loitering heirs of city directors," and, as for the bridals of Spenser's Elizabethan maidens, in the stanzas which follow we learn a great deal about those. At the end of the section the speech of the third of the Thames-nymphs summarizes the whole matter for us.

The waters of the Thames are also associated with those of Leman—the poet in the contemporary waste land is in a sort of Babylonian Captivity.

The castle of the Fisher King was always located on the banks of a river or on the sea shore. The title "Fisher King," Miss Weston shows, originates from the use of the fish as a fertility or life symbol. This meaning, however, was often forgotten, and so the title in many of the later Grail romances is accounted for by describing the king as fishing. Eliot uses the reference to fishing for reverse effect. The reference to fishing is part of the realistic detail of the scene—"While I was fishing in the dull canal." But to the reader who knows the Weston references, the reference is to that of the Fisher King of the Grail legends. The protagonist is the maimed and impotent king of the legends.

Eliot proceeds now to tie the waste-land symbol to that of *The Tempest,* by quoting one of the lines spoken by Ferdinand, Prince of Naples, which occurs just before Ariel's song, "Full Fathom Five," is heard. But he alters the passage from *The Tempest* somewhat, writing not, "Weeping again the king my father's wreck," but

> Musing upon the king my brother's wreck
> And on the king my father's death before him.

It is possible that the alteration has been made to bring the account taken from *The Tempest* into accord with the situation in the Percival stories. In Wolfram von Eschenbach's *Parzival,* for instance, Trevrezent, the hermit, is the brother of the Fisher King, Anfortas. He tells Parzival, "His name all men know as Anfortas, and I weep for him evermore." Their father, Frimutel, is, of course, dead.

The protagonist in the poem, then, imagines himself not only in the situation of Ferdinand in *The Tempest* but also in that of one of the characters in the Grail legend; and the wreck, to be applied literally in the first instance, applies metaphorically in the second.

After the lines from *The Tempest* appears again the image of a sterile death from which no life comes, the bones, "rattled by the rat's foot only, year to year." (The collocation of this figure with the vision of the death by water in Ariel's song has already been commented on. The lines quoted from *The Tempest* come just before the song.)

The allusion to Marvell's *To His Coy Mistress* is of course one of the easiest allusions in the poem. Instead of "Time's winged chariot" the poet hears "the sound of horns and motors" of contemporary London. But the passage has been further complicated. The reference has been combined with an allusion to Day's *Parliament of Bees*. "Time's winged chariot" of Marvell has not only been changed to the modern automobile; Day's "sound of horns and hunting" has changed to the horns of the motors. And Actaeon will not be brought face to face with Diana, goddess of chastity; Sweeney, type of the vulgar bourgeois, is to be brought to Mrs. Porter, hardly a type of chastity. The reference in the ballad to the feet "washed in soda water" reminds the poet ironically of another sort of foot-washing, the sound of the children singing in the dome heard at the ceremony of the foot-washing which precedes the restoration of the wounded Anfortas (the Fisher King) by Parzival and the taking away of the curse from the waste land. The quotation thus completes the allusion to the Fisher King commenced in line 189—"While I was fishing in the dull canal."

The pure song of the children also reminds the poet of the song of the nightingale which we have heard in "The Game of Chess." The recapitulation of symbols is continued with a repetition of "Unreal city" and with the reference to the one-eyed merchant.

Mr. Eugenides, the Smyrna merchant, is the one-eyed merchant mentioned by Madame Sosostris. The fact that the merchant is one-eyed apparently means in Madame Sosostris's speech no more than that the merchant's face on the card is shown in profile. But Eliot applies the term to Mr. Eugenides for a totally different effect. The defect corresponds somewhat to Madame Sosostris's bad cold. The Syrian merchants, we learn from Miss Weston's book, were, with slaves and soldiers, the principal carriers of the mysteries which lie at the core of the Grail legends. But in the modern world we find both the representatives of the Tarot divining and the mystery cults in decay. What he carries on his back and what the fortune-teller was forbidden to see is evidently the knowledge of the mysteries (although Mr. Eugenides himself is hardly likely to be more aware of it than Madame Sosostris is aware of the importance of her function). Mr. Eugenides, in terms of his former function, ought to be inviting the protagonist to an initiation into the esoteric cult which holds the secret of life, but on the realistic surface of the poem, in his invitation to "a weekend at the Metropole" he is really inviting him to a homosexual debauch. The homosexuality is "secret" and now a "cult," but a very different cult from that which Mr. Eugenides ought to represent. The end of the new cult is not life but, ironically, sterility.

In the modern waste land, however, even the relation between man and woman is also sterile. The incident between the typist and the carbuncular young man is a picture of "love" so exclusively and practically pursued that it is not love at all. The scene, as Allen Tate puts it, is one of our most terrible insights into Western civilization. The tragic chorus to the scene is Tiresias, into whom perhaps Mr. Eugenides may be said to modulate, Tiresias, the historical "expert" on the relation between the sexes.

The allusions to Sappho's lines and to Goldsmith's made in this passage need little comment. The hour of evening, which in Sappho's poem brings rest to all and brings the sailor home, brings the typist to her travesty of home—"On the divan . . . at night her bed"—and brings the carbuncular young man, the meeting with whom ends not in peace but in sterile burning.

The reminiscence of the lines from Goldsmith's song in the description of the young woman's actions after the departure of her lover gives concretely and ironically the utter breakdown of traditional standards.

It is the music of her gramophone which the protagonist hears "creep by" him "upon the waters." Far from the music which Ferdinand heard bringing him to Miranda and love, it is, one is tempted to think, the music of "O O O O that Shakespeherian Rag" of "A Game of Chess."

But the protagonist says that he *sometimes* hears "The pleasant whining of a mandoline." Significantly enough, it is the music of the fishmen (the fish again as a life symbol) and it comes from beside a church (though—if this is not to rely too much on Eliot's note—the church has been marked for

destruction). Life on Lower Thames Street, if not on the
Strand, still has meaning as it cannot have meaning for either
the typist or the rich woman of "A Game of Chess."

The song of the Thames-daughters brings us back to the
opening section of "The Fire Sermon" again, and once more
we have to do with the river and the river-nymphs. Indeed,
the typist incident is framed by the two river-nymph scenes.

The connection of the river-nymphs with the Rhine-
daughters of Wagner's *Götterdämmerung* is easily made. In
the passage in Wagner's opera to which Eliot refers in his
note, the opening of Act III, the Rhine-daughters bewail the
loss of the beauty of the Rhine occasioned by the theft of the
gold, and then beg Siegfried to give them back the Ring
made from this gold, finally threatening him with death if he
does not give it up. Like the Thames-daughters they too have
been violated; and like the maidens mentioned in the Grail
legend, the violation has brought a curse on gods and men.
The first of the songs depicts the modern river, soiled with
oil and tar. (Compare also with the description of the river in
the first part of "The Fire Sermon." The second song depicts
the Elizabethan river, also evoked in the first part of "The
Fire Sermon." (Leicester and Elizabeth ride upon it in a
barge of state. Incidentally, Spenser's *Prothalamion,* from
which quotation is made in the first part of "The Fire Sermon," mentions Leicester as having formerly lived in the
house which forms the setting of that poem.)

In this second song there is also a definite allusion to the
passage in *Antony and Cleopatra* already referred to in the
opening line of "A Game of Chess."

> Beating oars
> The stern was formed
> A gilded shell.

And if we still have any doubt of the allusion, Eliot's note on
the passage with its reference to the "barge" and "poop"
should settle the matter. We have already commented on the
earlier allusion to Cleopatra as the prime example of love for
love's sake. The symbol bears something of the same meaning

here, and the note which Eliot supplies does something to reinforce the "Cleopatra" aspect of Elizabeth. Elizabeth in the presence of the Spaniard De Quadra, though negotiations were going on for a Spanish marriage, "went so far that Lord Robert at last said, as I [De Quadra was a bishop] was on the spot there was no reason why they should not be married if the queen pleased." The passage has a sort of double function. It reinforces the general contrast between Elizabethan magnificence and modern sordidness: in the Elizabethan age love for love's sake had some meaning and therefore some magnificence. But the passage gives something of an opposed effect too: the same sterile love, emptiness of love, obtained in this period too: Elizabeth and the Typist are alike as well as different.

The third Thames-daughter's song depicts another sordid "love" affair, and unites the themes of the first two songs. It begins "Trams and *dusty* trees." With it we are definitely in the waste land again. Pia, whose words she echoes in saying "Highbury bore me. Richmond and Kew/Undid me" was in Purgatory and had hope. The woman speaking here has no hope—she too is in the Inferno: "I can connect/Nothing with nothing." She has just completed, floating down the river in the canoe, what Eliot has described in *Murder in the Cathedral* as

. . . the effortless journey, to the empty land

Where the soul is no longer deceived, for there are no objects, no tones,
Where those who were men can no longer turn the mind
To distraction, delusion, escape into dream, pretence,
No colours, no forms to distract, to divert the soul
From seeing itself, foully united forever, nothing with nothing,
Nor what we call death, but what beyond death is not death. . . .

Now, "on Margate sands," like the Hollow Men, she stands "on this beach of the tumid river."

The songs of the three Thames-daughters, as a matter of

fact, epitomize this whole section of the poem. With reference
to the quotations from St. Augustine and Buddha at the end
of "The Fire Sermon" Eliot states that "The collocation of
these two representatives of eastern and western asceticism,
as the culmination of this part of the poem, is not an accident."

It is certainly not an accident. The moral of all the incidents which we have been witnessing is that there must be an
asceticism—something to check the drive of desire. The wisdom of the East and the West comes to the same thing on this
point. Moreover, the image which both St. Augustine and
Buddha use for lust is fire. What we have witnessed in the
various scenes of "The Fire Sermon" is the sterile burning of
lust. Modern man, freed from all restraints, in his cultivation
of experience for experience's sake burns, but not with a "hard
and gemlike flame." One ought not to pound the point home
in this fashion, but to see that the imagery of this section of
the poem furnishes illustrations leading up to "The Fire
Sermon" is the necessary requirement for feeling the force of
the brief allusions here at the end to Buddha and St. Augustine.

IV

Whatever the specific meaning of the symbols, the general
function of the section, "Death by Water," is readily apparent. The section forms a contrast with "The Fire Sermon"
which precedes it—a contrast between the symbolism of fire
and that of water. Also readily apparent is its force as a
symbol of surrender and relief through surrender.

Some specific connections can be made, however. The
drowned Phoenician Sailor recalls the drowned god of the
fertility cults. Miss Weston tells that each year at Alexandria
an effigy of the head of the god was thrown into the water as
a symbol of the death of the powers of nature, and that this
head was carried by the current to Byblos where it was taken
out of the water and exhibited as a symbol of the reborn god.

Moreover, the Phoenician Sailor is a merchant—"Forgot . . .

the profit and loss." The vision of the drowned sailor gives a statement of the message which the Syrian merchants originally brought to Britain and which the Smyrna merchant, unconsciously and by ironical negatives, has brought. One of Eliot's notes states that the "merchant . . . melts into the Phoenician Sailor, and the latter is not wholly distinct from Ferdinand Prince of Naples." The death by water would seem to be equated with the death described in Ariel's song in *The Tempest*. There is a definite difference in the tone of the description of this death—"A current under sea/Picked his bones in whispers," as compared with the "other" death—"bones cast in a little low dry garret,/Rattled by the rat's foot only, year to year."

Farther than this it would not be safe to go, but one may point out that whirling (the whirlpool here, the Wheel of Madame Sosostris' palaver) is one of Eliot's symbols frequently used in other poems (*Ash Wednesday, Gerontion, Murder in the Cathedral*, and *Burnt Norton*) to denote the temporal world. And one may point out the following passage from *Ash Wednesday*:

> Although I do not hope to *turn* again
>
> . . . . . .
>
> Wavering between the *profit and the loss*
> In this brief transit where the dreams cross
> The dreamcrossed twilight *between birth and dying.*

At least, with a kind of hindsight, one may suggest that Section IV gives an instance of the conquest of death and time— the "perpetual recurrence of determined seasons," the "world of spring and autumn, birth and dying"—through death itself.

V

The reference to the "torchlight red on sweaty faces" and to the "frosty silence in the gardens" obviously associates, as we have already pointed out, Christ in Gethsemane with the other hanged gods. The god has now died, and in referring to this, the basic theme finds another strong restatement:

> He who was living is now dead
> We who were living are now dying
> With a little patience

The poet does not say "We who *are* living." It is "We who *were* living." It is the death-in-life of Dante's Limbo. Life in the full sense has been lost.

The passage on the sterility of the waste land and the lack of water which follows, provides for the introduction later of two highly important passages:

> There is not even silence in the mountains
> But dry sterile thunder without rain

—lines which look forward to the introduction later of "what the thunder said" when the thunder, no longer sterile, but bringing rain speaks.

The second of these passages is, "There is not even solitude in the mountains," which looks forward to the reference to the Journey to Emmaus theme a few lines later: "Who is the third who walks always beside you?" The god has returned, has risen, but the travellers cannot tell whether it is really he, or mere illusion induced by their delirium.

The parallelism between the "hooded" figure who walks "always . . . beside you," and the "hooded hordes" is another instance of the sort of parallelism that is really a contrast, one of the type of which Eliot is fond. In the first case, the figure is indistinct because spiritual; in the second, the hooded hordes are indistinct because completely *unspiritual*—they are the people of the waste land—

> Shape without form, shade without colour,
> Paralysed force, gesture without motion

—to take two lines from "The Hollow Men," where the people of the waste land once more appear. Or to take another line from the same poem, perhaps their hoods are the "deliberate disguises" which the Hollow Men, the people of the waste land, wear.

Eliot, as his notes tell us, has particularly connected the description here with the "decay of eastern Europe." The hordes represent then the general waste land of the modern world with a special application to the break-up of Eastern Europe, the region with which the fertility cults were especially connected and in which to-day the traditional values are thoroughly discredited. The cities, Jerusalem, Athens, Alexandria, Vienna, like the London of the first section of the poem, are "unreal," and for the same reason.

The passage which immediately follows develops the unreality into nightmare, but it is a nightmare vision which is not only an extension of the passage beginning, "What is the city over the mountains"—in it appear other figures from earlier in the poem: the lady of "A Game of Chess" who, surrounded by the glory of history and art, sees no meaning in either and threatens to rush out into the street "With my hair down, so," has here let down her hair and fiddles "whisper music on those strings." One remembers in "A Game of Chess" that it was the woman's hair that spoke:

                                                      . . . her hair
>   Spread out in fiery points
>   Glowed into words, then would be savagely still.

The hair has been immemorially a symbol of fertility, and Miss Weston and Frazer mention sacrifices of hair in order to aid the fertility god.

As we have pointed out earlier in dealing with "The Burial of the Dead," this whole passage is to be connected with the twelfth chapter of Ecclesiastes. The doors "of mudcracked houses," and the cisterns in this passage are to be found in Ecclesiastes, and the woman fiddling music from her hair is one of "the daughters of music" brought low. The towers and bells from the Elizabeth and Leicester passage of "The Fire Sermon" also appear here, but the towers are upside down, and the bells, far from pealing for an actual occasion or ringing the hours, are "reminiscent." The civilization is breaking up.

The "violet light" also deserves comment. In "The Fire Sermon" it is twice mentioned as the "violet hour," and there it has little more than a physical meaning. It is a description of the hour of twilight. Here it indicates the twilight of the civilization, but it is perhaps something more. Violet is one of the liturgical colors of the Church. It symbolizes repentance and it is the color of baptism. The visit to the Perilous Chapel, according to Miss Weston, was an initiation—that is, a baptism. In the nightmare vision, the bats wear baby faces.

The horror built up in this passage is a proper preparation for the passage on the Perilous Chapel which follows it. The journey has not been merely an agonized walk in the desert, though it is that, or merely the journey after the god has died and hope has been lost; it is also the journey to the Perilous Chapel of the Grail story. In Miss Weston's account, the Chapel was part of the ritual, and was filled with horrors to test the candidate's courage. In some stories the perilous cemetery is also mentioned. Eliot has used both: "Over the tumbled graves, about the chapel." In many of the Grail stories the Chapel was haunted by demons.

The cock in the folk-lore of many peoples is regarded as the bird whose voice chases away the powers of evil. It is significant that it is after his crow that the flash of lightning comes and the "damp gust/Bringing rain." It is just possible that the cock has a connection also with *The Tempest* symbols. The first song which Ariel sings to Ferdinand as he sits "Weeping again the king my father's wreck" ends

> The strain of strutting chanticleer,
> Cry, cock-a-doodle-doo.

The next stanza is the "Full Fathom Five" song which Eliot has used as a vision of life gained through death. If this relation holds, here we have an extreme instance of an allusion, in itself innocent, forced into serious meaning through transference to a new context.

As Miss Weston has shown, the fertility cults go back to a very early period and are recorded in Sanskrit legends. Eliot has been continually in the poem linking up the Christian doctrine with the beliefs of as many peoples as he can. Here he goes back to the very beginnings of Aryan culture, and tells the rest of the story of the rain's coming, not in terms of the setting already developed but in its earliest form. The passage is thus a perfect parallel in method to the passage in "The Burial of the Dead."

> You who were with me in the ships *at Mylae!*
> That corpse you planted *last year* in your garden. . . .

The use of Sanskrit in what the thunder says is thus accounted for. In addition, there is of course a more obvious reason for casting what the thunder said into Sanskrit here: onomatopoeia.

The comments on the three statements of the thunder imply an acceptance of them. The protagonist answers the first question, "What have we given?" with the statement:

> The awful daring of a moment's surrender
> Which an age of prudence can never retract
> By this, and this only, we have existed.

Here the larger meaning is stated in terms which imply the sexual meaning. Man cannot be absolutely self-regarding. Even the propagation of the race—even mere "existence"—calls for such a surrender. Living calls for—see the passage already quoted from Eliot's essay on Baudelaire—belief in something more than "life."

The comment on *dayadhvam* (sympathize) is obviously connected with the foregoing passage. The surrender to something outside the self is an attempt (whether on the sexual level or some other) to transcend one's essential isolation. The passage gathers up the symbols previously developed in the poem just as the foregoing passage reflects, though with a different implication, the numerous references to sex made earlier in the poem. For example, the woman in the first part of "A Game of Chess" has also heard the key turn in the door, and confirms her prison by thinking of the key:

> Speak to me. Why do you never speak. Speak.
> What are you thinking of? What thinking? What?
> I never know what you are thinking. Think.

The third statement made by the thunder, *damyata* (control) follows the logical condition for control, sympathy. The figure of the boat catches up the figure of control already given in "Death by Water"—"O you who turn the wheel and look to windward"—and from "The Burial of the Dead" the figure of happy love in which the ship rushes on with a fair wind behind it: *Frisch weht der Wind. . . .*

I cannot accept Mr. Leavis's interpretation of the passage, "I sat upon the shore/Fishing, with the arid plain behind me," as meaning that the poem "exhibits no progression." The comment upon what the thunder says would indicate, if other passages did not, that the poem does not "end where it began." It is true that the protagonist does not witness a revival of the waste land; but there are two important relationships involved in his case: a personal one as well as a general one. If secularization has destroyed, or is likely to destroy, modern civilization, the protagonist still has a private obligation to fulfil. Even if the civilization is breaking up—"London Bridge is falling down falling down falling down"—there remains the personal obligation: "Shall I at least set my lands in order?" Consider in this connection the last sentences of Eliot's "Thoughts After Lambeth": "The World is trying the experiment of attempting to form a civilized but non-Christian mentality. The experiment will fail; but we must be very patient in awaiting its collapse; meanwhile redeeming the time: so that the Faith may be preserved alive through the dark ages before us; to renew and rebuild civilization, and save the World from suicide."

The bundle of quotations with which the poem ends has a very definite relation to the general theme of the poem and to several of the major symbols used in the poem. Before Arnaut leaps back into the refining fire of Purgatory with joy he says: "I am Arnaut who weep and go singing; contrite I see my past folly, and joyful I see before me the day I hope for. Now I pray you by that virtue which guides you to the summit of the stair, at times be mindful of my pain." This note is carried forward by the quotation from *Pervigilium Veneris:* "When shall I be like the swallow?" The allusion also connects with the Philomela symbol. (Eliot's note on the passage indicates this clearly.) The sister of Philomela was changed into a swallow as Philomela was changed into a nightingale. The protagonist is asking therefore when shall the spring, the time of love return, but also when will he be reborn out of his sufferings, and—with the special meaning which the symbol takes on from the preceding Dante quotation and from the earlier contexts already discussed—he is asking what is asked at the end of one of the minor poems: "When will Time flow away?"

The quotation from "El Desdichado," as Edmund Wilson has pointed out, indicates that the protagonist of the poem has been disinherited, robbed of his tradition. The ruined tower is perhaps also the Perilous Chapel, "only the wind's home," and it is also the whole tradition in decay. The protagonist resolves to claim his tradition and rehabilitate it.

The quotation from *The Spanish Tragedy*—"Why then Ile fit you. Hieronymo's mad againe"—is perhaps the most puzzling of all these quotations. It means, I believe, this: the protagonist's acceptance of what is in reality the deepest truth will seem to the present world mere madness. ("And still she cried, and still the world pursues,/'Jug Jug' to dirty ears.") Hieronymo in the play, like Hamlet, was "mad" for a purpose. The protagonist is conscious of the interpretation which will be placed on the words which follow—words which will seem to many apparently meaningless babble, but which contain the oldest and most permanent truth of the race:

> Datta. Dayadhvam. Damyata.

After this statement comes the benediction:

> Shantih Shantih Shantih

The foregoing account of *The Waste Land* is, of course, not to be substituted for the poem itself. Moreover, it certainly is not to be considered as representing *the method by which the poem was composed*. Much which the prose expositor must represent as though it had been consciously contrived obviously was arrived at unconsciously and concretely.

The account given above is a statement merely of the "prose

meaning," and bears the same relation to the poem as does the "prose meaning" of any other poem. But one need not perhaps apologize for setting forth such a statement explicitly, for *The Waste Land* has been almost consistently misinterpreted since its first publication. Even a critic so acute as Edmund Wilson has seen the poem as essentially a statement of despair and disillusionment, and this account sums up the stock interpretation of the poem. Indeed, the phrase, "the poetry of drouth," has become a *cliché* of left-wing criticism. It is such a misrepresentation of *The Waste Land* as this which allows Eda Lou Walton to entitle an essay on contemporary poetry, "Death in the Desert"; or which causes Waldo Frank to misconceive of Eliot's whole position and personality. But more than the meaning of one poem is at stake. If *The Waste Land* is not a world-weary cry of despair or a sighing after the vanished glories of the past, then not only the popular interpretation of the poem will have to be altered but also the general interpretations of post-war poetry which begin with such a misinterpretation as a premise.

Such misinterpretations involve also misconceptions of Eliot's technique. Eliot's basic method may be said to have passed relatively unnoticed. The popular view of the method used in *The Waste Land* may be described as follows: Eliot makes use of ironic contrasts between the glorious past and the sordid present—the crashing irony of

> But at my back from time to time I hear
> The sound of horns and motors, which shall bring
> Sweeney to Mrs Porter in the spring.

But this is to take the irony of the poem at the most superficial level, and to neglect the other dimensions in which it operates. And it is to neglect what are essentially more important aspects of his method. Moreover, it is to over-emphasize the difference between the method employed by Eliot in this poem and that employed by him in later poems.

The basic method used in *The Waste Land* may be described as the application of the principle of complexity. The poet works in terms of surface parallelisms which in reality make ironical contrasts, and in terms of surface contrasts which in reality constitute parallelisms. (The second group set up effects which may be described as the obverse of irony.) The two aspects taken together give the effect of chaotic experience ordered into a new whole though the realistic surface of experience is faithfully retained. The complexity of the experience is not violated by the apparent forcing upon it of a predetermined scheme.

The fortune-telling of "The Burial of the Dead" will illustrate the general method very satisfactorily. On the surface of the poem the poet reproduces the patter of the charlatan, Madame Sosostris, and there is the surface irony: the contrast between the original use of the Tarot cards and the use made here. But each of the details (justified realistically in the palaver of the fortune-teller) assumes a new meaning in the general context of the poem. There is then in addition to the surface irony something of a Sophoclean irony too, and the "fortune-telling" which is taken ironically by a twentieth-century audience becomes *true* as the poem develops—true in a sense in which Madame Sosostris herself does not think it true. The surface irony is thus reversed and becomes an irony on a deeper level. The items of her speech have only one reference in terms of the context of her speech: the "man with three staves," the "one-eyed merchant," the "crowds of people, walking round in a ring," etc. But transferred to other contexts they become loaded with special meanings. To sum up, all the central symbols of the poem head up here, but here, in the only section in which they are explicitly bound together, the binding is slight and accidental. The deeper lines of association only emerge in terms of the total context as the poem develops—and this is, of course, exactly the effect which the poet intends.

This transference of items from an "innocent" context into a context in which they become charged and transformed in meaning will account for many of the literary allusions in the poem. For example, the "change of Philomel" is merely one of

the items in the decorative detail in the room in the opening
of "A Game of Chess." But the violent change of tense—"And
still she cried, and still the world pursues"—makes it a comment upon, and a symbol of, the modern world. And further
allusions to it through the course of the poem gradually equate
it with the general theme of the poem. The allusions to *The
Tempest* display the same method. The parallelism between
Dante's Hell and the waste land of the Grail legends is fairly
close; even the equation of Baudelaire's Paris to the waste
land is fairly obvious. But the parallelism between the death
by drowning in *The Tempest* and the death of the fertility god
is, on the surface, merely accidental, and the first allusion to
Ariel's song is merely an irrelevant and random association of
the stream-of-consciousness:

> Is your card, the drowned Phœnician Sailor,
> (Those are pearls that were his eyes. Look!)

And on its second appearance in "A Game of Chess" it is still
only an item in the protagonist's abstracted reverie. Even the
association of *The Tempest* symbol with the Grail legends in
the lines

> While I was fishing in the dull canal
>
> .   .   .   .   .   .
>
> Musing upon the king my brother's wreck.

and in the passage which follows, is ironical merely. But the
associations have been established, even though they may
seem to be made in ironic mockery, and when we come to the
passage, "Death by Water," with its change of tone, they assert themselves positively. We have a sense of revelation out
of material apparently accidentally thrown together. I have
called the effect the obverse of irony, for the method, like that
of irony, is indirect, though the effect is positive rather than
negative.

The "melting" of the characters into each other is, of course,
an aspect of this general process. Elizabeth and the girl born
at Highbury both ride on the Thames, one in the barge of

state, the other supine in a narrow canoe, and they are both Thames-nymphs, who are violated and thus are like the Rhine-nymphs who have also been violated, etc. With the characters as with the other symbols, the surface relationships may be accidental and apparently trivial and they may be made either ironically or through random association or in hallucination, but in the total context of the poem the deeper relationships are revealed. The effect is a sense of the oneness of experience, and of the unity of all periods, and with this, a sense that the general theme of the poem is true. But the theme has not been imposed—it has been revealed.

This complication of parallelisms and contrasts makes, of course, for ambiguity, but the ambiguity, in part, resides in the poet's fidelity to the complexity of experience. The symbols resist complete equation with a simple meaning. To take an example, "rock" throughout the poem seems to be one of the "desert" symbols. For example, the "dry stone" gives "no sound of water"; woman in the waste land is "the Lady of the Rocks," and most pointed of all, there is the long delirium passage in "What the Thunder Said": "Here is no water but only rock," etc. So much for its general meaning, but in "The Burial of the Dead" occur the lines

> Only
> There is shadow under this red rock,
> (Come in under the shadow of this red rock).

Rock here is a place of refuge. (Moreover, there may also be a reference to the Grail symbolism. In *Parzival*, the Grail is a stone: "And this stone all men call the grail. . . . As children the Grail doth call them, 'neath its shadow they wax and grow." The paradox, life through death, penetrates the symbol itself.

To take an even clearer case of this paradoxical use of symbols, consider the lines which occur in the hyacinth-girl passage. The vision gives obviously a sense of the richness and beauty of life. It is a moment of ecstasy (the basic imagery is obviously sexual); but the moment in its intensity is like death.

The protagonist looks in that moment into the "heart of light, the silence," and so looks into—not richness—but blankness: he is neither "living nor dead." The symbol of life stands also for a kind of death. This duality of function may, of course, extend to a whole passage. For example, consider:

> Where fishmen lounge at noon: where the walls
> Of Magnus Martyr hold
> Inexplicable splendour of Ionian white and gold.

The function of the passage is to indicate the poverty into which religion has fallen: the splendid church now surrounded by the poorer districts. But the passage has an opposed effect also: the fishmen in the "public bar in Lower Thames Street" next to the church have a meaningful life which has been largely lost to the secularized upper and middle classes.

The poem would undoubtedly be "clearer" if every symbol had one, unequivocal, meaning; but the poem would be thinner, and less honest. For the poet has not been content to develop a didactic allegory in which the symbols are two-dimensional items adding up directly to the sum of the general scheme. They represent dramatized instances of the theme, embodying in their own nature the fundamental paradox of the theme.

We shall better understand why the form of the poem is right and inevitable if we compare Eliot's theme to Dante's and to Spenser's. Eliot's theme is not the statement of a faith held and agreed upon (Dante's *Divine Comedy*) nor is it the projection of a "new" system of beliefs (Spenser's *Færie Queene*). Eliot's theme is the rehabilitation of a system of beliefs, known but now discredited. Dante did not have to "prove" his statement; he could assume it and move within it about a poet's business. Eliot does not care, like Spenser, to force the didacticism. He prefers to stick to the poet's business. But, unlike Dante, he cannot assume acceptance of the statement. A direct approach is calculated to elicit powerful "stock responses" which will prevent the poem's being *read* at all. Consequently, the only method is to work by indirection. The "Christian" material is at the center, but the poet never deals with it directly. The theme of resurrection is made on the surface in terms of the fertility rites; the words which the thunder speaks are Sanskrit words.

We have been speaking as if the poet were a strategist trying to win acceptance from a hostile audience. But of course this is true only in a sense. The poet himself is audience as well as speaker; we state the problem more exactly if we state it in terms of the poet's integrity rather than in terms of his strategy. He is so much a man of his own age that he can indicate his attitude toward the Christian tradition without falsity only in terms of the difficulties of a rehabilitation; and he is so much a poet and so little a propagandist that he can be sincere only as he presents his theme concretely and dramatically.

To put the matter in still other terms: the Christian terminology is for the poet here a mass of *clichés*. However "true" he may feel the terms to be, he is still sensitive to the fact that they operate superficially as *clichés*, and his method of necessity must be a process of bringing them to life again. The method adopted in *The Waste Land* is thus violent and radical, but thoroughly necessary. For the renewing and vitalizing of symbols which have been crusted over with a distorting familiarity demands the type of organization which we have already commented on in discussing particular passages: the statement of surface similarities which are ironically revealed to be dissimilarities, and the association of apparently obvious dissimilarities which culminates in a later realization that the dissimilarities are only superficial—that the chains of likeness are in reality fundamental. In this way the statement of beliefs emerges *through* confusion and cynicism—not in spite of them.

The Historical Interpretation of Literature

EDMUND WILSON

I WANT to talk about the historical interpretation of literature
—that is, about the interpretation of literature in its social, economic and political aspects.

To begin with, it will be worth while to say something about
the kind of criticism which seems to be furthest removed from
this. There is a kind of comparative criticism which tends to
be non-historical. The essays of T. S. Eliot, which have had
such an immense influence in our time, are, for example, fundamentally non-historical. Eliot sees, or tries to see, the whole
of literature, so far as he is acquainted with it, spread out
before him under the aspect of eternity. He then compares the
work of different periods and countries, and tries to draw from
it general conclusions about what literature ought to be. He
understands, of course, that our point of view in connection
with literature changes, and he has what seems to me a very
sound conception of the whole body of writing of the past as
something to which new works are continually being added,
and which is not thereby merely increased in bulk but modified as a whole—so that Sophocles is no longer precisely what
he was for Aristotle, or Shakespeare what he was for Ben
Jonson or for Dryden or for Dr. Johnson, on account of all the
later literature that has intervened between them and us. Yet
at every point of this continual accretion, the whole field may
be surveyed, as it were, spread out before the critic. The critic
tries to see it as God might; he calls the books to a Day of
Judgment. And, looking at things in this way, he may arrive
at interesting and valuable conclusions which could hardly be
reached by approaching them in any other way. Eliot was able
to see, for example—what I believe had never been noticed
before—that the French Symbolist poetry of the nineteenth
century had certain fundamental resemblances to the English

poetry of the age of Donne. Another kind of critic would draw certain historical conclusions from these purely esthetic findings, as the Russian D. S. Mirsky did; but Eliot does not draw them.

Another example of this kind of non-historical criticism, in a somewhat different way and on a somewhat different plane, is the work of the late George Saintsbury. Saintsbury was a connoisseur of wines; he wrote an entertaining book on the subject. And his attitude toward literature, too, was that of the connoisseur. He tastes the authors and tells you about the vintages; he distinguishes the qualities of the various wines. His palate was as fine as could be, and he possessed the great qualification that he knew how to take each book on its own terms without expecting it to be some other book and was thus in a position to appreciate a great variety of kinds of writing. He was a man of strong social prejudices and peculiarly intransigent political views, but, so far as it is humanly possible, he kept them out of his literary criticism. The result is one of the most agreeable and most comprehensive commentaries on literature that has ever been written in English. Most scholars who have read as much as Saintsbury do not have Saintsbury's discriminating taste. Here is a critic who has covered the whole ground like any academic historian, yet whose account of it is not merely a chronology but a record of fastidious enjoyment. Since enjoyment is the only thing he is looking for, he does not need to know the causes of things, and the historical background of literature does not interest him very much.

There is, however, another tradition of criticism which dates from the beginning of the eighteenth century. In the year 1725, the Neapolitan philosopher Vico published *La Scienza Nuova*, a revolutionary work on the philosophy of history, in which he asserted for the first time that the social world was certainly the work of man, and attempted what is, so far as I know, the first social interpretation of a work of literature. This is what Vico says about Homer: "Homer composed the *Iliad* when Greece was young and consequently burning with

sublime passions such as pride, anger and vengeance—passions
which cannot allow dissimulation and which consort with generosity; so that she then admired Achilles, the hero of force.
But, grown old, he composed the *Odyssey,* at a time when the
passions of Greece were already somewhat cooled by reflection, which is the mother of prudence—so that she now admired Ulysses, the hero of wisdom. Thus also, in Homer's
youth, the Greek people liked cruelty, vituperation, savagery,
fierceness, ferocity; whereas, when Homer was old, they were
already enjoying the luxuries of Alcinoüs, the delights of Ca-
lypso, the pleasures of Circe, the songs of the sirens and the
pastimes of the suitors, who went no further in aggression and
combat than laying siege to the chaste Penelope—all of which
practices would appear incompatible with the spirit of the
earlier time. The divine Plato is so struck by this difficulty
that, in order to solve it, he tells us that Homer had foreseen
in inspired vision these dissolute, sickly and disgusting cus-
toms. But in this way he makes Homer out to have been but
a foolish instructor for Greek civilization, since, however much
he may condemn them, he is displaying for imitation these
corrupt and decadent habits which were not to be adopted till
long after the foundation of the nations of Greece, and ac-
celerating the natural course which human events would take
by spurring the Greeks on to corruption. Thus it is plain that
the Homer of the *Iliad* must have preceded by many years the
Homer who wrote the *Odyssey;* and it is plain that the former
must belong to the northeastern part of Greece, since he celebrates the Trojan War, which took place in his part of the
country, whereas the latter belongs to the southeastern part,
since he celebrates Ulysses, who reigned there."

You see that Vico has here explained Homer in terms both
of historical period and of geographical origin. The idea that
human arts and institutions were to be studied and elucidated
as the products of the geographical and climatic conditions in
which the people who created them lived, and of the phase
of their social development through which they were passing
at the moment, made great progress during the eighteenth
century. There are traces of it even in Dr. Johnson, that most

orthodox and classical of critics—as, for example, when he accounts for certain characteristics of Shakespeare by the relative barbarity of the age in which he lived, pointing out, just as Vico had done, that "nations, like individuals, have their infancy." And by the eighties of the eighteenth century Herder, in his *Ideas on the Philosophy of History,* was writing of poetry that it was a kind of "Proteus among the people, which is always changing its form in response to the languages, manners, and habits, to the temperaments and climates, nay even to the accents of different nations." He said —what could still seem startling even so late as that—that "language was not a divine communication, but something men had produced themselves." In the lectures on the philosophy of history that Hegel delivered in Berlin in 1822-23, he discussed the national literatures as expressions of the societies which had produced them—societies which he conceived as great organisms continually transforming themselves under the influence of a succession of dominant ideas.

In the field of literary criticism, this historical point of view came to its first complete flower in the work of the French critic Taine, in the middle of the nineteenth century. The whole school of historian-critics to which Taine belonged— Michelet, Renan, Sainte-Beuve—had been occupied in interpreting books in terms of their historical origins. But Taine was the first of these to attempt to apply such principles systematically and on a large scale in a work devoted exclusively to literature. In the Introduction to his *History of English Literature,* published in 1863, he made his famous pronouncement that works of literature were to be understood as the upshot of three interfusing factors: *the moment, the race and the milieu.* Taine thought he was a scientist and a mechanist, who was examining works of literature from the same point of view as the chemist's in experimenting with chemical compounds. But the difference between the critic and the chemist is that the critic cannot first combine his elements and then watch to see what they will do: he can only examine phenomena which have already taken place. The procedure that Taine actually follows is to pretend to set the stage for the experiment by describing the moment, the race and the milieu, and then to say: "Such a situation demands such and such a kind of writer." He now goes on to describe the kind of writer that the situation demands, and the reader finds himself at the end confronted with Shakespeare or Milton or Byron or whoever the great figure is—who turns out to prove the accuracy of Taine's prognosis by precisely living up to this description.

There was thus a certain element of imposture in Taine; but it was the rabbits he pulled out that saved him. If he had really been the mechanist that he thought he was, his work on literature would have had little value. The truth was that Taine loved literature for its own sake—he was at his best himself a brilliant artist—and he had very strong moral convictions which give his writing emotional power. His mind, to be sure, was an analytic one, and his analysis, though terribly oversimplified, does have an explanatory value. Yet his work was what we call creative. Whatever he may say about chemical experiments, it is evident when he writes of a great writer that the moment, the race and the milieu have combined, like the three sounds of the chord in Browning's poem about Abt Vogler, to produce not a fourth sound but a star.

To Taine's set of elements was added, dating from the middle of the century, a new element, the economic, which was introduced into the discussion of historical phenomena mainly by Marx and Engels. The non-Marxist critics themselves were at the time already taking into account the influence of the social classes. In his chapters on the Norman conquest of England, Taine shows that the difference between the literatures produced respectively by the Normans and by the Saxons was partly the difference between a ruling class, on the one hand, and a vanquished and repressed class, on the other. And Michelet, in his volume on the Regency, which was finished the same year that the *History of English Literature* appeared, studies the *Manon Lescaut* of the Abbé Prévost as a document representing the point of view of the small gentry before the French Revolution. But Marx and Engels derived the social classes from the way that people made or got their livings—from what they called the *methods of production;* and they tended to regard these economic processes as fundamental to civilization.

The Dialectical Materialism of Marx and Engels was not really so materialistic as it sounds. There was in it a large element of the Hegelian idealism that Marx and Engels thought they had got rid of. At no time did these two famous materialists take so mechanistic a view of things as Taine began by professing; and their theory of the relation of works of literature to what they called the *economic base* was a good deal less simple than Taine's theory of the moment, the race and the milieu. They thought that art, politics, religion, philosophy and literature belonged to what they called the *superstructure* of human activity; but they saw that the practitioners of these various professions tended also to constitute social groups, and that they were always pulling away from the kind of solidarity based on economic classes in order to establish a professional solidarity of their own. Furthermore, the activities of the superstructure could influence one another, and they could influence the economic base. It may be said of Marx and Engels in general that, contrary to the popular impression, they were tentative, confused and modest when it came down to philosophical first principles, where a materialist like Taine was cocksure. Marx once made an attempt to explain why the poems of Homer were so good when the society that produced them was from his point of view—that is, from the point of view of its industrial development—so primitive; and this gave him a good deal of trouble. If we compare his discussion of this problem with Vico's discussion of Homer, we see that the explanation of literature in terms of a philosophy of social history is becoming, instead of simpler and easier, more difficult and more complex.

Marx and Engels were deeply imbued, moreover, with the German admiration for literature, which they had learned from the age of Goethe. It would never have occurred to either of them that *der Dichter* was not one of the noblest and most beneficent of humankind. When Engels writes about

Goethe, he presents him as a man equipped for "practical life," whose career was frustrated by the "misery" of the historical situation in Germany in his time, and reproaches him for allowing himself to lapse into the "cautious, smug and narrow" philistinism of the class from which he came; but Engels regrets this, because it interfered with the development of the "mocking, defiant, world-despising genius," "der geniale Dichter," "der gewaltige Poet," of whom Engels would not even, he says, have asked that he should have been a political liberal if Goethe had not sacrificed to his bourgeois shrinkings his truer esthetic sense. And the great critics who were trained on Marx—Franz Mehring and Bernard Shaw— had all this reverence for the priesthood of literature. Shaw deplores the absence of political philosophy and what he regards as the middle-class snobbery in Shakespeare; but he celebrates Shakespeare's poetry and his dramatic imagination almost as enthusiastically as Swinburne does, describing even those potboiling comedies, *Twelfth Night* and *As You Like It*—the themes of which seem to him most trashy—as "the Crown Jewels of English dramatic poetry." Such a critic may do more for a writer by showing him as a real man dealing with a real world at a definite moment of time than the impressionist critic of Swinburne's type who flourished in the same period of the late nineteenth century. The purely impressionist critic approaches the whole of literature as an exhibit of belletristic jewels, and he can only write a rhapsodic catalogue. But when Shaw turned his spotlight on Shakespeare as a figure in the Shavian drama of history, he invested him with a new interest as no other English critic had done.

The insistence that the man of letters should play a political role, the disparagement of works of art in comparison with political action, were thus originally no part of Marxism. They only became associated with it later. This happened by way of Russia, and it was due to special tendencies in that country that date from long before the Revolution or the promulgation of Marxism itself. In Russia there have been very good reasons why the political implications of literature should particularly occupy the critics. The art of Pushkin itself, with its marvelous power of implication, had certainly been partly created by the censorship of Nicholas I, and Pushkin set the tradition for most of the great Russian writers that followed him. Every play, every poem, every story, must be a parable of which the moral is *implied.* If it were stated, the censor would suppress the book as he tried to do with Pushkin's *Bronze Horseman,* where it was merely a question of the packed implications protruding a little too plainly. Right down through the writings of Chekhov and up almost to the Revolution, the imaginative literature of Russia presents the peculiar paradox of an art that is technically objective and yet charged with social messages. In Russia under the Tsar, it was inevitable that social criticism should lead to political conclusions, because the most urgent need from the point of view of any kind of improvement was to get rid of the tsarist regime. Even the neo-Christian moralist Tolstoy, who pretended to be non-political, was to exert a subversive influence, because his independent preaching was bound to embroil him with the Church, and the Church was an integral part of the tsardom. Tolstoy's pamphlet called *What Is Art?,* in which he throws overboard Shakespeare and a large part of modern literature, including his own novels, in the interest of his intransigent morality, is the example which is most familiar to us of the moralizing Russian criticism; but it was only the most sensational expression of a kind of approach which had been prevalent since Belinsky and Chernyshevsky in the early part of the century. The critics, who were usually journalists writing in exile or in a contraband press, were always tending to demand of the imaginative writers that they should dramatize bolder morals.

Even after the Revolution had destroyed the tsarist government, this state of things did not change. The old habits of censorship persisted in the new socialist society of the Soviets, which was necessarily made up of people who had been stamped by the die of the despotism. We meet here the peculiar phenomenon of a series of literary groups that attempt, one after the other, to obtain official recognition or to make themselves sufficiently powerful to establish themselves as arbiters of literature. Lenin and Trotsky and Lunacharsky had the sense to oppose these attempts: the comrade-dictators of Proletcult or Lev or Rapp would certainly have been just as bad as the Count Benckendorff who made Pushkin miserable, and when the Stalin bureaucracy, after the death of Gorky, got control of this department as of everything else, they instituted a system of repression that made Benckendorff and Nicholas I look like Lorenzo de' Medici. In the meantime, Trotsky, who was Commissar of War but himself a great political writer with an interest in belles-lettres, attempted, in 1924, apropos of one of these movements, to clarify the situation. He wrote a brilliant and valuable book called *Literature and Revolution,* in which he explained the aims of the government, analyzed the work of the Russian writers, and praised or rebuked the latter as they seemed to him in harmony or at odds with the former. Trotsky is intelligent, sympathetic; it is evident that he is really fond of literature and that he knows that a work of art does not fulfill its function in terms of the formulas of party propaganda. But Mayakovsky, the Soviet poet, whom Trotsky had praised with reservations, expressed himself in a famous joke when he was asked what he thought of Trotsky's book—a pun which implied that a Commissar turned critic was inevitably a Commissar still;[1] and what a foreigner cannot accept in Trotsky is his assumption that it is the duty of the government to take a hand in the direction of literature.

This point of view, indigenous to Russia, has been imported to other countries through the permeation of Communist influence. The Communist press and its literary followers have reflected the control of the Kremlin in all the phases through which it has passed, down to the wholesale imprisonment of Soviet writers which has been taking place since 1935. But it has never been a part of the American system that our Republican or Democratic administration should lay down a political line for the guidance of the national literature. A recent

---

[1] Первый блин лег наркомом, *The first pancake lies like a narkom* (people's commissar)—a parody of the Russian saying, Первый блин комом, *The first pancake lies like a lump.*

gesture in this direction on the part of Archibald MacLeish, who seems a little carried away by his position as Librarian of Congress, was anything but cordially received by serious American writers. So long as the United States remains happily a non-totalitarian country, we can very well do without this aspect of the historical criticism of literature.

Another element of a different order has, however, since Marx's time been added to the historical study of the origins of works of literature. I mean the psychoanalysis of Freud. This appears as an extension of something which had already got well started before, which had figured even in Johnson's *Lives of the Poets*, and of which the great exponent had been Sainte-Beuve: the interpretation of works of literature in the light of the personalities behind them. But the Freudians made this interpretation more exact and more systematic. The great example of the psychoanalysis of an artist is Freud's own essay on Leonardo da Vinci; but this has little critical interest: it is an attempt to construct a case history. One of the best examples I know of the application of Freudian analysis to literature is in Van Wyck Brooks's book, *The Ordeal of Mark Twain*, in which Mr. Brooks uses an incident of Mark Twain's boyhood as a key to his whole career. Mr. Brooks has since repudiated the method he resorted to here, on the ground that no one but an analyst can ever know enough about a writer to make a valid psychoanalytic diagnosis. This is true, and it is true of the method that it has led to bad results where the critic has built a Freudian mechanism out of very slender evidence, and then given us what is really merely a romance exploiting the supposed working of this mechanism, in place of an actual study that sticks close to the facts and the documents of the writer's life and work. But I believe that Van Wyck Brooks really had hold of something important when he fixed upon that childhood incident of which Mark Twain gave so vivid an account to his biographer—that scene at the deathbed of his father when his mother had made him promise that he would not break her heart. If it was not one of those crucial happenings that are supposed to determine the complexes of Freud, it has certainly a typical significance in relation to Mark Twain's whole psychology. The stories that people tell about their childhood are likely to be profoundly symbolic even when they have been partly or wholly made up in the light of later experience. And the attitudes, the compulsions, the emotional "patterns" that recur in the work of a writer are of great interest to the historical critic.

These attitudes and patterns are embedded in the community and the historical moment, and they may indicate its ideals and its diseases as the cell shows the condition of the tissue. The recent scientific experimentation in the combining of Freudian with Marxist method, and of psychoanalysis with anthropology, has had its parallel development in criticism. And there is thus another element added to our equipment for analyzing literary works, and the problem grows still more complex.

The analyst, however, is of course not concerned with the comparative values of his patients any more than the surgeon is. He cannot tell you why the neurotic Dostoevsky produces work of immense value to his fellows while another man with the same neurotic pattern would become a public menace. Freud himself emphatically states in his study of Leonardo that his method can make no attempt to account for Leonardo's genius. The problems of comparative artistic value still remain after we have given attention to the Freudian psychological factor just as they do after we have given attention to the Marxist economic factor and to the racial and geographical factors. No matter how thoroughly and searchingly we may have scrutinized works of literature from the historical and biographical points of view, we must be ready to attempt to estimate, in some such way as Saintsbury and Eliot do, the relative degrees of success attained by the products of the various periods and the various personalities. We must be able to tell good from bad, the first-rate from the second-rate. We shall not otherwise write literary criticism at all, but merely social or political history as reflected in literary texts, or psychological case histories from past eras, or, to take the historical point of view in its simplest and most academic form, merely chronologies of books that have been published.

And now how, in these matters of literary art, do we tell the good art from the bad? Norman Kemp Smith, the Kantian philosopher, whose courses I was fortunate enough to take at Princeton twenty-five years ago, used to tell us that this recognition was based primarily on an emotional reaction. For purposes of practical criticism this is a safe assumption on which to proceed. It is possible to discriminate in a variety of ways the elements that in any given department go to make a successful work of literature. Different schools have at different times demanded different things of literature: *unity, symmetry, universality, originality, vision, inspiration, strangeness, suggestiveness, improving morality, socialist realism,* etc. But you could have any set of these qualities that any school of writing has called for and still not have a good play, a good novel, a good poem, a good history. If you identify the essence of good literature with any one of these elements or with any combination of them, you simply shift the emotional reaction to the recognition of the element or elements. Or if you add to your other demands the demand that the writer must have *talent,* you simply shift this recognition to the talent. Once people find some grounds of agreement in the coincidence of their emotional reactions to books, they may be able to discuss these elements profitably; but if they do not have this basic agreement, the discussion will make no sense.

But how, you may ask, can we identify this élite who know what they are talking about? Well, it can only be said of them that they are self-appointed and self-perpetuating, and that they will compel you to accept their authority. Imposters may try to put themselves over, but these quacks will not last. The implied position of the people who know about literature (as is also the case in every other art) is simply that they know what they know, and that they are determined to impose their opinions by main force of eloquence or assertion on the people who do not know. This is not a question, of course, of professional workers in literature—such as editors, professors and critics, who very often have no real understanding of the products with which they deal—but of readers of all kinds in all walks of life. There are moments when a first-rate writer, unrecognized or out of fashion with the official chalkers-up for the market, may find his support in the demand for his work of an appreciative cultivated public.

But what is the cause of this emotional reaction which is the critic's divining rod? This question has long been a subject of study by the branch of philosophy called esthetics, and it has recently been made a subject of scientific experimentation. Both these lines of inquiry are likely to be prejudiced in the eyes of the literary critic by the fact that the inquiries are sometimes conducted by persons who are obviously deficient in literary feeling or taste. Yet one should not deny the possibility that something of value might result from the speculations and explorations of men of acute minds who take as their given data the esthetic emotions of other men.

Almost everybody interested in literature has tried to explain to himself the nature of these emotions that register our approval of artistic works; and I of course have my own explanation.

In my view, all our intellectual activity, in whatever field it takes place, is an attempt to give a meaning to our experience —that is, to make life more practicable; for by understanding things we make it easier to survive and get around among them. The mathematician Euclid, working in a convention of abstractions, shows us relations between the distances of our unwieldy and cluttered-up environment upon which we are able to count. A drama of Sophocles also indicates relations between the various human impulses, which appear so confused and dangerous, and it brings out a certain justice of Fate—that is to say, of the way in which the interaction of these impulses is seen in the long run to work out—upon which we can also depend. The kinship, from this point of view, of the purposes of science and art appears very clearly in the case of the Greeks, because not only do both Euclid and Sophocles satisfy us by making patterns, but they make much the same kind of patterns. Euclid's *Elements* takes simple theorems and by a series of logical operations builds them up to a climax in the square on the hypotenuse. A typical drama of Sophocles develops in a similar way.

Some writers (as well as some scientists) have a different kind of explicit message beyond the reassurance implicit in the mere feat of understanding life or of molding the harmony of artistic form. Not content with such an achievement as that of Sophocles—who has one of his choruses tell us that it is better not to be born, but who, by representing life as noble and based on law, makes its tragedy easier to bear—such writers attempt, like Plato, to think out and recommend a procedure for turning it into something better. But other departments of literature—lyric poetry such as Sappho's, for example —have *less* philosophical content than Sophocles. A lyric gives us nothing but a pattern imposed on the expression of a feeling; but this pattern of metrical quantities and of consonants and vowels that balance has the effect of reducing the feeling, however unruly or painful it may seem when we experience it in the course of our lives, to something orderly, symmetrical and pleasing; and it also relates this feeling to the more impressive scheme, works it into the larger texture, of the body of poetic art. The discord has been resolved, the anomaly subjected to discipline. And this control of his emotion by the poet has the effect at second-hand of making it easier for the reader to manage his own emotions. (Why certain sounds and rhythms gratify us more than others, and how they are connected with the themes and ideas that they are chosen as appropriate for conveying, are questions that may be passed on to the scientist.)

And this brings us back again to the historical point of view. The experience of mankind on the earth is always changing as man develops and has to deal with new combinations of elements; and the writer who is to be anything more than an echo of his predecessors must always find expression for something which has never yet been expressed, must master a new set of phenomena which has never yet been mastered. With each such victory of the human intellect, whether in history, in philosophy or in poetry, we experience a deep satisfaction: we have been cured of some ache of disorder, relieved of some oppressive burden of uncomprehended events.

This relief that brings the sense of power, and, with the sense of power, joy, is the positive emotion which tells us that we have encountered a first-rate piece of literature. But stay! you may at this point warn: are not people often solaced and exhilarated by literature of the trashiest kind? They are: crude and limited people do certainly feel some such emotion in connection with work that is limited and crude. The man who is more highly organized and has a wider intellectual range will feel it in connection with work that is finer and more complex. The difference between the emotion of the more highly organized man and the emotion of the less highly organized one is a matter of mere gradation. You sometimes discover books—the novels of John Steinbeck, for example—that seem to mark precisely the borderline between work that is definitely superior and work that is definitely bad. When I was speaking a little while back of the genuine connoisseurs who establish the standards of taste, I meant, of course, the people who can distinguish Grade A and who prefer it to the other grades.

Art and Neurosis

LIONEL TRILLING

THE QUESTION of the mental health of the artist has engaged the attention of our culture since the beginning of the Romantic Movement. Before that time it was commonly said that the poet was "mad," but this was only a manner of speaking, a way of saying that the mind of the poet worked in different fashion from the mind of the philosopher; it had no real reference to the mental hygiene of the man who was the poet. But in the early nineteenth century, with the development of a more elaborate psychology and a stricter and more literal view of mental and emotional normality, the statement was more strictly and literally intended. So much so, indeed, that Charles Lamb, who knew something about madness at close quarters and a great deal about art, undertook to refute in his brilliant essay, "On the Sanity of True Genius," the idea that the exercise of the imagination was a kind of insanity. And some eighty years later, the idea having yet further entrenched itself, Bernard Shaw felt called upon to argue the sanity of art, but his cogency was of no more avail than Lamb's. In recent years the connection between art and mental illness has been formulated not only by those who are openly or covertly hostile to art, but also and more significantly by those who are most intensely partisan to it. The latter willingly and even eagerly accept the idea that the artist is mentally ill and go on to make his illness a condition of his power to tell the truth.

This conception of artistic genius is indeed one of the characteristic notions of our culture. I should like to bring it into question. To do so is to bring also into question certain early ideas of Freud's and certain conclusions which literary laymen have drawn from the whole tendency of the Freudian psychology. From the very start it was recognized that psychoanalysis was likely to have important things to say about art and artists. Freud himself thought so, yet when he first addressed himself to the subject he said many clumsy and misleading things. I have elsewhere and at length tried to separate the useful from the useless and even dangerous statements about art that Freud has made.[1] To put it briefly here, Freud had some illuminating and even beautiful insights into certain particular works of art which made complex use of the element of myth. Then, without specifically undertaking to do so, his "Beyond the Pleasure Principle" offers a brilliant and comprehensive explanation of our interest in tragedy. And what is of course most important of all—it is a point to which I shall return—Freud, by the whole tendency of his psychology, establishes the *naturalness* of artistic thought. Indeed, it is possible to say of Freud that he ultimately did more for our understanding of art than any other writer since Aristotle; and this being so, it can only be surprising that in his early work he should have made the error of treating the artist as a neurotic who escapes from reality by means of "substitute gratifications."

As Freud went forward he insisted less on this simple formulation. Certainly it did not have its original force with him when, at his seventieth birthday celebration, he disclaimed the right to be called the discoverer of the unconscious, saying that whatever he may have done for the systematic understanding of the unconscious, the credit for its discovery properly belonged to the literary masters. And psychoanalysis has inherited from him a tenderness for art which is real although sometimes clumsy, and nowadays most psychoanalysts of any personal sensitivity are embarrassed by occasions which seem to lead them to reduce art to a formula of mental illness. Nevertheless Freud's early belief in the essential neuroticism of the artist found an all too fertile ground—found, we might say, the very ground from which it first sprang, for, when he spoke of the artist as a neurotic, Freud was adopting one of the popular beliefs of his age. Most readers will see this belief

[1] See "Freud and Literature," *The Liberal Imagination.*

as the expression of the industrial rationalization and the bourgeois philistinism of the nineteenth century. In this they are
partly right. The nineteenth century established the basic
virtue of "getting up at eight, shaving close at a quarter-past,
breakfasting at nine, going to the City at ten, coming home at
half-past five, and dining at seven." The Messrs. Podsnap who
instituted this scheduled morality inevitably decreed that the
arts must celebrate it and nothing else. "Nothing else to be
permitted to these . . . vagrants the Arts, on pain of excommunication. Nothing else To Be—anywhere!" We observe that
the virtuous day ends with dinner—bed and sleep are naturally not part of the Reality that Is, and nothing must be set
forth which will, as Mr. Podsnap put it, bring a Blush to the
Cheek of a Young Person.

The excommunication of the arts, when it was found necessary, took the form of pronouncing the artist mentally degenerate, a device which eventually found its theorist in Max
Nordau. In the history of the arts this is new. The poet was
always known to belong to a touchy tribe—*genus irritabile* was
a tag anyone would know—and ever since Plato the process
of the inspired imagination, as we have said, was thought to
be a special one of some interest, which the similitude of madness made somewhat intelligible. But this is not quite to say
that the poet was the victim of actual mental aberration. The
eighteenth century did not find the poet to be less than other
men, and certainly the Renaissance did not. If he was a professional, there might be condescension to his social status, but
in a time which deplored all professionalism whatever, this
was simply a way of asserting the high value of poetry, which
ought not to be compromised by trade. And a certain good
nature marked even the snubbing of the professional. At any
rate, no one was likely to identify the poet with the weakling.
Indeed, the Renaissance ideal held poetry to be, like arms or
music, one of the signs of manly competence.

The change from this view of things cannot be blamed
wholly on the bourgeois or philistine public. Some of the
"blame" must rest with the poets themselves. The Romantic
poets were as proud of their art as the vaunting poets of the

sixteenth century, but one of them talked with an angel in a tree and insisted that Hell was better than Heaven and sexuality holier than chastity; another told the world that he wanted to lie down like a tired child and weep away this life of care; another asked so foolish a question as "Why did I laugh tonight?"; and yet another explained that he had written one of his best poems in a drugged sleep. The public took them all at their word—they were not as other men. Zola, in the interests of science, submitted himself to examination by fifteen psychiatrists and agreed with their conclusion that his genius had its source in the neurotic elements of his temperament. Baudelaire, Rimbaud, Verlaine found virtue and strength in their physical and mental illness and pain. W. H. Auden addresses his "wound" in the cherishing language of a lover, thanking it for the gift of insight it has bestowed. "Knowing you," he says, "has made me understand." And Edmund Wilson in his striking phrase, "the wound and the bow," has formulated for our time the idea of the characteristic sickness of the artist, which he represents by the figure of Philoctetes, the Greek warrior who was forced to live in isolation because of the disgusting odor of a suppurating wound and who yet had to be sought out by his countrymen because they had need of the magically unerring bow he possessed.

The myth of the sick artist, we may suppose, has established itself because it is of advantage to the various groups who have one or another relation with art. To the artist himself the myth gives some of the ancient powers and privileges of the idiot and the fool, half-prophetic creatures, or of the mutilated priest. That the artist's neurosis may be but a mask is suggested by Thomas Mann's pleasure in representing his untried youth as "sick" but his successful maturity as senatorially robust. By means of his belief in his own sickness, the artist may the more easily fulfill his chosen, and assigned, function of putting himself into connection with the forces of spirituality and morality; the artist sees as insane the "normal" and "healthy" ways of established society, while aberration and illness appear as spiritual and moral health if only because they controvert the ways of respectable society.

Then too, the myth has its advantage for the philistine—a double advantage. On the one hand, the belief in the artist's neuroticism allows the philistine to shut his ears to what the artist says. But on the other hand it allows him to listen. For we must not make the common mistake—the contemporary philistine does want to listen, at the same time that he wants to shut his ears. By supposing that the artist has an interesting but not always reliable relation to reality, he is able to contain (in the military sense) what the artist tells him. If he did not want to listen at all, he would say "insane"; with "neurotic," which hedges, he listens when he chooses.

And in addition to its advantage to the artist and to the philistine, we must take into account the usefulness of the myth to a third group, the group of "sensitive" people, who, although not artists, are not philistines either. These people form a group by virtue of their passive impatience with philistinism, and also by virtue of their awareness of their own emotional pain and uncertainty. To these people the myth of the sick artist is the institutional sanction of their situation; they seek to approximate or acquire the character of the artist, sometimes by planning to work or even attempting to work as the artist does, always by making a connection between their own powers of mind and their consciousness of "difference" and neurotic illness.

The early attempts of psychoanalysis to deal with art went on the assumption that, because the artist was neurotic, the content of his work was also neurotic, which is to say that it did not stand in a correct relation to reality. But nowadays, as I have said, psychoanalysis is not likely to be so simple in its transactions with art. A good example of the psychoanalytical development in this respect is Dr. Saul Rosenzweig's well-known essay, "The Ghost of Henry James."[2] This is an admirable piece of work, marked by accuracy in the reporting of the literary fact and by respect for the value of the literary object. Although Dr. Rosenzweig explores the element of neurosis in James's life and work, he nowhere suggests that this element

[2] First published in *Character and Personality*, December 1943, and reprinted in *Partisan Review*, Fall, 1944.

in any way lessens James's value as an artist or moralist. In effect he says that neurosis is a way of dealing with reality which, in real life, is uncomfortable and uneconomical, but that this judgment of neurosis in life cannot mechanically be transferred to works of art upon which neurosis has had its influence. He nowhere implies that a work of art in whose genesis a neurotic element may be found is for that reason irrelevant or in any way diminished in value. Indeed, the manner of his treatment suggests, what is of course the case, that every neurosis deals with a real emotional situation of the most intensely meaningful kind.

Yet as Dr. Rosenzweig brings his essay to its close, he makes use of the current assumption about the causal connection between the psychic illness of the artist and his power. His investigation of James, he says, "reveals the aptness of the Philoctetes pattern." He accepts the idea of "the sacrificial roots of literary power" and speaks of "the unhappy sources of James's genius." "The broader application of the inherent pattern," he says, 'is familiar to readers of Edmund Wilson's recent volume *The Wound and the Bow*. . . . Reviewing the experience and work of several well-known literary masters, Wilson discloses the sacrificial roots of their power on the model of the Greek legend. In the case of Henry James, the present account . . . provides a similar insight into the unhappy sources of his genius. . . ."

This comes as a surprise. Nothing in Dr. Rosenzweig's theory requires it. For his theory asserts no more than that Henry James, predisposed by temperament and family situation to certain mental and emotional qualities, was in his youth injured in a way which he believed to be sexual; that he unconsciously invited the injury in the wish to identify himself with his father, who himself had been similarly injured—"castrated": a leg had been amputated—and under strikingly similar circumstances; this resulted for the younger Henry James in a certain pattern of life and in a preoccupation in his work with certain themes which more or less obscurely symbolize his sexual situation. For this I think Dr. Rosenzweig makes a sound case. Yet I submit that this is not the same thing as disclosing the roots of James's power or discovering the sources of his genius. The essay which gives Edmund Wilson's book its title and cohering principle does not explicitly say that the roots of power are sacrificial and that the source of genius is unhappy. Where it is explicit, it states only that "genius and disease, like strength and mutilation, may be inextricably bound up together," which of course, on its face, says no more than that personality is integral and not made up of detachable parts; and from this there is no doubt to be drawn the important practical and moral implication that we cannot judge or dismiss a man's genius and strength because of our awareness of his disease or mutilation. The Philoctetes legend in itself does not suggest anything beyond this. It does not suggest that the wound is the price of the bow, or that without the wound the bow may not be possessed or drawn. Yet Dr. Rosenzweig has accurately summarized the force and, I think, the intention of Mr. Wilson's whole book; its several studies do seem to say that effectiveness in the arts does depend on sickness.

An examination of this prevalent idea might well begin with the observation of how pervasive and deeply rooted is the notion that power may be gained by suffering. Even at relatively high stages of culture the mind seems to take easily to the primitive belief that pain and sacrifice are connected with strength. Primitive beliefs must be treated with respectful alertness to their possible truth and also with the suspicion of their being magical and irrational, and it is worth noting on both sides of the question, and in the light of what we have said about the ambiguous relation of the neurosis to reality, that the whole economy of the neurosis is based exactly on this idea of the *quid pro quo* of sacrificial pain: the neurotic person unconsciously subscribes to a system whereby he gives up some pleasure or power, or inflicts pain on himself in order to secure some other power or some other pleasure.

In the ingrained popular conception of the relation between suffering and power there are actually two distinct although related ideas. One is that there exists in the individual a fund of power which has outlets through various organs or faculties, and that if its outlet through one organ or faculty be prevented, it will flow to increase the force or sensitivity of another. Thus it is popularly believed that the sense of touch is intensified in the blind not so much by the will of the blind person to adapt himself to the necessities of his situation as, rather, by a sort of mechanical redistribution of power. And this idea would seem to explain, if not the origin of the ancient mutilation of priests, then at least a common understanding of their sexual sacrifice.

The other idea is that a person may be taught by, or proved by, the endurance of pain. There will easily come to mind the ritual suffering that is inflicted at the tribal initiation of youths into full manhood or at the admission of the apprentice into the company of journeyman adepts. This idea in sophisticated form found its way into high religion at least as early as Aeschylus, who held that man achieves knowledge of God through suffering, and it was from the beginning an important element of Christian thought. In the nineteenth century the Christianized notion of the didactic suffering of the artist went along with the idea of his mental degeneration and even served as a sort of countermyth to it. Its doctrine was that the artist, a man of strength and health, experienced and suffered, and thus learned both the facts of life and his artistic craft. "I am the man, I suffered, I was there," ran his boast, and he derived his authority from the knowledge gained through suffering.

There can be no doubt that both these ideas represent a measure of truth about mental and emotional power. The idea of didactic suffering expresses a valuation of experience and of steadfastness. The idea of natural compensation for the sacrifice of some faculty also says something that can be rationally defended: one cannot be and do everything and the wholehearted absorption in any enterprise, art for example, means that we must give up other possibilities, even parts of ourselves. And there is even a certain validity to the belief that the individual has a fund of undifferentiated energy which presses the harder upon what outlets are available to it when it has been deprived of the normal number.

Then, in further defense of the belief that artistic power is connected with neurosis, we can say that there is no doubt that what we call mental illness may be the source of psychic knowledge. Some neurotic people, because they are more apprehensive than normal people, are able to see more of certain parts of reality and to see them with more intensity. And many neurotic or psychotic patients are in certain respects in closer touch with the actualities of the unconscious than are normal people. Further, the expression of a neurotic or psychotic conception of reality is likely to be more intense than a normal one.

Yet when we have said all this, it is still wrong, I believe, to find the root of the artist's power and the source of his genius in neurosis. To the idea that literary power and genius spring from pain and neurotic sacrifice there are two major objections. The first has to do with the assumed uniqueness of the artist as a subject of psychoanalytical explanation. The second has to do with the true meaning of power and genius.

One reason why writers are considered to be more available than other people to psychoanalytical explanation is that they tell us what is going on inside them. Even when they do not make an actual diagnosis of their malaises or describe "symptoms," we must bear it in mind that it is their profession to deal with fantasy in some form or other. It is in the nature of the writer's job that he exhibit his unconscious. He may disguise it in various ways, but disguise is not concealment. Indeed, it may be said that the more a writer takes pains with his work to remove it from the personal and subjective, the more—and not the less—he will express his true unconscious, although not what passes with most for the unconscious.

Further, the writer is likely to be a great hand at personal letters, diaries, and autobiographies: indeed, almost the only good autobiographies are those of writers. The writer is more aware of what happens to him or goes on in him and often finds it necessary or useful to be articulate about his inner states, and prides himself on telling the truth. Thus, only a man as devoted to the truth of the emotions as Henry James was would have informed the world, despite his characteristic reticence, of an accident so intimate as his. We must not of course suppose that a writer's statements about his intimate life are equivalent to true statements about his unconscious, which, by definition, he doesn't consciously know; but they may be useful clues to the nature of an entity about which we can make statements of more or less cogency, although never statements of certainty; or they at least give us what is surely related to a knowledge of his unconscious—that is, an insight into his personality.[3]

But while the validity of dealing with the writer's intellectual life in psychoanalytical terms is taken for granted, the psychoanalytical explanation of the intellectual life of scientists is generally speaking not countenanced. The old myth of the mad scientist, with the exception of an occasional mad psychiatrist, no longer exists. The social position of science requires that it should cease, which leads us to remark that those partisans of art who insist on explaining artistic genius by means of psychic imbalance are in effect capitulating to the dominant mores which hold that the members of the respectable professions are, however dull they may be, free from neurosis. Scientists, to continue with them as the best example of the respectable professions, do not usually give us the clues to their personalities which writers habitually give. But no one who has ever lived observantly among scientists will claim that they are without an unconscious or even that they are

---

[3] I am by no means in agreement with the statements of Dr. Edmund Bergler about "the" psychology of the writer, but I think that Dr. Bergler has done good service in warning us against taking at their face value a writer's statements about himself, the more especially when they are "frank." Thus, to take Dr. Bergler's notable example, it is usual for biographers to accept Stendhal's statements about his open sexual feelings for his mother when he was a little boy, feelings which went with an intense hatred of his father. But Dr. Bergler believes that Stendhal unconsciously used his consciousness of his love of his mother and of his hatred of his father to mask an unconscious love of his father, which frightened him. ("Psychoanalysis of Writers and of Literary Productivity" in *Psychoanalysis and the Social Sciences*, vol. I.)

free from neurosis. How often, indeed, it is apparent that the
devotion to science, if it cannot be called a neurotic manifestation, at least can be understood as going very cozily with
neurotic elements in the temperament, such as, for example,
a marked compulsiveness. Of scientists as a group we can say
that they are less concerned with the manifestations of personality, their own or others', than are writers as a group. But
this relative indifference is scarcely a sign of normality—indeed, if we choose to regard it with the same sort of eye with
which the characteristics of writers are regarded, we might
say the indifference to matters of personality is in itself a suspicious evasion.

It is the basic assumption of psychoanalysis that the acts of
every person are influenced by the forces of the unconscious.
Scientists, bankers, lawyers, or surgeons, by reason of the traditions of their professions, practice concealment and conformity; but it is difficult to believe that an investigation according to psychoanalytical principles would fail to show that
the strains and imbalances of their psyches are not of the
same frequency as those of writers, and of similar kind. I do
not mean that everybody has the same troubles and identical
psyches, but only that there is no special category for writers.[4]

If this is so, and if we still want to relate the writer's power
to his neurosis, we must be willing to relate all intellectual
power to neurosis. We must find the roots of Newton's power
in his emotional extravagances, and the roots of Darwin's
power in his sorely neurotic temperament, and the roots of
Pascal's mathematical genius in the impulses which drove him
to extreme religious masochism—I choose but the classic examples. If we make the neurosis-power equivalence at all, we
must make it in every field of endeavor. Logician, economist,

---

[4] Dr. Bergler believes that there is a particular neurosis of writers,
based on an oral masochism which makes them the enemy of the
respectable world, courting poverty and persecution. But a later
development of Dr. Bergler's theory of oral masochism makes it
the basic neurosis, not only of writers but of everyone who is
neurotic.

botanist, physicist, theologian—no profession may be so respectable or so remote or so rational as to be exempt from the psychological interpretation.[5]

Further, not only power but also failure or limitation must be accounted for by the theory of neurosis, and not merely failure or limitation in life but even failure or limitation in art. Thus it is often said that the warp of Dostoevski's mind accounts for the brilliance of his psychological insights. But it is

[5] In his interesting essay, "Writers and Madness" (*Partisan Review*, January-February 1947), William Barrett has taken issue with this point and has insisted that a clear distinction is to be made between the relation that exists between the scientist and his work and the relation that exists between the artist and his work. The difference, as I understand it, is in the claims of the ego. The artist's ego makes a claim upon the world which is personal in a way that the scientist's is not, for the scientist, although he does indeed want prestige and thus "responds to one of the deepest urges of his ego, it is only that his prestige may come to attend his person through the public world of other men; and it is not in the end his own being that is exhibited or his own voice that is heard in the learned report to the Academy." Actually, however, as is suggested by the sense which mathematicians have of the *style* of mathematical thought, the creation of the abstract thinker is as deeply involved as the artist's—see *An Essay on the Psychology of Invention in the Mathematical Field* by Jacques Hadamard, Princeton University Press, 1945—and he quite as much as the artist seeks to impose *himself*, to *express* himself. I am of course not maintaining that the processes of scientific thought are the same as those of artistic thought, or even that the scientist's creation is involved with his total personality *in the same way* that the artist's is—I am maintaining only that the scientist's creation is as *deeply* implicated with his total personality as is the artist's.

This point of view seems to be supported by Freud's monograph on Leonardo. One of the problems that Freud sets himself is to discover why an artist of the highest endowment should have devoted himself more and more to scientific investigation, with the result that he was unable to complete his artistic enterprises. The particular reasons for this that Freud assigns need not be gone into here; all that I wish to suggest is that Freud understands these reasons to be the working out of an inner conflict, the attempt to deal with the difficulties that have their roots in the most primitive situations. Leonardo's scientific investigations were as necessary and "compelled" and they constituted as much of a claim on the whole personality as anything the artist undertakes; and so far from being carried out for the sake of public prestige, they were largely private and personal, and were thought by the public of his time to be something very like insanity.

never said that the same warp of Dostoevski's mind also accounted for his deficiency in insight. Freud, who greatly admired Dostoevski, although he did not like him, observed that "his insight was entirely restricted to the workings of the abnormal psyche. Consider his astounding helplessness before the phenomenon of love; he really only understands either crude, instinctive desire or masochistic submission or love from pity."[6] This, we must note, is not merely Freud's comment on the extent of the province which Dostoevski chose for his own, but on his failure to understand what, given the province of his choice, he might be expected to understand.

And since neurosis can account not only for intellectual success and for failure or limitation but also for mediocrity, we have most of society involved in neurosis. To this I have no objection—I think most of society is indeed involved in neurosis. But with neurosis accounting for so much, it cannot be made exclusively to account for one man's literary power.

We have now to consider what is meant by genius when its source is identified as the sacrifice and pain of neurosis.

In the case of Henry James, the reference to the neurosis of his personal life does indeed tell us something about the latent intention of his work and thus about the reason for some large part of its interest for us. But if genius and its source are what we are dealing with, we must observe that the reference to neurosis tells us nothing about James's passion, energy, and devotion, nothing about his architectonic skill, nothing about the other themes that were important to him which are not connected with his unconscious concern with castration. We cannot, that is, make the writer's inner life exactly equivalent to his power of expressing it. Let us grant for the sake of argument that the literary genius, as distinguished from other men, is the victim of a "mutilation" and that his fantasies are neurotic.[7] It does not then follow as the inevitable next step that

[6] From a letter quoted in Theodor Reik's *From Thirty Years with Freud*, p. 175.

[7] I am using the word *fantasy*, unless modified, in a neutral sense. A fantasy, in this sense, may be distinguished from the representation of something that actually exists, but it is not opposed to

his ability to express these fantasies and to impress us with them is neurotic, for that ability is what we mean by his genius. Anyone might be injured as Henry James was, and even respond within himself to the injury as James is said to have done, and yet not have his literary power.

The reference to the artist's neurosis tells us something about the material on which the artist exercises his powers, and even something about his reasons for bringing his powers into play, but it does not tell us anything about the source of his power, it makes no causal connection between them and the neurosis. And if we look into the matter, we see that there is in fact no causal connection between them. For, still granting that the poet is uniquely neurotic, what is surely not neurotic, what indeed suggests nothing but health, is his power of using his neuroticism. He shapes his fantasies, he gives them social form and reference. Charles Lamb's way of putting this cannot be improved. Lamb is denying that genius is allied to insanity; for "insanity" the modern reader may substitute "neurosis." "The ground of the mistake," he says, "is, that men, finding in the raptures of the higher poetry a condition of exaltation, to which they have no parallel in their own experience, besides the spurious resemblance of it in dreams and fevers, impute a state of dreaminess and fever to the poet. But the true poet dreams being awake. He is not possessed by his subject but has dominion over it. . . . Where he seems most to recede from humanity, he will be found the truest to it. From beyond the scope of nature if he summon possible existences, he subjugates them to the law of her consistency. He is beautifully loyal to that sovereign directress, when he appears most to betray and desert her. . . . Herein the great and the little wits are differenced; that if the latter wander ever so little from nature or natural existence, they lose themselves and their readers. . . . They do not create, which implies shaping and consistency. Their imaginations are not active—for to

---

"reality" and not an "escape" from reality. Thus the idea of a rational society, or the image of a good house to be built, as well as the story of something that could never really happen, is a fantasy. There may be neurotic or non-neurotic fantasies.

be active is to call something into act and form—but passive
as men in sick dreams."

The activity of the artist, we must remember, may be ap-
proximated by many who are themselves not artists. Thus, the
expressions of many schizophrenic people have the intense appearance of creativity and an inescapable interest and significance. But they are not works of art, and although Van Gogh
may have been schizophrenic he was in addition an artist.
Again, as I have already suggested, it is not uncommon in our
society for certain kinds of neurotic people to imitate the artist
in his life and even in his ideals and ambitions. They follow
the artist in everything except successful performance. It was,
I think, Otto Rank who called such people half-artists and confirmed the diagnosis of their neuroticism at the same time that
he differentiated them from true artists.

Nothing is so characteristic of the artist as his power of
shaping his work, of subjugating his raw material, however
aberrant it be from what we call normality, to the consistency
of nature. It would be impossible to deny that whatever disease or mutilation the artist may suffer is an element of his
production which has its effect on every part of it, but disease
and mutilation are available to us all—life provides them with
prodigal generosity. What marks the artist is his power to
shape the material of pain we all have.

At this point, with our recognition of life's abundant provi-
sion of pain, we are at the very heart of our matter, which is
the meaning we may assign to neurosis and the relation we
are to suppose it to have with normality. Here Freud himself
can be of help, although it must be admitted that what
he tells us may at first seem somewhat contradictory and
confusing.

Freud's study of Leonardo da Vinci is an attempt to understand why Leonardo was unable to pursue his artistic enterprises, feeling compelled instead to advance his scientific investigations. The cause of this Freud traces back to certain
childhood experiences not different in kind from the experiences which Dr. Rosenzweig adduces to account for certain
elements in the work of Henry James. And when he has com-

pleted his study Freud makes this *caveat:* "Let us expressly emphasize that we have never considered Leonardo as a neurotic. . . . We no longer believe that health and disease, normal and nervous, are sharply distinguished from each other. We know today that neurotic symptoms are substitutive formations for certain repressive acts which must result in the course of our development from the child to the cultural man, that we all produce such substitutive formations, and that only the amount, intensity, and distribution of these substitutive formations justify the practical conception of illness. . . ." The statement becomes the more striking when we remember that in the course of his study Freud has had occasion to observe that Leonardo was both homosexual and sexually inactive. I am not sure that the statement that Leonardo was not a neurotic is one that Freud would have made at every point in the later development of psychoanalysis, yet it is in conformity with his continuing notion of the genesis of culture. And the *practical,* the quantitative or economic, conception of illness he insists on in a passage in the *Introductory Lectures.* "The neurotic symptoms," he says, ". . . are activities which are detrimental, or at least useless, to life as a whole; the person concerned frequently complains of them as obnoxious to him or they involve suffering and distress for him. The principal injury they inflict lies in the expense of energy they entail, and, besides this, in the energy needed to combat them. Where the symptoms are extensively developed, these two kinds of effort may exact such a price that the person suffers a very serious impoverishment in available mental energy which consequently disables him for all the important tasks of life. This result depends principally upon the amount of energy taken up in this way; therefore you will see that "illness" is essentially a practical conception. But if you look at the matter from a theoretical point of view and ignore this question of degree, you can very well see that we are all ill, i.e., neurotic; for the conditions required for symptom-formation are demonstrable also in normal persons."

We are all ill: the statement is grandiose, and its implications—the implications, that is, of understanding the totality of human nature in the terms of disease—are vast. These implications have never been properly met (although I believe that a few theologians have responded to them), but this is not the place to attempt to meet them. I have brought forward Freud's statement of the essential sickness of the psyche only because it stands as the refutation of what is implied by the literary use of the theory of neurosis to account for genius. For if we are all ill, and if, as I have said, neurosis can account for everything, for failure and mediocrity—"a very serious impoverishment of available mental energy"—as well as for genius, it cannot uniquely account for genius.

This, however, is not to say that there is no connection between neurosis and genius, which would be tantamount, as we see, to saying that there is no connection between human nature and genius. But the connection lies wholly in a particular and special relation which the artist has to neurosis.

In order to understand what this particular and special connection is we must have clearly in mind what neurosis is. The current literary conception of neurosis as a *wound* is quite misleading. It inevitably suggests passivity, whereas, if we follow Freud, we must understand a neurosis to be an *activity*, an activity with a purpose, and a particular kind of activity, a *conflict*. This is not to say that there are no abnormal mental states which are not conflicts. There are; the struggle between elements of the unconscious may never be instituted in the first place, or it may be called off. As Freud says in a passage which follows close upon the one I last quoted, "If regressions do not call forth a prohibition on the part of the ego, no neurosis results; the libido succeeds in obtaining a real, although not a normal, satisfaction. But if the ego . . . is not in agreement with these regressions, conflict ensues." And in his essay on Dostoevski Freud says that "there are no neurotic complete masochists," by which he means that the ego which gives way completely to masochism (or to any other pathological excess) has passed beyond neurosis; the conflict has ceased, but at the cost of the defeat of the ego, and now some other name than that of neurosis must be given to the condition of the person who thus takes himself beyond the pain of the neurotic conflict. To understand this is to become aware of the curious complacency with which literary men regard mental disease. The psyche of the neurotic is not equally complacent; it regards with the greatest fear the chaotic and destructive forces it contains, and it struggles fiercely to keep them at bay.[8]

We come then to a remarkable paradox: we are all ill, but we are ill in the service of health, or ill in the service of life, or, at the very least, ill in the service of life-in-culture. The form of the mind's dynamics is that of the neurosis, which is to be understood as the ego's struggle against being overcome by the forces with which it coexists, and the strategy of this conflict requires that the ego shall incur pain and make sacrifices of itself, at the same time seeing to it that its pain and sacrifice be as small as they may.

But this is characteristic of all minds: no mind is exempt except those which refuse the conflict or withdraw from it; and we ask wherein the mind of the artist is unique. If he is not unique in neurosis, is he then unique in the significance and intensity of his neurosis? I do not believe that we shall go more than a little way toward a definition of artistic genius by answering this question affirmatively. A neurotic conflict cannot ever be either meaningless or merely personal; it must be understood as exemplifying cultural forces of great moment,

---

[8] In the article to which I refer in the note on page 156, William Barrett says that he prefers the old-fashioned term "madness" to "neurosis." But it is not quite for him to choose—the words do not differ in fashion but in meaning. Most literary people, when they speak of mental illness, refer to neurosis. Perhaps one reason for this is that the neurosis is the most benign of the mental ills. Another reason is surely that psychoanalytical literature deals chiefly with the neurosis, and its symptomatology and therapy have become familiar; psychoanalysis has far less to say about psychosis, for which it can offer far less therapeutic hope. Further, the neurosis is easily put into a causal connection with the social maladjustments of our time. Other forms of mental illness of a more severe and degenerative kind are not so widely recognized by the literary person and are often assimilated to neurosis with a resulting confusion. In the present essay I deal only with the conception of neurosis, but this should not be taken to imply that I believe that other pathological mental conditions, including actual madness, do not have relevance to the general matter of the discussion.

and this is true of any neurotic conflict at all. To be sure, some neuroses may be more interesting than others, perhaps because they are fiercer or more inclusive; and no doubt the writer who makes a claim upon our interest is a man who by reason of the energy and significance of the forces in struggle within him provides us with the largest representation of the culture in which we, with him, are involved; his neurosis may thus be thought of as having a connection of concomitance with his literary powers. As Freud says in the Dostoevski essay, "the neurosis . . . comes into being all the more readily the richer the complexity which has to be controlled by his ego." Yet even the rich complexity which his ego is doomed to control is not the definition of the artist's genius, for we can by no means say that the artist is pre-eminent in the rich complexity of elements in conflict within him. The slightest acquaintance with the clinical literature of psychoanalysis will suggest that a rich complexity of struggling elements is no uncommon possession. And that same literature will also make it abundantly clear that the devices of art—the most extreme devices of poetry, for example—are not particular to the mind of the artist but are characteristic of mind itself.

But the artist is indeed unique in one respect, in the respect of his relation to his neurosis. He is what he is by virtue of his successful objectification of his neurosis, by his shaping it and making it available to others in a way which has its effect upon their own egos in struggle. His genius, that is, may be defined in terms of his faculties of perception, representation, and realization, and in these terms alone. It can no more be defined in terms of neurosis than can his power of walking and talking, or his sexuality. The use to which he puts his power, or the manner and style of his power, may be discussed with reference to his particular neurosis, and so may such matters as the untimely diminution or cessation of its exercise. But its essence is irreducible. It is, as we say, a gift.

We are all ill: but even a universal sickness implies an idea of health. Of the artist we must say that whatever elements of neurosis he has in common with his fellow mortals, the one part of him that is healthy, by any conceivable definition of health, is that which gives him the power to conceive, to plan, to work, and to bring his work to a conclusion. And if we are all ill, we are ill by a universal accident, not by a universal necessity, by a fault in the economy of our powers, not by the nature of the powers themselves. The Philoctetes myth, when it is used to imply a causal connection between the fantasy of castration and artistic power, tells us no more about the source of artistic power than we learn about the source of sexuality when the fantasy of castration is adduced, for the fear of castration may explain why a man is moved to extravagant exploits of sexuality, but we do not say that his sexual power itself derives from his fear of castration; and further the same fantasy may also explain impotence or homosexuality. The Philoctetes story, which has so established itself among us as explaining the source of the artist's power, is not really an explanatory myth at all; it is a moral myth having reference to our proper behavior in the circumstances of the universal accident. In its juxtaposition of the wound and the bow, it tells us that we must be aware that weakness does not preclude strength nor strength weakness. It is therefore not irrelevant to the artist, but when we use it we will do well to keep in mind the other myths of the arts, recalling what Pan and Dionysius suggest of the relation of art to physiology and superabundance, remembering that to Apollo were attributed the bow and the lyre, two strengths together, and that he was given the lyre by its inventor, the baby Hermes—that miraculous infant who, the day he was born, left his cradle to do mischief: and the first thing he met with was a tortoise, which he greeted politely before scooping it from its shell, and, thought and deed being one with him, he contrived the instrument to which he sang "the glorious tale of his own begetting." These were gods, and very early ones, but their myths tell us something about the nature and source of art even in our grim, late human present.

The Responsibilities of the Critic

F. O. MATTHIESSEN

MY DELIBERATELY grave title is in the tradition from Matthew Arnold, my first critical enthusiasm as an undergraduate thirty years ago. But at that very time a new critical movement was rising, the critical movement in which we are living today. T. S. Eliot's first important essay, *Tradition and the Individual Talent,* was written in 1917, when he was twenty-nine; and I. A. Richards' first independent and most influential book, *The Principles of Literary Criticism,* came out in 1924, when he was in his early thirties. The talents and principles of those two then young men have been the most pervasive forces upon the criticism of the past quarter century.

We know now what a revolution they instigated, if one may use such a violent word as "revolution" in the field of the arts, where all victories fortunately are bloodless, and where what was overthrown remains undestroyed and capable of being rediscovered at the next turn of the wheel of taste. When Eliot was growing up, the tastes and standards of Arnold were still prevailing; and Eliot found himself wholly dissatisfied with Arnold's preoccupation with the spirit of poetry rather than with its form. The form of Eliot's own first poems was deceptively radical, since he was really rejecting the easily flowing forms of the romantics and the Elizabethans for the more intricately weighted forms of the symbolists and the metaphysicals.

When Richards, as a psychologist who believed in the basic importance of the words with which men try to fathom their meanings, began to read Eliot's poems, he encountered the kind of language that proved most compelling to readers just after the First World War. The immense loosening of speech that had accompanied the rapid expansions in mass education and mass communication had reached the point where, if the artist was again to communicate the richness and denseness of real experience, he must use a language that compelled the reader to slow down, to be concerned once more with the trip rather than with the arrival. As the young English critic T. E. Hulme had been arguing, before he was killed in battle in 1917, poetry must always endeavor thus "to arrest you . . . to make you continuously see a physical thing, to prevent you gliding through an abstract process."

What resulted from the joint influence of Eliot and Richards was a criticism that aimed to give the closest possible attention to the text at hand, to both the structure and texture of the language. You are all familiar with the names of its practitioners, who, if we confine ourselves to America alone, have already produced a more serious and exacting body of work than we had previously witnessed in this country. To be sure, Richards' most gifted follower was one of his own students at Cambridge, England. William Empson, in his precocious *Seven Types of Ambiguity* (1929), begun when he was still an undergraduate, pushed to its subtle extreme Richards' kind of linguistic analysis. Empson in turn has had a particular vogue here among the critics whom we now associate with the newly founded Kenyon School of Criticism, most notably with John Crowe Ransom, Robert Penn Warren, and Cleanth Brooks. Others whose names are linked with that school, Kenneth Burke, R. P. Blackmur, Allen Tate, Austin Warren, and Yvor Winters, however divergent their methods and emphases, reveal throughout their work how they have had to reckon with Eliot and Richards, whether in concord or belligerence.

The effect of this new movement upon the study of literature in our universities has been by now considerable. Although opposed by both the old guards of philologists and literary historians, most of the critics I have mentioned now hold academic appointments, which may or may not have been good for their work. But their work has thereby become instrumental in the revolt against concentrating exclusively on the past, and against concentrating on literary history instead of on literature. As a result both teachers and students are more

capable of close analysis and lively appreciation than they
were a generation ago.

But by now we have reached the stage where revolt has be-
gotten its own set of conventions, to use the terms of one of
Harvard's great former teachers, John Livingston Lowes. As
we watch our own generation producing whole anthologies of
criticism devoted to single contemporary authors and more and
more detailed books of criticism of criticism, we should realize
that we have come to the unnatural point where textual analysis seems to be an end in itself. The so-called little magazines
have been essential and valiant outposts of revolt in our time
when the magazines of wide circulation, in decline from their
standards in the nineteenth century, have abandoned serious
discussion of literature almost entirely.

But the little magazines seem now to be giving rise to the
conventions and vocabulary of a new scholasticism and to be
not always distinguishable from the philological journals which
they abhor. The names of the authors may be modern, but the
smell is old. The trouble is that the terms of the new criticism,
its devices and strategies and semantic exercises, can become
as pedantic as any other set of terms if they are handled not
as the means to fresh discoveries but as counters in a stale
game. In too many recent articles literature seems to be regarded merely as a puzzle to be solved.

This is not to underestimate the great and continuing service performed by the few quarterlies devoted to criticism, or
by those even littler magazines that often last only long
enough to introduce one or two new talents in poetry or fiction. The important experimental work of our time has again
and again been able to secure its first publication only through
their pages. This is one of the consequences of what F. R.
Leavis, the editor of *Scrutiny*, has called the split between
"mass civilization" and "minority culture." But to recognize
that phenomenon in our democracy should only be to combat it.

There is potentially a much greater audience in America for
the art of literature than the blurb writers, who often pass for

reviewers in the Sunday supplements, would seem to suspect. The effectiveness of the critics in the little magazines in having by now prepared a wider public for, say, Joyce or Kafka or Eliot, amply testifies to that. But the dilemma for the serious critic in our dangerously split society is that, feeling isolated, he will become serious in the wrong sense, aloof and finally taking an inverted superiority in his isolation. At that point criticism becomes a kind of closed garden.

My views are based on the conviction that the land beyond the garden's walls is more fertile, and that the responsibilities of the critic lie in making renewed contact with that soil. William James used to insist that the first duty of any thinker is to know as much as possible about life in his own time. Such an exhortation may seem too general to be of much use, but it can be grasped more concretely if we envisage the particular responsibilities of the critic in a whole series of awarenesses. These awarenesses may encompass some of the breadth and comprehensiveness which James assumed to be the thinker's goal, and some of the feeling of being drenched with actual life, which he believed to be the thinker's best reward. Much of the ground that we will traverse was also implied to be within the critic's scope by the early work of Eliot and Richards, though some of it has been lost sight of by their followers.

The first awareness for the critic should be of the works of art of our own time. This applies even if he is not primarily a critic of modern literature. One of Eliot's observations which has proved most salutary is that of the inescapable interplay between past and present: that the past is not what is dead, but what is already living; and that the present is continually modifying the past, as the past conditions the present. If one avails himself of the full resources latent in that perception, one is aware that it is not possible to be a good critic of Goethe today without knowing Mann, or of Stendhal or Balzac without knowing Proust, or of Donne or Dryden without knowing Eliot.

The converse is equally true, if less necessary to be argued in the academy. But once outside, particularly in the rapid and rootless life of our cities, the tendency even for practitioners in the arts is to be immersed wholly in the immediate. This is not what James foresaw, since he took for granted the constant meeting point between what was already known and what was still to be known. But today we can take no tradition for granted, we must keep repossessing the past for ourselves if we are not to lose it altogether. The value in this urgency is that what we manage to retain will really belong to us, and not on authority at second hand. The proper balance, even for the critic who considers his field to be the present, is to bring to the elucidation of that field as much of the art of the past as he can command.

A recently dead critic, Paul Rosenfeld, was a heartening example of this balance. Prolonging in this country the rich cultural life of his German-Jewish forebears, he moved naturally among the arts, and it would never have occurred to him that a critic of contemporary music would try to speak without having all the great composers of the past at his finger tips. But he regarded the work of the present, especially in America, as his particular province, and often said that if our younger composers were to have a sense of possessing any audience, someone must make it his function to listen to them all. In complete modesty and selflessness he took that task upon himself. As his friends knew, Paul Rosenfeld gave himself away to his generation, a very unusual act in our fiercely competitive world, where even our intellectual life seems so often to become poisoned by the habits of our business civilization.

I have cited Rosenfeld because his generous openness to all the arts and his devoted impressions of what he found now seem so foreign to the grimly thin-lipped disciples of a more rigorous analysis. Indeed, one of them, writing currently in the *Hudson Review,* has declared that the recent volume of tribute by Rosenfeld's contemporaries from the twenties and thirties praised him for a "thoroughly degraded function." Such total lack of comprehension is a devastating illustration of what Auden meant by saying that one of the worst symptoms of sterility in our present culture is that of "intellectuals without love."

No incapacity could be less fruitful in the presence of the arts. Its recent frequency may be another unhappy by-product of the sort of specialization that leaves the student knowing only his own field. Such self-enclosed knowledge may often mean that he really knows nothing at all. At least it is hard to conceive of a good critic of literature who does not have an alert curiosity about other fields and techniques. Anyone understands his own subject and discipline better if he is aware of some other subject and discipline. To what extent this awareness should lead to mastery will vary greatly with individual aptitude. It does not seem profitable to insist that any given critic should also be expert in linguistic theory or mathematical logic or Marx or Freud, but I can hardly think of a critic today being indifferent to the access of power his mind could gain from a close study of one or more of these.

This does not mean that the misapplication of theory from one field to another is not as big a pitfall as it always was, or that fads don't often outrun facts. But as one instance of valuable cross-fertilization between fields there is cultural anthropology. Utilizing the disciplines of history and sociology, it has proved a particularly stimulating ally to the study of literature in a period when literature itself, in the hands of Joyce and Mann, has been rediscovering the vitality of primitive myth. Through our renewed awareness of folk patterns we now realize that the fertility rites which solemnize the death and rebirth of the year are equally germane to our understanding of *The Waste Land* or *The Winter's Tale* or *The Peace* of Aristophanes or the *Bacchae* of Euripides.

Another awareness which our split society makes it hard for us to keep in the right proportion is that of the popular arts of our technological age. The consequences for all our lives of the mass media of communication become ever more insistent, so that we must either channel them to socially valuable ends or be engulfed by them. The first results of our new discoveries are often as discouraging as when Thoreau scorned the transatlantic cable on the grounds that the initial news that would "leak through into the broad, flapping American ear" would be that the Princess Adelaide had the whooping cough.

The first results of television would appear to be that it has made conversation impossible in one of its few remaining American strongholds, the barroom, and is debauching the customers with entertainment that is a long throwback to the juvenile days of the penny arcade. But then one recalls how the radio, despite its intolerable deal of soap, has during the past twenty-five years built up a taste for the best symphony music among millions of listeners who would not otherwise have ever heard it. The chief art form of our age, the moving picture, is the compelling reminder of our immense potentialities and continual corruptions. Even now when, in its postwar doldrums, Hollywood seems again to have forgotten that standardization through mass production is more suitable for soup than for art, the great new Italian films are demonstrating the important access of social truth that the art of the film can gain by utilizing some of the solid techniques of the documentary.

I have mentioned these disparate examples of good and bad as a way of enforcing my conviction that we in the universities cannot afford to turn our backs upon them or upon the world from which they come. The proper place for the thinker, as William James conceived it, was at the central point where a battle is being fought. It is impossible for us to take that metaphor with the lightness that he could. Everywhere we turn in these few fateful years since the first atom bomb dropped on Hiroshima we seem menaced by such vast forces that we may well feel that we advance at our peril. But even greater peril would threaten us if those whose prime responsibility as critics is to keep open the life-giving communications between art and society should waver in their obligations to provide ever fresh thought for our own society.

In using metaphors of battle here and now, I am not thinking in an academic void. If we believe that freedom of thought and of speech are the distinguishing features of the culture of democracy, we must realize by what a thin margin they now survive in this country. Within the past year there have been the most serious violations of academic freedom, caused, ironically, by officials who are determined to prove that the United States is so much better than any other country that it is above criticism. We must recognize the full gravity of these casualties of the cold war, for they are a product of the very kind of blind suppression that their instigators declare exists only behind what they denounce as "the iron curtain."

The most flagrant recent case of national importance has nothing to do with the issue of communism, and thus furnishes a concrete demonstration of how, once official opinion embarks on the course of stamping out dangerous views, every shade of dissent becomes dangerous. Olivet College, as you all here know, was founded in the great pioneering period of our education, when Americans were expanding the frontiers of their thought as well as of their territory. Its recent career, particularly in the period between two world wars, added a notable chapter to our experiments with education by tutorial work and group discussion. When members of its faculty of such national distinction as a Pulitzer-prize winner for biography and the candidate for vice-president on the Socialist ticket are dismissed, none of us can stand aloof or feel that we are not implicated.

If what I have just been saying seems an unwarranted digression from the responsibilities of the critic of the arts, I want to correct that impression. The series of awarenesses which I believe the critic must possess lead ineluctably from literature to life, and I do not see how the responsible intellectual in our time can avoid being concerned with politics. It is at this point that my divergence becomes most complete from the formalists who have followed in the wake of Eliot, as well as from Eliot himself, whose reverence for the institutions of monarchy and aristocracy seems virtually meaningless for life in America.

I would like to recall the atmosphere of the early 1930's, of the first years of the last depression, when the critical pendulum had swung to the opposite pole, from the formalists to the Marxists. I am not a Marxist myself but a Christian, and I have no desire to repeat the absurdities of the moment when literary men, quite oblivious theretofore of economics, were finding sudden salvation in a dogma that became more rigid the less they had assimilated it. But I believe the instinct of that moment was right, as our greatest recent cultural historian, Vernon Parrington's instinct was right, insisting upon the primacy of economic factors in society. Most artists and students of literature remain amateurs in the field of economics, but that does not prevent them from utilizing some of the basic and elementary truths which economists have made available for our culture.

Emerson held that a principle is an eye to see with, and despite all the excesses and exaggerated claims of the Marxists of the thirties, I still believe that the principles of Marxism—so much under fire now—can have an immense value in helping us to see and comprehend our literature. Marx and Engels were revolutionary in many senses of that word. They were pioneers in grasping the fact that the industrial revolution had brought about—and would continue to bring about—revolutionary changes in the whole structure of society. By cutting through political assumptions to economic realities, they revolutionized the way in which thinking men regarded the modern state. By their rigorous insistence upon the economic foundations underlying any cultural superstructure, they drove, and still drive, home the fact that unless the problems rising from the economic inequalities in our own modern industrialized society are better solved, we cannot continue to build democracy. Thus the principles of Marxism remain at the base of much of the best social and cultural thought of our century. No educated American can afford to be ignorant of them, or to be delinquent in realizing that there is much common ground between these principles and any healthily dynamic America.

This is not to say that Marxism gives what I consider an adequate view of the nature of man, or that it or any other economic theory can provide a substitute for the critic's essential painstaking discipline in the interplay between form and content in concrete works of art. But a concern with economics can surely quicken and enlarge the questions that a critic asks about the content of any new work of art with which he is faced, about the fullness to which it measures and reveals the forces that have produced both it and its author. Walt Whitman might have said, in *Democratic Vistas:* "Man becomes free, not by realizing himself in opposition to society, but by realizing himself through society." That sentence was actually written by Christopher Caudwell, a young English Marxist who was killed fighting for the Loyalists in Spain. His book *Illusion and Reality,* published in 1937, has recently been re-issued, and is having a renewed vogue now with younger writers and students. Their enthusiasm for it, I gather, springs from the fact that Caudwell, despite the sweeping immaturity of many of his judgments, keeps asking the big questions about man in society that the school of close textual analysis has tended to ignore.

I do not mean for a moment to underestimate the value of that school. It has taught us in particular how to read poetry with an alertness and resilience of attention that were in danger of being altogether lost through the habits set up by an age of quick journalism. All I would suggest is that analysis itself can run to seed unless the analyzing mind is also absorbed in a wider context than the text before it.

Mention of Caudwell's name has brought me to the last of the awarenesses that I would urge upon the critic: that of the wide gap which still exists between America and Europe. Henry James discovered long ago his leading theme in the contrast between American innocence and European experience. Although the world that he contemplated has been altered beyond recognition, that theme is still peculiarly urgent when we are faced with the difference between a Europe which has undergone fascism and destructive war at first hand and an America which has come out of the war richer and more powerful than ever before. Stephen Spender has noticed the difference in reading Randall Jarrell's book of poems called *Losses.* For the American, as Spender observes, even when the losses are those of our own fliers, they are something that happens far away on distant continents, they are not yet immediately overhead and inescapable. Allen Tate has described the kind of false superiority that can be engendered by such special isolation:

> The American people fully armed
> With assurance policies, righteous and harmed,
> Battle the world of which they're not at all.

How do Americans become part of that greater world? Not by pretending to be something they are not, nor by being either proud or ashamed of their vast special fortune. It does no good, for example, to adopt the vocabulary of the Paris existentialists in order to emulate the crisis of occupation which we have not passed through. The ironic lines of Tate's *Sonnet at Christmas* suggest a more mature way of meeting experience. None of us can escape what we are, but by recognizing our limitations, and comprehending them, we can transcend them by the span of that knowledge.

Here is the area where breadth of concern becomes most rewarding for the critic. By perceiving what his country is and is not in comparison with other countries, he can help contribute, in this time of fierce national tensions, to the international understanding without which civilization will not survive. He will also find that he has come to know his own country better.

The art of a country always becomes richer by being open to stimulus from outside, and criticism can find a particularly fertile field in observing the results of that interchange. For one fascinating instance, how much we can learn about both Europe and America from the high estimation that French writers are now giving to the novels of Faulkner. At a period when the French have felt a debilitation in their own tradition, they have turned to the new world for an access of vitality. But what has seemed to them most real in America is not our surface optimism, but the terrible underlying violence that has possessed the imaginations of nearly all our naturalistic novelists. It may seem a strange paradox that America, spared so far the worst violences of fascism and war, has imagined violence in a way that impresses men who have experienced the savage brutality of both.

But as we look back at America through French eyes, we become more conscious of what the preponderantly genteel reviewers for our organs of mass circulation have done their best to obscure: that Faulkner is not a writer of meaningless sensationalism, but one who has seized upon basic forces in our history, particularly upon the tensions resulting from our initial injustice to the Negro. Faulkner may often overwrite and use some of the cheap devices of melodrama, but we should not allow these to deflect us from the truth of his record. If we prefer a more smiling version of ourselves, we are liable to the peculiarly American dilemma of passing from innocence to corruption without ever having grasped maturity. By which I mean the maturity that comes from the knowledge of both good and evil.

In proposing an ever widening range of interests for the ideal critic, I have moved from his central responsibility to the text before him out to an awareness of some of the world-wide struggles of our age. We must come back to where we started, to the critic's primary function. He must judge the work of art as work of art. But knowing form and content to be inseparable, he will recognize his duty to both. Judgment of art is unavoidably both an aesthetic and a social act, and the critic's sense of social responsibility gives him a deeper thirst for meaning.

This is not a narrow question of the wrong right or right left politics. The *locus classicus* on this matter was furnished by Marx's judgment of Balzac, who as a monarchist and Catholic reactionary supported the very forces to which Marx was most opposed. Yet Marx could perceive that, no matter what this novelist's views, his vision of the deep corruption of French society by money made him the most searching historian of his time. Engels proceeded to evolve the principle inherent in this judgment: "The father of tragedy, Aeschylus, and the father of comedy, Aristophanes, were both very clearly poets with a thesis. . . . But I believe that the thesis must inhere in the situation and the action, without being explicitly formulated; and it is not the poet's duty to supply the reader in advance with the future historical solution of the conflict he describes."

A poet describes many other things besides conflict, yet without some sense of conflict there is no drama to engage us. The way in which the artist implies social judgments and entices the critic to meditate upon them may be elucidated by a pair of examples. Wallace Stevens' second book, *Ideas of Order,* appeared in 1935. Until then he had been known by his richly musical *Harmonium,* by what he himself had called "the essential gaudiness of poetry." The besetting weakness of criticism, when faced with a new writer, is to define his work too narrowly, and then to keep applying that definition like a label. Stevens had been bracketed as "a dandy of poetry," as an epicurean relisher of "sea surfaces full of clouds," as one who had found his role in discovering "thirteen ways of looking at a blackbird," as identical with his own Crispin in his relish of "good, fat, guzzly fruit."

He was, to be sure, all these enchanting things. But no one seemed to have been prepared for the fact that his imagination was so fecund and robust that it would compel him to launch forth, in his mid-fifties, upon the new territory indicated by his explicitly philosophical title. He was also making his own response to the vast disequilibrium that every sensitive mind had to feel at the pit of the depression. He had come to recognize that "a violent order is disorder." Or, as Horace Gregory put it more explicitly, Stevens' new poems were demonstrating that he was not merely a connoisseur of nuances, but—not unlike Henry James—a shrewdly trained observer of "the decadence that follows upon the rapid acquisition of wealth and power."

Stevens' kind of symbolist poetry never makes the explicit approach. So far as he has any political or social views, they would appear to be conservative. Yet in *Sad Strains of a Gay Waltz,* the second poem in *Ideas of Order,* he gave to a then young radical like myself a sudden clarification of the clouded time in which we are living. It is this kind of "momentary stay against confusion," as Robert Frost has said, that a poem is designed to give, and that becomes one of the measures of its authenticity.

In listening to almost any poem by Stevens, the first thing that strikes you is his past-masterly command of rhetoric, a reminder that, unlike the poets of the imagist movement, he is still rooted in the older tradition that leads from Bridges back to Milton. In this poem his rhetoric is formed into three-lined unrhymed stanzas of a basically iambic pentameter pattern, but with many irregular line lengths which quicken but do not break that pattern. The conflict that constitutes his theme is between an age that is dying and a hazardous potential new birth. He adumbrates this by offsetting a character whom he calls Hoon, a lover of solitude like Thoreau, against the rising masses of men in a still formless society. But his controlling symbols are more oblique, they are "waltzes" and "shadows." Music that has become played out seems to its listeners to be "empty of shadows," and by a very effective repetition of the phrase, "Too many waltzes have ended," Stevens sets up his counterpoise for a new, more dynamic music that will again be full of shadows:

> The truth is that there comes a time
> When we can mourn no more over music
> That is so much motionless sound.
>
> There comes a time when the waltz
> Is no longer a mode of desire, a mode
> Of revealing desire and is empty of shadows.
>
> Too many waltzes have ended. And then
> There's that mountain-minded Hoon,
> For whom desire was never that of the waltz,
>
> Who found all form and order in solitude,
> For whom the shapes were never the figures of men.
> Now, for him, his forms have vanished.
>
> There is order in neither sea nor sun.
> The shapes have lost their glistening.
> There are these sudden mobs of men,

These sudden clouds of faces and arms,
An immense suppression, freed,
These voices crying without knowing for what,

Except to be happy, without knowing how,
Imposing forms they cannot describe,
Requiring order beyond their speech.

Too many waltzes have ended. Yet the shapes
For which the voices cry, these, too, may be
Modes of desire, modes of revealing desire.

Too many waltzes—The epic of disbelief
Blares oftener and soon, will soon be constant.
Some harmonious skeptic soon in a skeptical music

Will unite these figures of men and their shapes
Will glisten again with motion, the music
Will be motion and full of shadows.

The extension of our sense of living by compelling us to contemplate a broader world is the chief gift that literature holds out to us. This sense is never limited to our own place or time. What makes the art of the past still so full of undiscovered wealth is that each age inevitably turns to the past for what it most wants, and thereby tends to remake the past in its own image. The cardinal example is Shakespeare. What the nineteenth century saw in Hamlet was what Coleridge saw, the figure of a transcendental philosopher absorbed in himself. What we see is a man inextricably involved with his own society, as may be suggested in brief by one of the scenes which nineteenth-century producers usually cut. This is the scene in the fourth act where Hamlet, on his way to England, encounters a Captain from Fortinbras' army. The Captain is bitter at what his orders are compelling him to do:

> Truly to speak, and with no addition,
> We go to gain a little patch of ground
> That hath in it no profit but the name.
> To pay five ducats, five, I would not farm it.

The effect of this speech upon Hamlet is to heighten his awareness of the difference between the Captain's situation

and his own, of how he, Hamlet, has every reason for action
and yet cannot bring himself to act:

> Examples gross as earth exhort me;
> Witness this army of such mass and charge
> Led by a delicate and tender prince,
> Whose spirit with divine ambition puff'd
> Makes mouths at the invisible event,
> Exposing what is mortal and unsure
> To all that fortune, death, and danger dare,
> Even for an egg-shell. Rightly to be great
> Is not to stir without great argument,
> But greatly to find quarrel in a straw
> When honour's at the stake. How stand I then,
> That have a father kill'd, a mother stain'd,
> Excitements of my reason and my blood,
> And let all sleep, while to my shame I see
> The imminent death of twenty thousand men,
> That for a fantasy and trick of fame
> Go to their graves like beds, fight for a plot
> Whereon the numbers cannot try the cause,
> Which is not tomb enough and continent
> To hide the slain?

As John Gielgud speaks these lines, we feel what Shakespeare meant his audience to feel, the necessity for Hamlet's
revenge. But we also bring to the passage our own sense of
vast insecurity, our need of being engaged in the public issues
of our menaced time, and yet the need of making sure that
the seeming issues are the true issues, that we are not betrayed
into engagements that are merely "th'imposthume of much
wealth and peace."

There is a basic distinction between bringing everything in
your life to what you read and reading into a play of the past
issues that are not there. All I am suggesting is the extent to
which our awareness of ourselves as social beings is summoned
by the greatest art. That is the root of my reason for believing
that the good critic becomes fully equipped for his task by as
wide a range of interests as he can master. The great temptation for the young writer at the present moment is to think

that because the age is bad, the artist should escape from it and, as a superior being, become a law simply to himself. Some memorable romantic poetry has been written on that assumption, but not the great forms of drama or epic, nor the comparable great forms in prose. However, the critic should freely grant that the artist writes as he must. But for his own work the critic has to be both involved in his age and detached from it. This double quality of experiencing our own time to the full and yet being able to weigh it in relation to other times is what the critic must strive for, if he is to be able to discern and demand the works of art that we need most. The most mature function of the critic lies finally in that demand.

Literature and Morality:
A Crucial Question of Our Times

JAMES T. FARRELL

I

IN RECENT YEARS emphasis on moral questions has been increasingly apparent in all kinds of discussions—journalistic, political, literary, and philosophical. This interest in morality has developed at a time when the entire capitalist system, and with it the Soviet Union, has sunk into a deep moral impasse. Briefly and unmistakably, the modern world has fallen into a moral abyss. But despite the real moral conditions and practices of the times, there is a kind of petty pathos in the lack of seriousness with which a number of writers—ex-Marxists, journalists who have been styled "one-man revolutions," literary critics included—have tried to discuss these questions while they themselves have been so empty.

In dealing with moral questions, two polar approaches can be cited: the approach which emphasizes social morality, and that which stresses personal, or individual, morality. Social morality assumes that major evils are derivable from, or at least *decisively* influenced by, the structural character of society itself. Consequently the aim of social morality is to change society by changing and lifting moral practice to a higher level, or to eradicate those conditions and attitudes which sanction and contribute in manifold ways to the practices which result in social harm, in the deformation of human personalities, and in the oppression and exploitation of groups, classes, and nations. In other words, social morality conceives social change as the major means of creating better moral conditions. The real core of any social morality, and the establishment of the theoretical basis for the premises of such a morality, is to be found in revolutionary Marxism. For Marxism declares without equivocation that the exploitation of man by man is the major causative factor underlying social immorality.

Many recent moral discussions have presented critiques, of various importance and merit, of Marxian morality. In some cases these have attacked the practices of individuals or organizations working within the historical tradition of Marxism. Some of these attacks have been made on the ground that Marxists, or so-called Marxists, in practice have violated their own moral standards; others have been to the effect that immoral practices, real or alleged, on the part of Marxists, have been a necessary consequence of the essential ideas, the very basis, the seemingly ineradicable character of Marxian theory and practice itself. However, rarely have critics (well-intentioned or otherwise, intelligent and informed or obtuse and trivial) attacked the premise upon which a Marxian moral conception is, and must be, established: the condemnation of the exploitation of man by man. But here when I speak for Marxian morality, I do so on the basis of this premise: an overwhelming number of immoral practices in modern society are, directly or indirectly, a result of the exploitation of man by man; this, in turn, means the exploitation of social classes by other social classes, in order that the exploiting classes may reap the fruits produced by the exploited class; so often this goes on under conditions which barely permit more than a subsistence living for large numbers of the exploited. Subsidiary questions—questions of the practices of Marxians, criticism of the methods of certain organizations which are, or which style themselves, Marxian—are not an issue here and do not bear directly on this discussion.

Counterposed to the social conception of morality is the conception of individual morality: the assumption that the major moral problem facing man is the regeneration of the individual rather than the change of society. There are a number of variations of this attitude: sundry Christian attitudes, such as that of the Catholic Church (which holds that the purpose of life is death and that the aim of a good man on this earth should be to save his soul in the next world); Tolstoyism (which preaches passive resistance, pacifism, apoliticalism in general); the conceptions of various anarchists, ex-Marxists, Platonists, and pseudo-Platonists, of psychiatrists who see the curing of psychoneuroses as the major problem facing man, and so on. Although I do not wish arbitrarily to equate these various doctrines which are based on one or another form of personal or self-regeneration, it should be clear that they can be grouped together in the sense that they present the problem of the individual as prior to the social problem.

There is, however, no necessary polarity between a moral code based on what I here term social morality and one based on personal morality. When the individual and society are separated as polar opposites, moral problems are made less, not more, clear. For this kind of bifurcation results in a false picture of man in relation to society. Man (and this is also stressed in the best Marxian writing) lives out his personal drama on the plane of society; man's very self and his personality are socially directed, socially delimited, socially organized. The self is a social product, not a separate, individual entity, superior to, anterior to, separable from, society. Nor can one consider society as outside of man, superior to man, or the sole responsible agent for what is called immoral action. And it is equally misleading to consider and condemn immoral action on the assumption that the individual *qua* individual is solely responsible for the action so condemned, and that the society in which he lives is in no way responsible. Consequently, a social morality should not, and can not, base itself on such a bifurcation. The laws, the standards, the moral code, the *mores* of capitalist society sanction exploitation, grant individuals with money the legal and even the moral right to exploit others. But when a man is exploited he is not exploited by society in general; he is exploited by individual men. A careful reading of Marx's *Capital* should make it clear that Marx definitely shows that capitalist society creates the conditions which deform the human nature of both exploited and exploiter, who therefore pay a moral price. Other writers have made the same point and it has been dramatized in fiction.

Social morality should not conceive of society as a separate entity; it should not view society as a responsible agent divorced from the men of whom it is composed, who live by, in spite of, or in opposition to its values, and who affirm or attack its sanctions. If this is done, social morality is rendered *arbitrary* and can easily become nothing more than a sentimental and innocuous humanitarianism which preaches but does not practice. It can be, and has been, turned into a philosophy which substitutes social service for independent political action on the part of the workers, in behalf of all the oppressed and exploited.

But, on the other hand, a morality based solely on the conception of personal or self regeneration is usually limited, at best, and besides being incomplete, it is often used as a means of evading issues and expressing moral snobbery and moral priggishness, or as an excuse for moral escape and inactivity.

The problems of literature and morals have been dealt with or alluded to frequently in recent years. Conceptions of morality, moral judgments of literature, are ultimately inescapable, even if rendered on a solely hedonistic basis. Simply put, morality deals with what is considered to be either good or bad, and good or bad are determined, absolutely or relatively, in terms of some set of values or attitudes or standards. We all make moral judgments, and at times we offer moral judgment when we discuss literature. The recent revival of interest in problems of literature and morality is one manifestation of the alleged moral renaissance in our times. These problems have been presented and dealt with differently by various literary critics and writers. The current revival of the works of Henry James, the creation of what actually amounts to a James cult, has also brought to the fore the problems of literature and morality. In fact, some enthusiasts have presented James as a moralist. But there are moralists and moralists. In James, morals and manners are bound together; we can see this simply and clearly in one of his best stories, *Daisy Miller*. Daisy, a delightful, spontaneous, and wholly attractive American girl traveling in Europe (a characterization which, if nothing else could be cited, would be more than enough to establish James as an artist of extraordinary perception and adroitness) faces a

dual danger which arises from the fact that in her social relationships she is democratic—that in general she is direct, frank,
honest. The danger is that: (a) she may lose her virginity,
which in her world means ruin and degradation; and (b) she
may compromise herself and cause her own social ruin by
violating the code of etiquette of her social class.

James was not a moralist in the sense that Tolstoy was.
James did not write with an urgency, with an almost pitiless
consistency, urging change as a demanding necessity; he cannot be described as a man who fought vigorously for a code of
morals he saw as higher than that prevalent in his time nor did
he condemn the code of his time or the evils bound up with it
pitilessly, as Tolstoy did.

James's world is one of people deformed by the fear of violating etiquette. But the moral protest in James is relatively
pale. He was rather a reflector of the moral tone of sections of
the upper classes in his own time than a moralist in any serious
sense of the word. Those who have elevated James to the
stature of a major moralist of our time are fooling themselves
if not their readers. They are as unfair to the reputation of
James as an artist as to their readers. And they are helping to
make moral attitudes the special preoccupation of a literary
cult, composed of people who consider themselves to be *au
courant* and indisputably *advanced*. Morality then becomes a
special esthetic of literary people. The seeming newness of this
stylized and estheticized morality makes it appear as part of
the tone of the times. But actually the attitude it conceals is
one of the stalest of all reactionary tricks. Until reaction is
forced out into the open, where it must be nakedly violent, it
has to rely on all kinds of subterfuges; and these subterfuges
appear in literature, in literary criticism, in philosophy, in
ideology in general. The full or partial equation of morals and
manners, the stylization of morals into an esthetic-moral attitude, lead to a snobbery which glorifies the special apprecia-
tors of literature, of cultural value—how common, how banal!
In passing, I would remark that a parallel attitude in politics
was one of the major ideological weapons of the rebellious
slaveowners who tried to destroy the American Union in 1861

and to establish in perpetuity a slaveowners' republic in America. The ideologists of the slaveowners said their cause would win because Jefferson Davis was more educated than Abraham Lincoln, had better manners than The Rail Splitter, and—to cap the climax—was the better-looking of the two presidents. I cite this example not to equate the ideologists of the slaveowners with some of the current, advanced, *educated*, genteel, and undeniably competent literary people of the hour, but, rather, to point out that there are various manifestations of this reactionary subterfuge.

This kind of estheticized morality, then, is a variation of the moral attitude which demands personal regeneration in place of social change. But at best it is the most tenuous kind of morality. It is neither robust nor all-inclusive. To a great extent it is literary. And it functions, more or less, by dealing with moral reflection as it is to be grasped by reading and analyzing literary works of art. But there is more to be said concerning works of literature that deal with moral problems in terms of personal experience. In order to make my point plain, I shall refer to the writings of Dostoevsky and Ibsen.

Dostoevsky deals with moral problems from the standpoint of the personal experience of one or more of his protagonists. And these moral problems usually result from the behavior of a hero who causes serious and even irreparable injury to another human being, or else wishes to do so. Thus, Raskolnikov commits a murder. Thus, Ivan Karamazov wishes for the death of his father and acts on this wish by speaking with high suggestiveness to Smerdyakov, who is the actual murderer. Ivan then goes off in order to be away from the scene at the time of the murder—if it is to be committed at all. For Dostoevsky, an action of this kind poses a moral problem in the mind of the hero, and this problem becomes obsessive. It is expressed by a need for confession, a need for the resolution of a disturbing, painfully recurring, demanding sense of guilt. Thus Dostoevsky is concerned with problems in terms of consequences to others beside the agent of an act. And these problems arise from actions that are central to his stories. Dostoevsky meets moral problems head-on. Furthermore, he identifies himself,

directly and unmistakably, with sinners, criminals, the suffering—in short, with all the unfortunate. He was explicitly a
political reactionary, and he never masked this fact. But explicitly reactionary though he was, he nonetheless identified
himself not with those who benefited most from their advan-
tageous position in Tsarist society, but with some of those who
suffered most—with some of those who punished themselves as
well as others. His work expressed an urgent need for change
—for a psychological change which he perceived as a process
of purgation and regeneration. Thus it is to be noted that at
the end of *Crime and Punishment* Raskolnikov, a convicted
and confessed murderer, is described as bound for Siberia,
which the author presents as the stage for a possible drama of
Raskolnikov's regeneration. Finally, the moral problem posed
concerns the hero, the protagonist. I stress this fact because
the new tendency of stylized literary morality sometimes poses
the moral problem in terms of the spectator, who does not act
and who does not have to make responsible decisions demanding action.

For Ibsen, too, conscience was a recurrent problem. A representative Ibsen character such as Mrs. Alving or the wife of
John Gabriel Borkman is haunted by ghosts. The ghosts symbolize guilt as well as tragically recurring patterns and continuously poison the existence of one or more persons. The
action of someone in the past has resulted in a serious interfer-
ence with the destinies of other people. These other people
suffer; they are victims and they are not free. The yearning
and manly urge toward freedom expressed in Ibsen involves
a desire to be free of ghosts, which can be ultimately associated with bourgeois morality. In Ibsen's world it is usually a
bourgeois who in the past has been guilty of the actions which
cause serious problems in the present. It is the more favorably
situated persons who are morally guilty. In this connection,
one might remark in passing that Ibsen does not throw the
major burden of guilt on Jacob Engstrand or on his daughter,
Regina, who, in *Ghosts*, is a maid in the Alving household. The
fate of these two characters has been bound up with the actions of their superiors, the Alvings, who have a superior class

and social position: Regina suffers because she is the victim of the actions of her social superiors. This is unmistakable in *Ghosts*.

In general, features parallel to those we have noted briefly in the cases of Dostoevsky and Ibsen can be observed in many works of the past which deal with morality from the standpoint of personal experience and personal problems. In such writings the artist does not reveal these moral problems from the standpoint of the upper classes. He does not present the upper classes as morally superior. Rather, he often deals with the moral problems and the moral consequences confronting those who have a favored or a relatively favored position in society.

II

In *Partisan Review*, Fall, 1945, there is a story that throws some light on these problems: "The Other Margaret," by Lionel Trilling. It can be accepted as a representative literary expression of the stylized literary-moral tendency that exists in some of the advanced, cultural circles of contemporary New York. The protagonist of Mr. Trilling's story is named Stephen Elwin; he is a publisher of scientific works; he is married; and he has a thirteen-year-old daughter, Margaret, who evidently goes to a progressive school. Stephen lives in the East Nineties (in New York City), and the best feature of the story is the manner in which Trilling re-creates the genteel, cultivated, wistful atmosphere of an educated family in this vicinity. Stephen, a man of taste, is first seen buying a Rouault reproduction. He can be described as seeking wisdom, and, early in the story, he recalls that in high school a teacher had read to his class the following sentence from Hazlitt: "No young man believes he shall ever die." At that time Stephen hadn't fully understood the wisdom of this sentence but now, at the age of forty-one, he does understand. Thus, wisdom is to be defined basically as the comprehension of death. Stephen is wistful, gentle; and he is, presumably, a man of wisdom as well as taste. Moreover, he perceives what is ostensibly the moral problem of the present era.

This moral problem, which is at the heart of Trilling's story, concerns the question of responsibility. Is the individual responsible for his actions or is society responsible? Although Stephen sees this problem from the vantage point of an individual moral spectator, the problem is posed in class terms. In the course of the story three important incidents give data concerning the problem. As Stephen rides home on a Fifth Avenue bus, an Irish conductor is berating a small boy of the well-to-do classes—a boy who might have been Stephen when he couldn't comprehend the wisdom in the sentence "No young man believes he shall ever die." Then, after Stephen arrives home, and while his daughter, Margaret, ritualistically prepares a pre-supper cocktail for him, Stephen's wife, Lucy, tells him that while riding on a bus she heard the conductor speaking with anti-Semitic innuendoes to a Jewish person. Further, the Elwins are having difficulties with their Negro maid, The Other Margaret, who is very unpleasant. Today she has not appeared and Mrs. Elwin has to cook dinner.

While she cooks, Stephen has his drink. He shows his Rouault reproduction to their daughter who doesn't like it. They discuss morality, with special reference to their maid. The daughter disagrees with Stephen concerning the conduct of The Other Margaret, and declares that she isn't to be blamed for her rudeness (at school Margaret's teacher, who is a liberal, has explained to the students that society is responsible). Stephen, wistfully tolerant, does not press his objections to his daughter's view too strongly, but it is clear that he does not accept it. He points out that a former maid, after borrowing money in order to go South because of family illness, had paid it back; and thus, while also of the lower classes, she is different from The Other Margaret. Margaret has modeled a toy lamb at school to be given to her mother as a birthday present, and she now shows it to her father; he is pleased. Her mother sees it, and is touched by it.

The Other Margaret appears unexpectedly to serve dinner. She is again very rude to her employers. But this rudeness does not change the daughter's view that society is responsible. However, after dinner The Other Margaret—as is her wont—

breaks things. One of the things she breaks is the personally precious lamb Margaret has made for her mother. When this happens, the daughter cries in anger and denounces The Other Margaret. She declares that the maid broke the lamb on purpose and out of hatred for her, Margaret. As a result, the claim that society, and not the individual, is responsible is refuted: Margaret's liberal teacher is shown to be wrong on the basis of evidence to be found in personal experience. Margaret is hurt and begins to cry. Stephen gives her what comfort he can but cannot heal the child's spiritual wound. Furthermore, it is one of the scars of growing up. Like her father, Margaret, also, must bear the pains of growth and discovery, those pains which mark the journey through life whereby the child becomes the youth—the youth who believes he will never die—and only begins to attain wisdom when he goes on into the maturity of middle age. The attainment of wisdom is painful. It teaches us that we will die, that we are responsible agents, and that we must accept our responsibility. This, in substance, is the theme of Trilling's story.

Trilling's story was conceived and written with adroitness; but the author's careful selection of incidents reveals that it is also highly tendentious. Thus, all the middle-class people in the story are kind, civilized, tolerant. They want to be fair. On the other hand the workers, the lower classes, as represented by two bus conductors and a Negro maid, are shown acting with unjustifiable rudeness in street incidents and in the sphere of home life. And these incidents are used as illustrative data on the basis of which a conclusion is to be reached concerning the contemporary moral problem. Stephen Elwin believes that the individual is responsible; the opposite view, the claim that society is responsible, is presented in the words of an inexperienced thirteen-year-old girl who is still too young to appreciate the painting of Rouault. She has learned her moral lessons by rote from an off-stage teacher who never appears directly in the story. Moreover, the social view of morality is presented in a few generalized sentences. And opposed to the child who defends the ideas of social morality we have the moral spectator, the man who has grown to wisdom, Stephen

Elwin. Stephen is not even called upon to act morally. He perceives the data of experience necessary for drawing moral conclusions in much the same manner as he tastefully appreciates the work of Rouault.

Trilling exercises his genuine skill and cultivation on this pretentious triviality, which he masks by so organizing the story as to be able to draw an almost all-encompassing moral conclusion. Stephen Elwin's sadness over the rudeness and brutality of the world, manifest in the behavior of bus conductors and maids—what is this if not the attitude we find in contemporary criticism, among the Henry James cultists, among those critics and writers who were the literary Marxists of yesterday? There is further triviality in the pettiness of the incidents as compared to the grandeur of the conclusion, which affirms nothing less than that man is a free agent. For the claim that the individual is responsible presupposes a belief in free agency. Thus, while we can recognize the skill with which this story is written, and while we can concede it the merit of picturing a certain cultivated milieu of our time, we should realize that it is cleverly organized to present a reactionary moral view with insidious persuasiveness. I use the word reactionary here because Trilling's story establishes a conclusion concerning freedom and responsibility at the expense of those who most need to be free, and on the basis of citing relatively trivial incidents. This tendentiousness, expressed not by overt statement but in the selection of characters and incidents, dictates in this way the structure of the story. The rude lower classes are portrayed objectively, through action and dialogue. But with the author we penetrate the consciousness of the cultivated intellectual of the middle class, presented as a thoughtful man, a tolerant man. Further, this man is not an exploiting capitalist who brutally grinds down the workers; he is a man who performs a valuable social function: the publication of books of scientific value. His way of life and his sensibilities are intellectual; in fact, the style and tone of his thoughts suggest the man of literary rather than of scientific cultivation. He is curious about esthetics and morals, and a true seeker after wisdom. But he is not curious enough to ask himself what conditions in the lives of bus conductors and maids might contribute toward rudeness—a rudeness we are not trying to defend. If he were to pose this question to himself, he might be led to other questions and problems—among them the problem of identity. What would Stephen be like if he had come from the lower classes, and how would he differ from the rude representatives who insult children? Is it his cultural background which makes him more tolerant, and if so, how did he get it? These and a number of other questions might be asked. And it is legitimate for us to raise them here in the analysis of a short story for, let me repeat, this short story asserts the all-inclusive moral judgment that man has free will. In reality, the story is not what it seems; it is an expression of the general mood, the retreat from Marxism, the growing moral snobbery of the advanced and cultivated New York intellectual. As such, it is a revealing account of the escapism of what we might call the *Partisan Review* intellectual. It indicates the kind of hothouse creative literature we may expect from those of literary sensibilities who confuse morals and manners, and who see morality more or less as a kind of literary stylization.

Literature as Equipment for Living

KENNETH BURKE

HERE I shall put down, as briefly as possible, a statement in behalf of what might be catalogued, with a fair degree of accuracy, as a *sociological* criticism of literature. Sociological criticism in itself is certainly not new. I shall here try to suggest what partially new elements or emphasis I think should be added to this old approach. And to make the "way in" as easy as possible, I shall begin with a discussion of proverbs.

I

Examine random specimens in *The Oxford Dictionary of English Proverbs*. You will note, I think, that there is no "pure" literature here. Everything is "medicine." Proverbs are designed for consolation or vengeance, for admonition or exhortation, for foretelling.

Or they name typical, recurrent situations. That is, people find a certain social relationship recurring so frequently that they must "have a word for it." The Eskimos have special names for many different kinds of snow (fifteen, if I remember rightly) because variations in the quality of snow greatly affect their living. Hence, they must "size up" snow much more accurately than we do. And the same is true of social phenomena. Social structures give rise to "type" situations, subtle subdivisions of the relationships involved in competitive and coöperative acts. Many proverbs seek to chart, in more or less homey and picturesque ways, these "type" situations. I submit that such naming is done, not for the sheer glory of the thing, but because of its bearing upon human welfare. A different name for snow implies a different kind of hunt. Some names for snow imply that one should not hunt at all. And similarly, the names for typical, recurrent social situations are not developed out of "disinterested curiosity," but because the names imply a command (what to expect, what to look out for).

To illustrate with a few representative examples:

Proverbs designed for consolation: "The sun does not shine on both sides of the hedge at once." "Think of ease, but work on." "Little troubles the eye, but far less the soul." "The worst luck now, the better another time." "The wind in one's face makes one wise." "He that hath lands hath quarrels." "He knows how to carry the dead cock home." "He is not poor that hath little, but he that desireth much."

For vengeance: "At length the fox is brought to the furrier." "Shod in the cradle, barefoot in the stubble." "Sue a beggar and get a louse." "The higher the ape goes, the more he shows his tail." "The moon does not heed the barking of dogs." "He measures another's corn by his own bushel." "He shuns the man who knows him well." "Fools tie knots and wise men loose them."

Proverbs that have to do with foretelling (the most obvious are those to do with the weather): "Sow peas and beans in the wane of the moon, Who soweth them sooner, he soweth too soon." "When the wind's in the north, the skilful fisher goes not forth." "When the sloe tree is as white as a sheet, sow your barley whether it be dry or wet." "When the sun sets bright and clear, An easterly wind you need not fear. When the sun sets in a bank, A westerly wind we shall not want."

In short: "Keep your weather eye open": be realistic about sizing up today's weather, because your accuracy has bearing upon tomorrow's weather. And forecast not only the meteorological weather, but also the social weather: "When the moon's in the full, then wit's in the wane." "Straws show which way the wind blows." "When the fish is caught, the net is laid aside." "Remove an old tree, and it will wither to death." "The wolf may lose his teeth, but never his nature." "He that bites on every weed must needs light on poison." "Whether the pitcher strikes the stone, or the stone the pitcher, it is bad for the pitcher." "Eagles catch no flies." "The more laws, the more offenders."

In this foretelling category we might also include the recipes for wise living, sometimes moral, sometimes technical: "First thrive, and then wive." "Think with the wise but talk with the vulgar." "When the fox preacheth, then beware your geese." "Venture a small fish to catch a great one." "Respect a man, he will do the more."

In the class of "typical, recurrent situations" we might put such proverbs and proverbial expressions as: "Sweet appears sour when we pay." "The treason is loved but the traitor is hated." "The wine in the bottle does not quench thirst." "The sun is never the worse for shining on a dunghill." "The lion kicked by an ass." "The lion's share." "To catch one napping." "To smell a rat." "To cool one's heels."

By all means, I do not wish to suggest that this is the only way in which the proverbs could be classified. For instance, I have listed in the "foretelling" group the proverb, "When the fox preacheth, then beware your geese." But it could obviously be "taken over" for vindictive purposes. Or consider a proverb like, "Virtue flies from the heart of a mercenary man." A poor man might obviously use it either to console himself for being poor (the implication being, "Because I am poor in money I am rich in virtue") or to strike at another (the implication being, "When he got money, what else could you expect of him but deterioration?"). In fact, we could even say that such symbolic vengeance would itself be an aspect of solace. And a proverb like "The sun is never the worse for shining on a dunghill" (which I have listed under "typical recurrent situations") might as well be put in the vindictive category.

The point of issue is not to find categories that "place" the proverbs once and for all. What I want is categories that suggest their active nature. Here is no "realism for its own sake." Here is realism for promise, admonition, solace, vengeance, foretelling, instruction, charting, all for the direct bearing that such acts have upon matters of welfare.

II

Step two: Why not extend such analysis of proverbs to encompass the whole field of literature? Could the most complex and sophisticated works of art legitimately be considered somewhat as "proverbs writ large"? Such leads, if held admissible, should help us to discover important facts about literary organization (thus satisfying the requirements of technical criticism). And the kind of observation from this perspective should apply beyond literature to life in general (thus helping to take literature out of its separate bin and give it a place in a general "sociological" picture).

The point of view might be phrased in this way: Proverbs are *strategies* for dealing with *situations*. In so far as situations are typical and recurrent in a given social structure, people develop names for them and strategies for handling them. Another name for strategies might be *attitudes*.

People have often commented on the fact that there are *contrary* proverbs. But I believe that the above approach to proverbs suggests a necessary modification of that comment. The apparent contradictions depend upon differences in *attitude,* involving a correspondingly different choice of *strategy.* Consider, for instance, the *apparently* opposite pair: "Repentance comes too late" and "Never too late to mend." The first is admonitory. It says in effect: "You'd better look out, or you'll get yourself too far into this business." The second is consolatory, saying in effect: "Buck up, old man, you can still pull out of this."

Some critics have quarreled with me about my selection of the word "strategy" as the name for this process. I have asked them to suggest an alternative term, so far without profit. The only one I can think of is "method." But if "strategy" errs in suggesting to some people an overly *conscious* procedure, "method" errs in suggesting an overly *"methodical"* one. Anyhow, let's look at the documents:

Concise Oxford Dictionary: "Strategy: Movement of an army or armies in a campaign, art of so moving or disposing troops or ships as to impose upon the enemy the place and time and conditions for fighting preferred by oneself" (from a Greek word that refers to the leading of an army).

New English Dictionary: "Strategy: The art of projecting and directing the larger military movements and operations of a campaign."

André Cheron, *Traité Complet d'Echecs: "On entend par stratégie les manoeuvres qui ont pour but la sortie et le bon arrangement des pièces."*

Looking at these definitions, I gain courage. For surely, the most highly alembicated and sophisticated work of art, arising in complex civilizations, could be considered as designed to organize and command the army of one's thoughts and images, and to so organize them that one "imposes upon the enemy the time and place and conditions for fighting preferred by oneself." One seeks to "direct the larger movements and operations" in one's campaign of living. One "maneuvers," and the maneuvering is an "art."

Are not the final results one's "strategy"? One tries, as far as possible, to develop a strategy whereby one "can't lose." One tries to change the rules of the game until they fit his own necessities. Does the artist encounter disaster? He will "make capital" of it. If one is a victim of competition, for instance, if one is elbowed out, if one is willy-nilly more jockeyed against than jockeying, one can by the solace and vengeance of art convert this very "liability" into an "asset." One tries to fight on his own terms, developing a strategy for imposing the proper "time, place, and conditions."

But one must also, to develop a full strategy, be *realistic.* One must *size things up* properly. One cannot accurately know how things *will be,* what is promising and what is menacing, unless he accurately knows how things *are.* So the wise strategist will not be content with strategies of merely a self-gratifying sort. He will "keep his weather eye open." He will not too eagerly "read into" a scene an attitude that is irrelevant to it. He won't sit on the side of an active volcano and "see" it as a dormant plain.

Often, alas, he will. The great allurement in our present popular "inspirational literature," for instance, may be largely of this sort. It is a strategy for easy consolation. It "fills a need," since there is always a need for easy consolation—and in an era of confusion like our own the need is especially keen. So people are only too willing to "meet a man halfway" who will *play down* the realistic naming of our situation and *play up* such strategies as make solace cheap. However, I should propose a reservation here. We usually take it for granted that people who consume our current output of books on "How to Buy Friends and Bamboozle Oneself and Other People" are reading as *students* who will attempt applying the recipes given. Nothing of the sort. *The reading of a book on the attaining of success is in itself the symbolic attaining of that success.* It is *while they read* that these readers are "succeeding." I'll wager that, in by far the great majority of cases, such readers make no serious attempt to apply the book's recipes. The lure of the book resides in the fact that the reader, while reading it, is then living in the aura of success. What he wants is *easy* success; and he gets it in symbolic form by the mere reading itself. To attempt applying such stuff in real life would be very difficult, full of many disillusioning problems.

Sometimes a different strategy may arise. The author may remain realistic, avoiding too easy a form of solace—yet he may get as far off the track in his own way. Forgetting that realism is an aspect for foretelling, he may take it as an end in itself. He is tempted to do this by two factors: (1) an *ill-digested* philosophy of science, leading him mistakenly to assume that "relentless" naturalistic "truthfulness" is a proper end in itself, and (2) a merely *competitive* desire to outstrip other writers by being "more realistic" than they. Works thus made "efficient" by tests of competition internal to the book trade are a kind of academicism not so named (the writer usually thinks of it as the *opposite* of academicism). Realism thus stepped up competitively might be distinguished from the proper sort by the name of "naturalism." As a way of "sizing things up," the naturalistic tradition tends to become as inaccurate as the "inspirational" strategy, though at the opposite extreme.

Anyhow, the main point is this: A work like *Madame Bovary* (or its homely American translation, *Babbitt*) is the strategic naming of a situation. It singles out a pattern of experience that is sufficiently representative of our social structure, that recurs sufficiently often *mutatis mutandis,* for people to "need a word for it" and to adopt an attitude towards it. Each work of art is the addition of a word to an informal dictionary (or, in the case of purely derivative artists, the addition of a subsidiary meaning to a word already given by some originating artist). As for *Madame Bovary,* the French critic Jules de Gaultier proposed to add it to our *formal* dictionary by coining the word "Bovarysme" and writing a whole book to say what he meant by it.

Mencken's book on *The American Language,* I hate to say, is splendid. I console myself with the reminder that Mencken didn't write it. Many millions of people wrote it, and Mencken was merely the amanuensis who took it down from their dictation. He found a true "vehicle" (that is, a book that could be greater than the author who wrote it). He gets the royalties, but the job was done by a collectivity. As you read that book, you see a people who were up against a new set of typical recurrent situations, situations typical of their business, their politics, their criminal organizations, their sports. Either there were no words for these in standard English, or people didn't know them, or they didn't "sound right." So a new vocabulary arose, to "give us a word for it." I see no reason for believing that Americans are unusually fertile in word-coinage. American slang was not developed out of some exceptional gift. It was developed out of the fact that new typical situations had arisen and people needed names for them. They had to "size things up." They had to console and strike, to promise and admonish. They had to describe for purposes of forecasting. And "slang" was the result. It is, by this analysis, simply *proverbs not so named,* a kind of "folk criticism."

III

With what, then, would "sociological criticism" along these lines be concerned? It would seek to codify the various strategies which artists have developed with relation to the naming of situations. In a sense, much of it would even be "timeless," for many of the "typical, recurrent situations" are not peculiar to our own civilization at all. The situations and strategies framed in Aesop's Fables, for instance, apply to human relations now just as fully as they applied in ancient Greece. They are, like philosophy, sufficiently "generalized" to extend far beyond the particular combination of events named by them in any one instance. They name an "essence." Or, we could say that they are on a "high level of abstraction." One doesn't usually think of them as "abstract," since they are usually so concrete in their stylistic expression. But they invariably aim to discern the "general behind the particular" (which would suggest that they are good Goethe).

The attempt to treat literature from the standpoint of situations and strategies suggests a variant of Spengler's notion of the "contemporaneous." By "contemporaneity" he meant corresponding stages of different cultures. For instance, if modern New York is much like decadent Rome, then we are "contemporaneous" with decadent Rome, or with some corresponding decadent city among the Mayas, etc. It is in this sense that situations are "timeless," "non-historical," "contemporaneous." A given human relationship may be at one time named in terms of foxes and lions, if there are foxes and lions about; or it may now be named in terms of salesmanship, advertising, the tactics of politicians, etc. But beneath the change in particulars, we may often discern the naming of the one situation.

So sociological criticism, as here understood, would seek to assemble and codify this lore. It might occasionally lead us to outrage good taste, as we sometimes found exemplified in some great sermon or tragedy or abstruse work of philosophy the same strategy as we found exemplified in a dirty joke. At this point, we'd put the sermon and the dirty joke together, thus "grouping by situation" and showing the range of possible particularizations. In his exceptionally discerning essay, "A Critic's Job of Work," R. P. Blackmur says, "I think on the whole his (Burke's) method could be applied with equal fruitfulness to Shakespeare, Dashiell Hammett, or Marie Corelli." When I got through wincing, I had to admit that Blackmur was right. This article is an attempt to say for the method what can be said. As a matter of fact, I'll go a step further and maintain: You can't properly put Marie Corelli and Shakespeare apart until you have first put them together. First genus, then differentia. The strategy in common is the genus. The *range* or *scale* or *spectrum* of particularizations is the differentia.[1]

Anyhow, that's what I'm driving at. And that's why reviewers sometimes find in my work "intuitive" leaps that are dubious as "science." They are not "leaps" at all. They are classifications, groupings, made on the basis of some strategic element common to the items grouped. They are neither more nor less "intuitive" than *any* grouping or classification of social events. Apples can be grouped with bananas as fruits, and they can be grouped with tennis balls as round. I am simply proposing, in the social sphere, a method of classification with reference to *strategies*.

The method has these things to be said in its favor: It gives definite insight into the organization of literary works; and it automatically breaks down the barriers erected about literature as a specialized pursuit. People can classify novels by reference to three kinds, eight kinds, seventeen kinds. It doesn't matter. Students patiently copy down the professor's classification and pass examinations on it, because the range of possible academic* classifications is endless. Sociological classification, as herein suggested, would derive its relevance from the fact that it should apply both to works of art and to social situations outside of art.

[1] See footnote 1 (p. 225) of the essay, "Freud—and the Analysis of Poetry," *The Philosophy of Literary Form*.

It would, I admit, violate current pieties, break down current categories, and thereby "outrage good taste." But "good taste" has become *inert*. The classifications I am proposing would be *active*. I think that what we need is active categories.

These categories will lie on the bias across the categories of modern specialization. The new alignment will outrage in particular those persons who take the division of faculties in our universities to be an exact replica of the way in which God himself divided up the universe. We have had the Philosophy of Being; and we have had the Philosophy of Becoming. In typical contemporary specialization, we have been getting the Philosophy of the Bin. Each of these mental localities has had its own peculiar way of life, its own values, even its own special idiom for seeing, thinking, and "proving." Among other things, a sociological approach should attempt to provide a reintegrative point of view, a broader empire of investigation encompassing the lot.

What would such sociological categories be like? They would consider works of art, I think, as strategies for selecting enemies and allies, for socializing losses, for warding off evil eye, for purification, propitiation, and desanctification, consolation and vengeance, admonition and exhortation, implicit commands or instructions of one sort or another. Art forms like "tragedy" or "comedy" or "satire" would be treated as *equipments for living*, that size up situations in various ways and in keeping with correspondingly various attitudes. The typical ingredients of such forms would be sought. Their relation to typical situations would be stressed. Their comparative values would be considered, with the intention of formulating a "strategy of strategies," the "over-all" strategy obtained by inspection of the lot.

Language as Gesture

R. P. BLACKMUR

IF THERE IS A PUZZLE in my title, it is because, like Sweeney with his ladies in Eliot's *Fragment of an Agon*, "I've gotta use words when I talk to you." The puzzle is verbal, something we have made ourselves, and may be solved. Language is made of words, and gesture is made of motion. There is one half the puzzle. The other half is equally self-evident if only because it is an equally familiar part of the baggage of our thought. It is the same statement put the other way round. Words are made of motion, made of action or response, at whatever remove; and gesture is made of language—made of the language beneath or beyond or alongside of the language of words. When the language of words fails we resort to the language of gesture. If we stop there, we stop with the puzzle. If we go on, and say that when the language of words most succeeds it *becomes* gesture in its words, we shall have solved the verbal puzzle with which we began by discovering one approach to the central or dead-end mystery of meaningful expression in the language of the arts. We shall have made, too, I take it, an imaginative equivalent for Kenneth Burke's more nearly intellectual thesis, which I share, that the language of poetry may be regarded as symbolic action. The difference between Mr. Burke and myself is that where he is predominantly concerned with setting up methods for analyzing the actions as they are expressed in the symbol, I choose to emphasize the created or dead-end symbol. He explores the puzzle of the language in the process of becoming symbolic. I try to show in a series of varied and progressive examples how the symbol invests the actions in language with poetic actuality. Mr. Burke legislates; I would judge; the executive is between us.

There is a line in *Othello* which I think makes it all plain between us, not just between Mr. Burke and myself, but between all of us. "I understand a fury in your words/But not the words." I do not propose this language as itself a gesture, but it is proposed as a fair example of the situation in which language gains the force of gesture; and indeed it leads to the memory of my own earliest experience of language as gesture. As a small boy of six or seven walking the streets of Cambridge I used often to pass little dead-end streets, each with its signpost which at its top read, say, Trowbridge Place or Irving Terrace, and underneath in letters of a different color and on a separate board, the following mysterious legend: Private Way Dangerous Passing. The legend meant of course merely that the City of Cambridge, since it neither built nor maintained the roadbed of this place or this terrace, would not be responsible for injury to life or property sustained through its use. But to me it meant something else. It meant that there was in passing across its mouth a clear and present danger which might, and especially if it was dusk, suddenly leap out and overcome me. Thus, to say the least of it, I had the regular experience of that heightened, that excited sense of being which we find in poetry, whenever I passed one of those signs. I understood the fury in its words, but not the words. Yet I am not sure at this late and dejected day that in understanding the words I have not become indifferent to a fury of meaning that was actually there. There was a steady over-arching gesture in those words, Dangerous Passing, which because I was included within it and indeed partly created it, meant more and touched me more deeply than any merely communicative words, deprived of their native gesture, can ever do.

For gesture *is* native to language, and if you cut it out you cut roots and get a sapless and gradually a rotting if indeed not a petrifying language. (If I may quote a poem of my own in which there was some effort to make an image for standing dead timber, what in Maine we call dri-kai, "Ghostly, these gestures are beyond repair.") But gesture is not only native to language, it comes before it in a still richer sense, and must be, as it were, carried into it whenever the context is imaginative. Living in Belmont some ten years ago I used to go into Cambridge on an orange-yellow bus which made very good time the first half of the trip. If anyone were ahead of you getting on, you might jump from ten to twenty to forty or fifty miles an hour by the time you had paid your fare and found your seat. So it was for the woman I remember one very high bright noon. She got on with a friend whom I do not remember at all except that she sat directly behind me and no doubt looked over my shoulder seeing just what I saw. But the woman herself I remember very well. She was largish and of a French figure, that is with a noticeable waist and a more noticeable rear, and she had heels too high for her balance in a spurting bus. There she stood holding the chromium rail back of the driver's seat looking at her friend (and therefore at me) while the driver made her change. She fair yawed to leeward every few yards, each time knocking the great floppy hat, which women of such figure so often wear askew, against the upright post on which the coin box was set. She had much trouble getting the two fares in the box, and considerably more trouble getting herself from the box down the aisle, hauling from seat to seat by their shining handles against the momentum of the bus, lurching, as she had to, in all directions save the right one. During the whole business—and this is what I am getting at—she managed by sniffs and snorts, by smiles, by sticking her tongue out very sharp, by batting her very blue eyes about, and generally by cocking her head this way and that, she managed to express fully, and without a single word either uttered or wanted, the whole mixed, flourishing sense of her disconcertment, her discomfiture, her uncertainty, together with a sense of adventure and of gaiety, all of which she wanted to share with her companion behind me, who took it I was sure, as I did myself, all smiles. Because I was within the orbit of her gestures I felt myself, as I felt her, fairly playing in life as we say that water-lights play in the sun or moon.

That is an example of the gesture that comes before language; but reflecting upon it, it seems also an example of the gesture which when it goes with language crowns it, and so animates it as to make it independent of speaker or writer; reflecting upon it, it seems that the highest use of language cannot be made without incorporating some such quality of gesture within it. How without it could the novelist make his dialogue ring? how could the poet make his cry lyric, his incongruity comic, or his perspective tragic? The great part of our knowledge of life and of nature—perhaps all our knowledge of their play and interplay—comes to us as gesture, and we are masters of the skill of that knowledge before we can ever make a rhyme or a pun, or even a simple sentence. Nor can we master language purposefully without re-mastering gesture within it. Gesture, in language, is the outward and dramatic play of inward and imaged meaning. It is that play of meaningfulness among words which cannot be defined in the formulas in the dictionary, but which is defined in their use together; gesture is that meaningfulness which is moving, in every sense of that word: what moves the words and what moves us.

Before pursuing the means of access to the mystery of gesture in the art of poetry, let us see quickly how it behaves among the other arts. For if gesture is of such structural importance in poetry as I claim for it, then the other arts should attest for it an equivalent importance; it is in such matters that there must be a substantial unity in all art; there are not two, or three, much less seven, fundamental modes of imagination, but only one. We must use example, not argument, for we wish to remind ourselves not of formulas but of insights, and we wish to get back to poetry with our sense of gesture fortified rather than obstructed.

The clearest and most familiar example of gesture in architecture is the spire on a church, for we have all seen church spires whether we go to church or not. Bad spires weigh a church down and are an affair of carpentry rather than architecture, an example of formula stifling form. A good spire is weightless, springing, an arrow aimed at the Almighty, carrying, in its gesture, the whole church with it. Though it may have been as much made out of formula as the bad spire, it differs in that the formula has somehow seized enough life to become form again; which is one way of saying what gesture does in art—it is what happens to a form when it becomes identical with its subject. It does this, in the case of a spire, by giving the sense of movement, of aspiration, as a tree or a shrub gives the sense of process of growth, or as a beautiful room gives the effect of extending space rather than enclosing it. This sense of movement in "actually" inert mass and empty space is what we call gesture in architecture. So, too, we feel that pillars are mighty, that a bridge spans or leaps, that a dome covers us, or a crypt appalls us.

In sculpture we have much the same situation as in architecture except that the effects are more specifically human in character; for in sculpture we arrest or fix in physical mass and space those human or animal movements, or those essential shapes of body or object, which, arrested, move within themselves, whether from inward outward or outward inward, so as to make a timeless gesture. Here we get the difference between gestures and act. In bad sculpture, what bores us and annoys us and makes us feel that we are bumping our heads against stones, is the sense that the athlete wants to leap or that the horse is about to canter, or whatever it is; the arrested movement wants to go on and complete itself in action. In good sculpture there is none of this, but rather that in the movement arrested, in the moving stillness, there is a gesture completed at the moment of its greatest significance. Examples in sculpture are easy, as in architecture, but less conspicuous. A good vase shows all the gesture value of roundness; a good nude by Maillol or Lehmbruck or Lachaise gives a deep gesture of the body in some moment of meaningful balance. Let us say that good sculpture has a heaviness or lightness which has nothing to do with stone or wood or the carver's trade, but which has everything to do with the gesture which illumines the medium. It is gesture that makes a stone figure a sphinx, and it is gesture that makes the great Sphinx a smile. By which I mean that there is great momentum in great repose and inexhaustible meaningfulness in any image that makes the gesture, as the sphinx does, of the momentum and the repose in man's brooding upon himself. Sculpture is man breeding shapes out of his brooding.

Painting may combine the effect of the gestures in both sculpture and architecture, since it represents the feeling of physical mass and space, but it does so at a remove. The true play of meaning in painting lies rather in what it does with texture, with light, and especially with what it does with our great, and otherwise ineluctable, visual knowledge of human character. No knowledge is so great or so skilled and no knowledge has been so variously felt as our knowledge of what, literally, we *see* in people. But in our knowledges there is none, too, in which we so fumble when we try to say what we know as in this visual knowledge, except when we use the mode of imaginative painting in the field of the portrait or of figure painting. I think, to reach for things at hand, of Rembrandt's Polish Rider, in the Frick galleries, with all its golden gloom and the light gathering against the rider's face, or in the same galleries of Titian's young man in ermine alive in old air —both so full of that maximum human dignity, that rightness and fullness of being, of which no man, seen, can be deprived. Or again there are the portraits of El Greco, brimming, as Marianne Moore's poem says, with inner light—the portrait of the Cardinal in the Metropolitan or that of Brother Felix in the Boston Museum; haunted faces both, haunted with that spiritual life beyond dignity which the flesh cannot ever attain in fact but which is sometimes reached as a gesture of light in eyes and features. How does a painter come by such effects? Look at a society portrait, a prettified portrait, an official portrait—all faithful enough to their sitters; all too faithful, precisely—and is it not plain that their great lack, their yawning vacuity, the almost visible yawn of suppressed inattention, comes about because the painter has rendered them as the average of a long series of unresponsive moments. Nothing is left out but the vital gesture of the single, focal moment, the gesture of some particular state, some long perspective—say the lifelong heaviness of the head upon its little fulcrum—some deep inspiration of the flesh, say the desire *in weariness* for rest, or even, say, just the gaiety and radiance of the features in play with life; nothing is left out but what the great portrait painter puts in: some caught or imagined gesture of awareness that startles the features into a maximum life. The painter puts into his portraits the crossed gesture of knowledge and mystery, of the intolerably familiar and the impossibly alien, which we see in the looking-glass. That is why in great portraits we see ourselves.

In dancing we would seem to have the art that is most directly concerned with gesture, for when the gesture breaks down or does not communicate, the dance does not speak at all. Put the other way around, this means that the gesture in ballet must be built up and infused into what is otherwise "mere" movement. Gesture is what makes dancing buoyant and what makes it possible for it to end. Without gesture there cannot be a beginning or a middle or an end to a dance. Gesture is the means through which the movements of the dance complete themselves, and for these movements to become gesture they usually require ritual (as in the Mass), or music (as in the ballet) for both source and background. I think of a rehearsal of one of the ballets based on Mozart where all was dead cluttering movement until Balanchine, by his single example, brought the movements into tune with the music and so made them suddenly into gesture. Again to revert to the Mass, we have the nature of the ritual itself (consecration, sacrifice, communion) determining the scope of the gesture, and on the other hand we reflect that it is the gesture (the posture of prayer, the elevation of the host, the service of the cup and wafer) which transforms the "mere" movements into ritual. Gesture is perhaps the stable *and* moving element in ritual; it is both what is autochthonous—reborn out of the native soil of feeling—and what is autonomous—and independently controls the meaningfulness in ritual. Still again, and not actually far afield, there is Nijinski's remark that it is the costumes of a ballet that determine what the gestures shall be, as the cut of one's cloth determines one's stride; but it is in turn the gestures of the dancers that bring the costumes, or the nakedness, of the bodies to life. Dancing *delivers* gestures otherwise conceived. It is the natural wayward play of the body, controlled.

Control is the key word with regard to gesture in acting, too, and in much the same senses as in dancing; it is the purposive, conventional control of the body's movements that produces meaningful gesture. Or perhaps we should say that it is a kind of reduction, condensation, telescoping, of free instinctive movements that transforms them into residual gestures, almost as closely ordained as the gestures in ritual. Historically, we can remind ourselves, what we call playacting came out of dumb-show, which was conventionalized mimicry—in short, mummery. Mummery is what the actor calls on apart from his lines when he is making appropriate gestures, and what he calls on in spite of his lines when he is making bad gestures. Of course, as a matter of practice we seldom get familiar enough with a particular version of even a play of Shakespeare to be able to divorce the mummery of it from the lines, but if we could I think we should find that mummery alone is an extraordinarily resourceful and complex art, using the full personality of the actor, rising often through a great span of gesture. Our nearest approach is with a good actor making the best out of bad lines, an affair which, unless we are ourselves mummers, we enjoy apologetically. I recall once having seen Tolstoy's *Living Corpse,* a play which I had not read, produced in German, a language I do not know, with the lead acted by Alessandro Moissi, an actor with whose reputation I was at that time unfamiliar, and in conditions that were hardly propitious: with a straggling handful for audience in the great barn of the Boston Opera House. Yet the experience of the evening proved the case far more than seeing Bernhardt or Duse or Mantell or the Barrymores ever did. For what I saw and heard was nothing but the mummer at his work with movement and posture and voice; the words of the play were transparencies used to time and to bound the acting. What the mere words were, it seemed to me, must have been rubbish; they were so little needed in the face of the fast conventions of voice and movement, conventions that must have been universal to western man since I understood them so well, through which Moissi worked from beauty to lucid beauty of created gesture. The gamut of the actor showed as great as that of any art just because my attention was fastened upon it by being excluded from anything else. Yet I knew at the time that what I felt was good for training short of complete experience: I felt the effect of supreme control without feeling all the controlling force. I missed what the lines of the play called upon Moissi to create; but at least I learned why poor actors ruin the best plays: they have not the knowledge within them which can be called into play. How can a man understand the play of light who has not felt the sun aching in his bones? And how, similarly, can an actor understand the play of words unless they seem to rise and set within him as his own meaning? Great acting bodies forth the gestures only of great words: no more.

It is music that of all the arts does more. Like pure acting its medium may be thought of as entirely in time as time is filled with sound. It is purer than acting because all its movement is movement of sound. But its greatest purity lies in the fact that, although other arts may use some of its effects, it alone of the arts can proceed according to its own purpose without either anterior or subsequent obligation to any other art. Roger Sessions, in the essay which he contributed to *The Intent of the Artist,* says that the purpose of music is to create gestures of the human spirit, and as my argument is on this point only a lesser version of his I refer you to it for the completion and confirmation of my own. But I will say this. I do not know what constitutes the discipline of music from a composer's point of view, except that I am sure it is severe, yet I feel as a layman that the freedom which that discipline secures is the freedom of repetition, of development, of variation within or upon or around a theme to an extent which in any other major art would be not only ineffectual but boring: the freedom, in short, to play with the elements of musical meaning until they become gesture. This is no doubt why Pater said that all the arts tend to the condition of music; the condition is gesture. The rest of music is but the means for the delivery of gesture, and for the artist who rejoices at all in his work that is the most blessed circumstance possible to imagine. It is tantamount to saying that his means—his technique—may become almost the whole object of attention, both for himself and for his audience. It is not his theme, once he has it, but what happens to his theme, that counts; and what happens to it will be precisely and immitigably what he does within his means. His form and his substance will be united in process as well as at the end: united as gesture. No wonder we are happy when we sing and sing when we are sad. The other arts take us in parts, and give us roles to play with ourselves looking on; music takes us all round, gesture without remove.

So with gesture in the six arts of which poetry is surely the natural child, as it shows variously the stigmata of all six and yet makes a fiery gesture all its own. It is the gesture, I like to think, of poetic judgment, the judgment of all the gestures, all the play of meaning, which makes up full being. Poetry is the meaning of meaning, or at least the prophecy of it. "Behold, all ye that kindle a fire, that compass yourselves about with sparks: walk in the light of your fire, and in the sparks that ye have kindled." In these words of Isaiah there is a motto for poetry, a judgment of poetry, and a poetic gesture which carries the prophetic meaning of poetry. The words sound with music, make images which are visual, seem solid like sculpture and spacious like architecture, repeat themselves like the movements in a dance, call for a kind of mummery in the voice when read, and turn upon themselves like nothing but the written word. Yet it is the fury in the words which we understand, and not the words themselves. Let them serve as text for the rest of these remarks; for with them to buoy us up we can start on as low a level as we like.

That is the level of the writer who finds himself inarticulate because, as he thinks, the words in his pen are not as viable as the words in his mouth. He says in explanation of why he cannot write—at least one such writer said to me not long ago— "The trouble is I don't have the benefit of gesture in writing —or of inflection either." He is wrong; his trouble is that he has put himself in the position of the stenographer, and what he wants is what the stenographer cannot take down—on the one hand rhythm and cadence and interval, the gestures of the voice that speaks, and on the other hand the look and feel and movement of the man while speaking, whatever is necessary to render what we may call the whole gesture of the scene. What he has to do is to forget the whole theory of stenography or reporting and make the words of his pen do not only what the words of his mouth did, but also, and most of all, what they failed to do at those crucial moments when he went off into physical gesture with face and hands and vocal gesture in shifting inflections. And he must do this by making his written words sound in the inward ear of his reader, and so play upon each other by concert and opposition and pattern that they not only drag after them the gestures of life but produce a new gesture of their own. To make words play upon each other both in small units and large is one version of the whole technique of imaginative writing. Since what is being played with is meanings and congeries of meanings, what is wanted cannot be articulated in a formula, but on the other hand it cannot be articulated at all except when delivered within a form. The point is that contrary to the general view there are relatively few formulas and relatively many forms; exactly as many as there are gestures to require them; and for forms there are many rules of thumb. Let us look at a few where the means are small enough to handle.

In a sense any word or congeries of words can be pushed to the condition of gesture either by simple repetition or by a combination of repetition and varied preparation. Macbeth's "Tomorrow and tomorrow and tomorrow," or Lear's "Never never never never never," would seem good immediate examples of simple repetition metamorphosing the most familiar words into the most engulfing gesture. To emphasize what has happened in these lines, and to indicate how words sometimes get out of mere verbal meaning when they become gesture, it may be suggested that Macbeth might have said Today and today and today, and Lear said, Always always always always always, and much the same effect have transpired in either case. It is not at all the meaning the words *had* that counts, but the meaning that repetition, in a given situation, makes them take on. The repetition of the word "will" in the will sonnets, and also all the words that rhyme with will, does much the same thing; the resultant meaning has nothing to do with will, but is an obsessive gesture of Shakespeare the man himself, made out of the single iterated syllable intensified into a half-throttled cry.

A more complex and quite different type of repetition offers itself in Iago's exhortation to Roderigo to leave off thinking of suicide and take up thinking again of Desdemona. I truncate the passage somewhat for the production purposes of these remarks.

"Put money in thy purse; follow thou the wars; defeat thy favour with an usurped beard; I say, put money in thy purse. It cannot be that Desdemona should long continue her love to the Moor—put money in thy purse—nor he his to her: it was a violent commencement, and thou shalt see an answerable sequestration; put money in thy purse. These Moors are changeable in their wills:—fill thy purse with money. . . . She must change for youth: when she is sated with his body, she will find the error of her choice: she must have change, she must: therefore put money in thy purse. If thou wilt needs damn thyself, do it a more delicate way than drowning. Make all the money thou canst: if sanctimony and a frail vow betwixt an erring barbarian and a supersubtle Venetian be not too hard for my wits and all the tribe of Hell, thou shalt enjoy her; therefore make money." . . .

Roderigo questions him. "Wilt thou be fast to my hopes, if I depend on the issue?" and Iago resumes his charge.

"Thou art sure of me: go, make money: I have told thee often, and I re-tell thee again and again, I hate the Moor: my cause is hearted; thine hath no less reason. . . . There are many events in the womb of time, which will be delivered. Traverse; go; provide thy money."

Roderigo as he makes his exit says. "I am changed: I'll go sell all my land," and looking after him Iago begins, "Thus do I ever make my fool my purse."

So we see poor Roderigo bought and sold, bought cheap and sold dear, put on change and quite sold out, half a dozen ways at once, and always in terms of the iterated and focusing phrase, "Put money in thy purse," and the changes rung upon it. Roderigo is indeed a changed man in every sense of the word, and the dark, unclean, unconscious, equivocal nature of that change is made clearer and clearer, brought to a light of its own by Iago's phrase. Unlike the simple syllabic repetitions of Lear and Macbeth, Iago's phrase could not be altered without altering the gesture; it is rather that the material that comes between the different iterations could have been altered to almost anything else providing only that they followed the same general line. As Kenneth Burke remarked, money is a neutral symbol capable of bringing meaningful action into any situation. Money is in this situation the symbol of stored evil, and by rehearsing it Shakespeare has released the gesture of the evil.

In Hamlet's best-known soliloquy there is a passage in which the repetition of two words similarly draws upon the reservoir of chthonic meaning but with a different effect upon the words themselves:

> To die: to sleep;
> No more; and by a sleep to say we end
> The heartache, and the thousand natural shocks
> That flesh is heir to, 'tis a consummation
> Devoutly to be wish'd. To die, to sleep;
> To sleep: perchance to dream; aye, there's the rub;
> For in that sleep of death what dreams may come,
> When we have shuffled off this mortal coil,
> Must give us pause.

Here it is the context that determines the meaningfulness that the words *die* and *sleep* and their variants take on in the process of becoming gesture; but once determined, that meaningfulness, that over-arching gesture, carries on through the rest of the soliloquy and beyond, into Hamlet's answer to Ophelia's query how he is: "I humbly thank you: well, well, well," which as gesture moves us to other than the literal sense. It is all the ill of doubt and trepidation before the unknown prospect which the words "to die: to sleep" release as gesture, which in turn infect the triple, mutilating repetition: "Well, well, well."

But we should put this playing upon the meanings of sleep and death over against another kind of playing, this time from *Macbeth*, on the same words, where all the repetition comes at the beginning and is only implied, in the played-upon sense, through the rest of the passage.

> Methought I heard a voice cry, "Sleep no more
> Macbeth does murder sleep!" the innocent sleep,
> Sleep that knits up the ravell'd sleave of care,
> The death of each day's life, sore labour's bath,
> Balm of hurt minds, great nature's second course.
> Chief nourisher in life's feast.

Where Hamlet's play of gesture was toward condensation, a focusing of the gesture into action, a gesture invading the very plot of the play itself, in the lines from *Macbeth* the context only suggests the gesture and provides it a means to invoke an escape from the context of the action, and sets it, in its little freed world of words, to creating other gestures in the last four phrases, which themselves both play upon each other and all backwards upon sleep. Sore labour plays upon hurt minds, and great nature's second course (meaning a second round or lap in the sense of movement) plays upon the other sense of *course* in connection with life's feast, and life's feast plays directly back upon the death of each day's life: itself sleep, which has already been murdered by Macbeth. What we have here is part prayer and part imprecation, with gesture invoking its substance: the substance of what is lacking and cannot, except in the form of prayer, be had.

What these two passages do in common—and it is their most remarkable deed—is by the power of discovered or invoked gesture to transform the simple name of sleep into a rich and complex symbol. In a large way we are familiar with such metamorphoses in the titles of poems or plays or in the names of great imaginative figures, or sometimes—though very rarely—in the names of particular authors and artists. All the gestures in *Hamlet* combine to make a symbol which has become, with each fresh use, the more inexhaustible and the more complex; so much that we do not need to ask, when we say Hamlet, whether we mean the play as a whole or the figure of a man resolving the agony of doubt in gestures. So with Macbeth and Anna Karenina and Raskolnikov and Don Quixote; and so too with Villon and Dante and Michelangelo and Plato and Baudelaire and Poe. It is the same operation in a small way that we have been watching in the two passages about sleep: the creation of symbols. A symbol, I take it, is what we use to express meaningfulness in a permanent way which cannot be expressed in direct words or formulas of words with any completeness; a symbol is a cumulus of meaning which, once established, attracts further meanings to it until, overloaded, it collapses. The making of symbols is a steady occupation for minds at all aware, and they are especially the objects in which meaning is shared and transmitted by those who have life in common, by lovers, friends, and that version of society which we think of as fellowship. Gestures are the first steps toward the making of symbols, and those symbols which endure are the residuary legatees of the meanings earned through gesture. Returning to our passages about sleep it is only the accident that they are a little too long to be said all at once that has kept them as gestures only, just as, on the same argument, it is their brevity more than their residual possibilities that has made actual symbols out of "The rest is silence," or "Ripeness is all," or "Flesh is grass," quite independent of their original contexts in *Hamlet* and *Lear* and *Isaiah*.

Let us take next what at first appears an even smaller context of effort than the repetition of words or phrases, namely the effort to make one word act like another, or several; that is punning. Rhyme, which is the terminal form of punning, and alliteration, which the the initial form of punning, are the commonest uses of this mode of language and are of course the most effective to the widest audience, since they deal, on the surface, entirely with the sounds of the words played on: what we know without thought and cannot know better no matter how much thought we take. That rhyme and alliteration have other uses is not questioned; I merely want to emphasize how primitive and how pervasive is the pun in poetry. It is, taken in its fullest gamut as gesture (for any achieved pun is a gesture), the only direct avenue to undifferentiated sense that the poet has; it is what objectively joins the perceptions of the different senses together, heightening them into a single sensation. Not only that, but it also —and this is our chosen nexus—produces an undifferentiated gesture of meaning; under masterly hands punning is the onomatopoeia of meaning. Which is to say that the play upon words is both the most immediate and most final congeries of signs; it is the very gesture which identifies the elements of the sound with the elements of meaning.

Let us take three examples from Shakespeare, all short. The first centers in a single word spoken by Horatio to Hamlet. He says that the ghost had appeared two nights together "In the dead vast and middle of the night." *Vast* is of course the focal word, and it should be said at once that it appears in this form only in the first Quarto. In the second Quarto and the first Folio it was *wast*, and in the second, third and fourth folios it was *waste*. My contention (which I borrow in part from Empson in his *Seven Types of Ambiguity*) is that no matter which way the word is printed the effect of all three is evident and felt, with a strong possibility of a fourth sense, that of *waist*, as well. The accident of the recorded variations in printing forces the attention upon the variety of meanings bedded down to sleep in this single syllable. Let us read the line in the middle spelling: "In the dead wast and middle of the night," and do we not have all at once in the word the sense of the vast void of the night, the stretching and useless waste of the night, and the waist or middle and generative part of the night as well? And do we not have, finally, a kind of undifferentiated meaning which is a product of all three, a gesture of meaning which can only be less defined the more deeply it is experienced?

The second example is still shorter than the first and requires almost no exposition. There is a line in *Macbeth*, when murder is all acanter in the offing, which images "in his surcease, success." So far as the sound goes the words vary only enough to permit sharp play among them, but so far as the literal meaning goes there is almost direct contradiction, yet in the gesture or play which the two make together there is a new meaningfulness that could not be produced without the play. *Success* is so to speak the cadence that falls from *and* rounds out *surcease;* and with an evil omen in it unknown to the speaker.

The third example is from one of the sonnets most nearly packed with similar play of meaning ("The expense of spirit in a waste of shame"), but from which I take only the most obvious play. Speaking of lust, the poet says it is:

> Past reason hunted, and no sooner had,
> Past reason hated.

Reading these lines, the play of meaning between *hunted* and *hated* so grows upon me that I cannot help thinking somewhere between the two, as a kind of backward consequence, of the poet as past reason *haunted* as well, for that is what the whole sonnet gives as gesture out of the focus of the phrases quoted. Surely one is haunted by what one both hunts and hates.

To bring the three examples together, can we not say that the gesture of these plays upon and within words constitutes the revelation of the *sum* or *product* of all the meanings possible within the focus of the words played upon, even though we did not know what all those meanings were? Language as gesture creates meaning as conscience creates judgment, by feeling the pang, the inner bite, of things forced together.

Here is a good place to introduce, for relief from too high a tone, a conspicuous example of the superficially frivolous intellectual onomatopoeia. It is the first two lines from Wallace Stevens' poem, "Bantams in Pine-Woods," and conceals nothing which it does not also disclose.

> Chieftain Iffucan of Azcan in caftan
> Of tan with henna hackles, halt!

I should say that this was a maximum case of alliteration and rhyme taken as pun, and pun both of sound and meaning, for the sound of the lines presses into meaning and the meaning is pressed into sound. There is a kind of close roistering in the syllables, with such yelping at the heels of meaning and such a hullabaloo of meaning in the sound, which prevents one from knowing what is going on except in such a double and darting image as drunkards delight to see. More seriously we can say that these lines are an example of words which, by being momentarily deprived of their normal meanings, tend to become gesture, just as words which temporarily go beyond their normal meanings, such as the word *geo-politics* today, also tend to become gesture. That Stevens should practice such examples, and that we should delight in them, is altogether natural. The whole movement in the arts known progressively as dadaism and surrealism was devoted, in its poetry, to releasing such gestures from language by the deliberate obliteration of the normal modes of meaning from the context. The difference between Stevens and the surrealists is that Stevens writes his words in such a way that they are able to resume their natural modes so soon as the gesture is released. So with Eliot in such lines as "I should have been a pair of ragged claws, scuttling across the floors of silent seas," and so Shakespeare's "miching mallecho," which the glossary says means mouching mischief, but which means miching mallecho just the same. The Queen was much better informed than the glossary, when she said to Hamlet with regard to the invoked ghost:

> This is the very coinage of your brain:
> This bodiless creation ecstasy
> Is very cunning in.

The poet is likely to make his purest though not his profoundest gestures when most beside himself. If words fail they must serve just the same. Transformed into gesture, they carry the load, wield the load, lighten the load, and leap beyond the load of meaning.

But in this carrying, wielding, lightening, and leaping there are abler agents than that uncovered by the resort to nonsense; abler because, once mastered, they are always reliable.

I mean such formal agents as plot and meter and refrain. Plot is too large an order to discuss here, but it may be said that it is the stress and urgency of plot that determine *what* gestures are wanted and by its exigencies *when* they shall be released. Plot does in a large way pretty much the same sort of thing that meter and refrain do in the small; and if we cannot see infinity in the palm of the hand and eternity in an hour, we shall not see them at all.

Coleridge defined meter as the motion of meaning, and accepting that we must also for our present purposes turn it around and say that motion is the meter of meaning. That is, if meter as motion brings meaning to gesture, then motion as meter moors gesture to meaning. There is a mutual tying-down process, in the operation of meter, a strict and precise delivery of detail in an order of movement, which, well used, gives a sense of absolute speed and absolute position otherwise unavailable to the poet. Where would "Tiger tiger burning bright/ In the forest of the night" be if its wild syllables and wilder insights were not measured out in an expected, a conventionally recognizable, order? But on the other hand where would the speed of the meter be if it were not both initially and finally established by the movement to and from gesture that the words make? These are questions that could have been asked of every quotation we have dealt with, including those in prose, for there is a pattern to the rhythm of prose which has much the same function as meter in verse.

Refrain, like meter, has to do with the ordering of perceptions, and in that sense we may say that refrain is a means of emphatic ordering; but it is more than that, it modifies meaning itself by giving to gesture a conventional form. Refrain, or nearly identical repetition, gives particular form, on a general and dependable model, to gesture that might otherwise be formless. Refrain is the emphatic measure of all those gestures that have to do with the declaration of recurrence, return, rebirth and new birth, of motion in stillness and stillness in motion, of permanence in change, and change in permanence. It is the lyric gesture of recognition and the emphatic gesture of identity. The ballads are full of it and the songbooks, whether Elizabethan or cowboy or the latest collection of popular catches. I choose as free examples, Greene's "Weep not, my wanton, smile upon my knee," which upon its last recurrence identifies with the substance of the poem, and Spenser's "Sweet Thames! runne softly, till I end my Song," which makes a gesture of inclusiveness for all that mounts up to it, and Dunbar's "Timor mortis conturbat me," which in every repetition makes the gesture of focus. A more deliberate example where the refrain is used to modify the meaning backward and forward, would be Yeats's double refrain in "Crazy Jane and the Bishop." I give together the two lines that come four lines apart: "All find safety in the tomb/ The solid man and the coxcomb." Better still is the refrain in "Crazy Jane on God," for the effect of its developing action in recurrence can be briefly abstracted. The first stanza ends, "Men come, men go; *all things remain in God,*" the second emphasizes the same image, and the third contrasts it. The fourth stanza reads:

> I had wild Jack for a lover;
> Though like a road
> That men pass over
> My body makes no moan
> But sings on:
> *All things remain in God.*

Thus we see by the use of refrain insight become deepening gesture.

But refrain is a mere instrument or aid to order, and will flatten a poem like a burden if it is not constantly refreshed from the common resources of language itself. Let us end, then, with brief examinations of three examples, of which the first two are determined partly by the critical words themselves and partly by the order in which they occur, and of which the third makes a pretty complete use of all the devices of lyric poetry, including all those here discussed. The first is from *Hamlet,* and is found in the dialogue between Hamlet and Horatio, just before they go in for the final duel. The passage is in prose.

  Hor.   You will lose this wager, my lord.

  Ham. I do not think so; since he went into France, I have
               been in continual practice; I shall win at the odds.
               But thou wouldst not think how ill all's here about
               my heart: but it is no matter.

"But thou wouldst not think how ill all's here about my heart."
Do not these words rise from what is past and fall toward what
is coming, and both rise and fall as a gesture, almost his last,
out of Hamlet himself? We see how order and cadence and
the ear of the poet give the actor all that he has to do except
that most arduous thing, put the gesture in the words into the
gesture of his mere voice and body.

    The second example is from *Othello*. Othello is at swords'
points with himself over Desdemona's teasing request for him
to make up his quarrel with Cassio, and has just dismissed
her. Looking after her he exclaims:

> Excellent wretch! Perdition catch my soul,
> But I do love thee! and when I love thee not,
> Chaos is come again.

Here in the order both of the plot and of the lines, and in the
fall of the plot and of the lines, too, the word *chaos* acts to
pull into the context a whole realm of being not otherwise
present. Shakespeare had undoubtedly re-made this line from
its earlier version of *Venus and Adonis,* where "Black chaos
comes again when beauty is dead," and he had probably in
both instances the Graeco-Latin sense of chaos in mind; the
yawning gulf or gap, the abyss of night, the original dark, as
well as the sense of disorder and formlessness; both senses
were Elizabethan. We have thus the gesture of invoked prophecy made actual in the gesture of a word. The mere actor can
do no more than leave it alone to act itself.

    Our third example does not envisage an actor and could
not use one, if even the best offered, for more than its merely
immediate effects; its major effects transpire only in the inward ear. It is a poem which, using alliteration and rhyme and
meter and refrain, using symbol and making symbol, playing
upon its words as it runs, escapes all the mere meaning in

words and reaches the pure meaningfulness of gesture. You can do with it whatever you will, for with poems of this order all things are possible. It is Yeats's "I am of Ireland."

"I am of Ireland,
And the Holy Land of Ireland,
And time runs on," cried she.
"Come out of charity,
Come dance with me in Ireland."

One man, one man alone
In that outlandish gear,
One solitary man
Of all that rambled there
Had turned his stately head.
"That is a long way off,
And time runs on," he said,
"And the night grows rough."

"I am of Ireland,
And the Holy Land of Ireland,
And time runs on," cried she.
"Come out of charity
And dance with me in Ireland."

"The fiddlers are all thumbs,
Or the fiddle-string accursed,
The drums and the kettledrums
And the trumpets all are burst,
And the trombone," cried he,
"The trumpet and trombone,"
And cocked a malicious eye,
"But time runs on, runs on."

"I am of Ireland,
And the Holy Land of Ireland,
And time runs on," cried she.
"Come out of charity
And dance with me in Ireland."

With this poem as evidence I think it may be said in conclusion that we feel almost everything that deeply stirs us as if it were a gesture, the gesture of our uncreated selves. Thus as artists we would create great gestures; and if we most often fail to do so, it is because, as Shakespeare says, "The deep of night is crept upon our talk," which is a gesture that must overwhelm us even though we realize, as we consent to it, that we have made it ourselves.

Preliminary Problems

YVOR WINTERS

FIRST PROBLEM

IS IT POSSIBLE to say that Poem A (one of Donne's *Holy Sonnets,* or one of the poems of Jonson or of Shakespeare) is better than Poem B (Collins' *Ode to Evening*) or vice versa?

If not, is it possible to say that either of these is better than Poem C (*The Cremation of Sam Magee,* or something comparable)?

If the answer is no in both cases, then any poem is as good as any other. If this is true, then all poetry is worthless; but this obviously is not true, for it is contrary to all our experience.

If the answer is yes in both cases, then there follows the question of whether the answer implies merely that one poem is better than another for the speaker, or whether it means that one poem is intrinsically better than another. If the former, then we are impressionists, which is to say relativists; and are either mystics of the type of Emerson, or hedonists of the type of Stevens and Ransom. If the latter, then we assume that constant principles govern the poetic experience, and that the poem (as likewise the judge) must be judged in relationship to those principles. It is important, therefore, to discover the consequences of assuming each of these positions.

If our answer to the first question is no and to the second yes, then we are asserting that we can distinguish between those poems which are of the canon and those which are not, but that within the canon all judgment is impossible. This view, if adopted, will require serious elucidation, for on the face of it, it appears inexplicable. On the other hand, one cannot deny that within the canon judgment will become more difficult, for the nearer two poems may be to the high-

est degrees of excellence, the harder it will be to choose between them. Two poems, in fact, might be so excellent that
there would be small profit in endeavoring to say that one
was better, but one could arrive at this conclusion only after
a careful examination of both.

SECOND PROBLEM

If we accept the view that one poem can be regarded as
better than another, the question then arises whether this
judgment is a matter of inexplicable intuition, or whether it
is a question of intuition that can be explained, and consequently guided and improved by rational elucidation.

If we accept the view that the judgment in question is inexplicable, then we are again forced to confess ourselves impressionists and relativists, unless we can show that the
intuitions of all men agree at all times, or that the intuitions
of one man are invariably right and those of all others wrong
whenever they differ. We obviously can demonstrate neither
of these propositions.

If we start, then, with the proposition that one poem may
be intrinsically superior to another, we are forced to account
for differences of opinion regarding it. If two critics differ, it
is possible that one is right and the other wrong, more likely
that both are partly right and partly wrong, but in different
respects: neither the native gifts nor the education of any
man have ever been wholly adequate to many of the critical
problems he will encounter, and no two men are ever the
same in these respects or in any others. On the other hand,
although the critic should display reasonable humility and
caution, it is only fair to add that few men possess either the
talent or the education to justify their being taken very seriously, even of those who are nominally professional students
of these matters.

But if it is possible by rational elucidation to give a more
or less clear account of what one finds in a poem and why
one approves or disapproves, then communication between

two critics, though no doubt imperfect, becomes possible, and it becomes possible that they may in some measure correct each other's errors and so come more near to a true judgment of the poem.

THIRD PROBLEM

If rational communication about poetry is to take place, it is necessary first to determine what we mean by a poem.

A poem is first of all a statement in words.

But it differs from all such statements of a purely philosophical or theoretical nature, in that it has by intention a controlled content of feeling. In this respect, it does not differ from many works written in prose, however.

A poem differs from a work written in prose by virtue of its being composed in verse. The rhythm of verse permits the expression of more powerful feeling than is possible in prose when such feeling is needed, and it permits at all times the expression of finer shades of feeling.

A poem, then, is a statement in words in which special pains are taken with the expression of feeling. This description is merely intended to distinguish the poem from other kinds of writing; it is not offered as a complete description.

FOURTH PROBLEM

What, however, are words?

They are audible sounds, or their visual symbols, invented by man to communicate his thoughts and feelings. Each word has a conceptual content, however slight; each word, exclusive, perhaps, of the particles, communicates vague associations of feeling.

The word *fire* communicates a concept; it also connotes very vaguely certain feelings, depending on the context in which we happen to place it—depending, for example, on whether we happen to think of a fire on a hearth, in a furnace, or in a forest. These feelings may be rendered more and more precise as we render the context more and more precise; as we come more and more near to completing and perfecting our poem.

FIFTH PROBLEM

But if the poem, as compared to prose, pays especial attention to feeling, are we to assume that the rational content of the poem is unimportant to its success?

The rational content cannot be eliminated from words; consequently the rational content cannot be eliminated from poetry. It is there. If it is unsatisfactory in itself, a part of the poem is unsatisfactory; the poem is thus damaged beyond argument. If we deny this, we must surely explain ourselves very fully.

If we admit this, we are faced with another problem: is it conceivable that rational content and feeling-content may both be perfect, and yet that they may be unrelated to each other, or imperfectly related? To me this is inconceivable, because the emotional content of words is generated by our experience with the conceptual content, so that a relationship is necessary.

This fact of the necessity of such relationship may fairly return us for a moment to the original question: whether imperfection of rational content damages the entire poem. If there is a necessary relationship between concept and feeling, and concept is unsatisfactory, then feeling must be damaged by way of the relationship.

SIXTH PROBLEM

If there is a relationship between concept and feeling, what is the nature of that relationship?

To answer this, let us return to the basic unit, the word. The concept represented by the word motivates the feeling which the word communicates. It is the concept of fire which generates the feelings communicated by the word, though the sound of the word may modify these feelings very subtly, as may other accidental qualities, especially if the word be used skillfully in a given context. The accidental qualities of a word, however, such as its literary history, for example, can only modify, cannot essentially change, for these will be governed ultimately by the concept; that is, *fire* will seldom be used to signify *plum-blossom,* and so will have few opportunities to gather connotations from the concept, *plum-blossom.* The relationship, in the poem, between rational statement and feeling, is thus seen to be that of motive to emotion.

SEVENTH PROBLEM

But has not this reasoning brought us back to the proposition that all poems are equally good? For if each word motivates its own feeling, because of its intrinsic nature, will not any rational statement, since it is composed of words, motivate the feeling exactly proper to it?

This is not true, for a good many reasons, of which I shall enumerate only a few of the more obvious. In making a rational statement, in purely theoretical prose, we find that our statement may be loose or exact, depending upon the relationships of the words to each other. The precision of a word depends to some extent upon its surroundings. This is true likewise with respect to the connotations of words. Two words, each of which has several usably close rational synonyms, may reinforce and clarify each other with respect to their connotations or they may not do so.

Let me illustrate with a simple example from Browning's *Serenade at the Villa:*

> So wore night; the East was gray,
> White the broad-faced hemlock flowers.

The lines are marred by a crowding of long syllables and difficult consonants, but they have great beauty in spite of the fault. What I wish to point out, for the sake of my argument, is the relationship between the words *wore* and *gray.* The verb *wore* means literally that the night passed, but it carries with it connotations of exhaustion and attrition which belong to the condition of the protagonist; and grayness is a color which we associate with such a condition. If we change the phrase to read: "Thus night passed," we shall have the same rational meaning, and a meter quite as respectable, but no trace of the power of the line: the connotation of *wore* will be lost, and the connotation of *gray* will remain merely in a state of ineffective potentiality. The protagonist in seeing his feeling mirrored in the landscape is not guilty of motivating his feeling falsely, for we know his general motive from the poem as a whole; he is expressing a portion of the feeling motivated by the total situation through a more or less common psychological phenomenon. If the poem were such, however, that we did not know why the night *wore* instead of *passed,* we should have just cause for complaint; in fact, most of the strength of the word would probably be lost. The second line contains other fine effects, immediately with reference to the first line, ultimately with reference to the theme; I leave the reader to analyze them for himself, but he will scarcely succeed without the whole poem before him.

Concepts, as represented by particular words, are affected by connotations due to various and curious accidents. A word may gather connotations from its use in folk-poetry, in formal poetry, in vulgar speech, or in technical prose: a single concept might easily be represented by four words with these distinct histories; and any one of the words might prove to be proper in a given poetic context. Words gain connotation from etymological accidents. Something of this may be seen in the English word *outrage,* in which is commonly felt, in all likelihood, something associated with *rage,* although there is no rage whatever in the original word. Similarly the word *urchin,* in modern English, seldom connotes anything related to hedgehogs, or to the familiars of the witches, by whose intervention the word arrived at its modern meaning and feeling. Yet the connotation proper to any stage in the history of such a word might be resuscitated, or a blend of connotations effected, by skillful use. Further, the connotation of a word may be modified very strongly by its function in the metrical structure, a matter which I shall discuss at length in connection with the theories of Ransom.

This is enough to show that exact motivation of feeling by concept is not inherent in any rational statement. Any rational statement will govern the general possibilities of feeling derivable from it, but the task of the poet is to adjust feeling to motive precisely. He has to select words containing not only the right relationships within themselves, but the right relationships to each other. The task is very difficult; and this is no doubt the reason why the great poetry of a great poet is likely to be very small in bulk.

EIGHTH PROBLEM

Is it not possible, however, to escape from this relationship of motive to emotion by confining ourselves very largely to those words which denote emotion: love, envy, anger, and the like?

This is not possible, for these words, like others, represent concepts. If we should confine ourselves strictly to such a vocabulary, we should merely write didactic poetry: poetry about love in general, or about anger in general. The emotion communicated would result from our apprehension of the ideas in question. Such poetry is perfectly legitimate, but it is only one kind of poetry, and it is scarcely the kind which the Romantic theorist is endeavoring to define.

Such poetry has frequently been rendered particular by the use of allegory. The playful allegorizing of minor amoristic themes which one encounters in the Renaissance and which is possibly descended from certain neo-Platonic elements in medieval poetry may serve as illustration. Let us consider these and the subsequent lines by Thomas Lodge:

> Love in my bosom like a bee
>   Doth suck his sweet;
> Now with his wings he plays with me,
>   Now with his feet.

Love itself is a very general idea and might include many kinds of experience; the idea is limited by this allegory to the sentimental and sensual, but we still have an idea, the sub-division of the original idea, and the feeling must be appropriate to the concept. The concept is rendered concrete by the image of Cupid, whose actions, in turn, are rendered visible by comparison to the bee: it is these actions which make the poem a kind of anticipatory meditation on more or less sensual love, a meditation which by its mere tone of expression keeps the subject in its proper place as a very minor one. Sometimes the emphasis is on the mere description of the bee, sometimes on the description of Cupid, sometimes on the lover's feeling; but the feeling motivated in any passage is governed by this emphasis. The elements, once they are united in the poem, are never really separated, of course. In so far as the poet departs from his substantial theme in the direction of mere bees and flowers, he will achieve what Ransom calls irrelevance; but if there is much of this the poem will be weakened. Whether he so departs or not, the relation of motive to emotion must remain the same, within each passage. I have discussed this problem in my essay on Ransom.

A common romantic practice is to use words denoting emotions, but to use them loosely and violently, as if the very carelessness expressed emotion. Another is to make a general statement, but seem to refer it to a particular occasion, which, however, is never indicated: the poet thus seems to avoid the didactic, yet he is not forced to understand the particular motive. Both these faults may be seen in these lines from Shelley:

> Out of the day and night
> A joy has taken flight;
>   Fresh spring, and summer, and winter hoar,
> Move my faint heart with grief, but with delight
>   No more—oh, never more.

The poet's intention is so vague, however, that he achieves nothing but stereotypes of a very crude kind.

The Romantics often tried other devices. For example, it would be possible to write a poem on fear in general, but to avoid in some measure the effect of the purely didactic by illustrating the emotion along the way with various experiences which might motivate fear. There is a danger here, though it is merely a danger, that the general idea may not dominate the poem, and that the poem may thus fall apart into a group of poems on particular experiences. There is the alternative danger, that the particular quality of the experiences may be so subordinated to the illustrative function of the experiences, that within each illustration there is merely a stereotyped and not a real relationship of motive to feeling: this occurs in Collins' *Ode to Fear,* though a few lines in the Epode come surprisingly to life. But the methods which I have just described really offer no semblance of an escape from the theory of motivation which I am defending.

Another Romantic device, if it is conscious enough to be called a device, is to offer instead of a defensible motive a false one, usually culled from landscape. This kind of writing represents a tacit admission of the principle of motivation which I am defending, but a bad application of the principle. It results in the kind of writing which I have called pseudo-reference in my volume, *Primitivism and Decadence.* One cannot believe, for example, that Wordsworth's passions were charmed away by a look at the daffodils, or that Shelley's were aroused by the sight of the leaves blown about in the autumn wind. A motive is offered, and the poet wants us to accept it, but we recognize it as inadequate. In such a poem there may be fragments of good description, which motivate a feeling more or less purely appropriate to the objects described, and these fragments may sustain our liking for the poem: this happens in Collins' *Ode to Evening;* but one will find also an account of some kind of emotion essentially irrelevant to the objects described, along with the attempt, more or less explicit, to deduce the emotion from the object.

There remains the method of the Post-Romantics, whether French Symbolists or American Experimentalists: the method of trying to extinguish the rational content of language while retaining the content of association. This method I have dis-

cussed in *Primitivism and Decadence,* and I shall discuss it
again in this book [*In Defense of Reason*].

NINTH PROBLEM

The relationship in the poem of rational meaning to feeling
we have seen to be that of motive to emotion; and we have
seen that this must be a satisfactory relationship. How do we
determine whether such a relationship is satisfactory? We determine it by an act of moral judgment. The question then
arises whether moral judgments can be made, whether the
concept of morality is or is not an illusion.

If morality can be considered real, if a theory of morality
can be said to derive from reality, it is because it guides us
toward the greatest happiness which the accidents of life permit: that is, toward the fullest realization of our nature, in
the Aristotelian or Thomistic sense. But is there such a thing,
abstractly considered, as full realization of our nature?

To avoid discussion of too great length, let us consider the
opposite question: is there such a thing as obviously unful-
filled human nature? Obviously there is. We need only turn
to the feeble-minded, who cannot think and so cannot perceive or feel with any clarity; or to the insane, who sometimes perceive and feel with great intensity, but whose feelings and perceptions are so improperly motivated that they
are classed as illusions. At slightly higher levels, the criminal,
the dissolute, the unscrupulously selfish, and various types
of neurotics are likely to arouse but little disagreement as
examples.

Now if we are able to recognize the fact of insanity—if in
fact we are forced to recognize it—that is, the fact of the obvious maladjustment of feeling to motive, we are forced to
admit the possibility of more accurate adjustment, and, by
necessary sequence, of absolutely accurate adjustment, even
though we admit the likelihood that most people will attain
to a final adjustment but very seldom indeed. We can guide
ourselves toward such an adjustment in life, as in art, by

means of theory and the critical examination of special instances; but the final act of judgment is in both life and art a unique act—it is a relationship between two elements, the rational understanding and the feeling, of which only one is classificatory and of which the other has infinite possibilities of variation.

TENTH PROBLEM

If the final act of adjustment is a unique act of judgment, can we say that it is more or less right, provided it is demonstrably within the general limits prescribed by the theory of morality which has led to it? The answer to this question is implicit in what has preceded; in fact the answer resembles exactly that reached at the end of the first problem examined. We can say that it is more or less nearly right. If extreme deviation from right judgment is obvious, then there is such a thing as right judgment. The mere fact that life may be conducted in a fairly satisfactory manner, by means of inaccurate judgment within certain limits, and that few people ever bother to refine their judgment beyond the stage which enables them to remain largely within those limits, does not mean that accurate judgment has no reality. Implicit in all that has preceded is the concept that in any moral situation there is a right judgment as an ultimate possibility; that the human judge, or actor, will approximate it more or less nearly; that the closeness of his approximation will depend upon the accuracy of his rational understanding and of his intuition, and upon the accuracy of their interaction upon each other.

ELEVENTH PROBLEM

Nothing has thus far been said about human action, yet morality is supposed to guide human action. And if art is moral, there should be a relationship between art and human action.

The moral judgment, whether good, bad, or indifferent, is commonly the prelude and instigation to action. Hastily or carefully, intelligently or otherwise, one arrives at some kind of general idea of a situation calling for action, and one's idea motivates one's feeling: the act results. The part played by will, or the lack of it, between judgment and act, the possibility that action may be frustrated by some constitutional or habitual weakness or tendency, such as cowardice or a tendency to anger, in a person of a fine speculative or poetic judgment, are subjects for a treatise on ethics or psychology; a treatise on poetry stops with the consideration of the speculative judgment, which reaches its best form and expression in poetry. In the situations of daily life, one does not, as a rule, write a poem before acting: one makes a more rapid and simple judgment. But if the poem does not individually lead to a particular act, it does not prevent action. It gives us a better way of judging representative acts than we should otherwise have. It is thus a civilizing influence: it trains our power of judgment, and should, I imagine, affect the quality of daily judgments and actions.

Twelfth Problem

What, then, is the nature of the critical process?

It will consists (1) of the statement of such historical or biographical knowledge as may be necessary in order to understand the mind and method of the writer; (2) of such analysis of his literary theories as we may need to understand and evaluate what he is doing; (3) of a rational critique of the paraphrasable content (roughly, the motive) of the poem; (4) of a rational critique of the feeling motivated—that is, of the details of style, as seen in language and technique; and (5) of the final act of judgment, a unique act, the general nature of which can be indicated, but which cannot be communicated precisely, since it consists in receiving from the poet his own final and unique judgment of his matter and in judging that judgment. It should be noted that the purpose of the first four processes is to limit as narrowly as possible the region in which the final unique act is to occur.

In the actual writing of criticism, a given task may not require all of these processes, or may not require that all be given equal emphasis; or it may be that in connection with a certain writer, whether because of the nature of the writer or because of the way in which other critics have treated him previously, one or two of these processes must be given so much emphasis that others must be neglected for lack of space. These are practical matters to be settled as the occasions arise.

A *Symbolic Reading of the* Ancient Mariner

Elder Olson

The *Ancient Mariner* is one of those poems the interpretations of which have rather illustrated the different methods of interpretation than explained the poem itself. Mr. Warren's essay[1] seems to me to be valuable principally as exhibiting what happens to poetry in interpretation, and not particularly valuable as a comment upon the poem. His argument may be summarized as follows. The famous passage in the *Table Talk,* recording Mrs. Barbauld's criticism of the poem and the poet's response, may not be taken as evidence that the poem is without theme or moral. Warren is severe, thus, with Griggs and with Lowes. The former has, according to Warren, first "misread his text," since he interprets the passage as excluding a moral intention and, second, asserted that the poem is without theme or meaning. The latter asserts that the poem has a theme but "reverses his argument" in considering that it has no moral or, at any rate, none which will "hold water" outside the poem. Both men consequently make the poem "nothing more than a pleasant but meaningless dream." Yet dreams in Coleridge's view contain nothing absurd or nonsensical or causeless; and, similarly, the inferences of Griggs and Lowes from the remark that the poem was a work of "pure imagination" can be corrected by the restatement of Coleridge's concept of the imagination.

The *Ancient Mariner,* then, has a meaning—not a literal one, not an allegorical one, but a symbolic one. A symbol for Coleridge, says Warren, is "focal, massive, and not arbitrary"; that is, according to our critic, it combines idea and feeling, it implies a body of ideas and does not stand for a single

[1] Samuel Taylor Coleridge, *The Rime of the Ancient Mariner,* with an essay by Robert Penn Warren (New York: Reynal & Hitchcock, 1946).

idea, and "it is not a mere sign" but "contains within itself
the appeal which makes it serviceable as a symbol." Read as
a symbolic poem, the *Ancient Mariner* has two basic themes:
the primary (not the more important but merely the more
obvious) is that of the "One Life" or of "sacramental vision";
the secondary, the theme of the imagination. Discussion of
the first turns on the nature of the Mariner's act: literally, he
killed a bird; symbolically, he commits murder. Why is the
crime unmotivated? It "symbolizes the Fall"; we are here
"confronting the mystery of the corruption of the will." But
the sin of the will is the expression of the essence of the will;
the crime is the crime of pride.

The secondary theme is the theme of the imagination; in
it the Mariner appears as one who is driven from a "world of
comfortable familiarity" by a storm, which is "the creative
urge," to a land of ice, which is "both beautiful and terrible,
as is proper for the spot where the acquaintance with the
imagination is to be made." Like the storm, it "shakes man
from his routine of life"; but out of this apparent indifference
to man "comes the first response to man—the Albatross."
Wind and bird, according to Warren, are associated with the
moon or the half-light, which is the symbol of the imagination; the sun, on the other hand, symbolizes the "light of the
'understanding.'" These symbols, we are told, are ambivalent,
i.e., now hostile, now beneficial, to man. The crime is a crime
against the imagination; the imagination obtains its terrible
redress but also "heals" the Mariner; the wandering is also a
blessing and a curse, for the Mariner is the *poète maudit* as
well as the "prophet of universal charity."

I trust this much of summary will be sufficient—not perhaps to Warren, who, if he is like most authors, must feel
that his best summary is his own work—but to most serious
readers of his essay. On the supposition that it *is* sufficient,
what can be said of his interpretations?

We may begin by noting how Warren so easily subverts
the positions of Griggs and Lowes. "Obviously, only the
reader who cannot enjoy this journey into the realm of the

supernatural finds it necessary to seek out a moral," said Griggs; and Warren remarks: "I take it that Griggs uses the word *moral* in a broad, general sense, equating it with theme understood as a comment on human conduct and values. . . . And if this . . . is what he means, he is saying that the poem has no theme." Now, this "taking it" is precisely what Warren has no title to do, if, indeed, it be such sheer absurdity to assert that a poem has no theme,[2] especially since Griggs very obviously means something quite different, and something perfectly sensible. He means that the pleasure arising from the poem *as a poem* is so great that only one incapable of feeling that pleasure would ask for anything more. And this "equating" is a gratuity of Warren's, not of Griggs's; for, even granting that every poem must have a theme, it is by no means the case that every theme is a comment on human conduct and values; and even if that were the case, it would not follow that such comment would be *ethical* comment; and even if that, too, were granted, it would not follow that every ethical comment is a *moral*. The rout of Griggs, in short, is accomplished by incorrect interpretation followed by illicit inference. Even the passage of which Griggs has, according to Warren, "reversed the undebatable sense," suffers a similar fate; for, having just cited Coleridge's remark that the poem "ought to have had no more moral than the Arabian

MEANING

[2] We may indeed worry about whether, ~~on the contrary,~~ it is not an absurdity to conceive of a poem—i.e., any imitative poem—as *having* a theme or meaning. The words have a meaning; they mean the poem; but why should the poem itself have any further meaning? What sense is there in asking about the meaning of something which is itself a meaning? And, if there is any point to this asking, shall we not have a further meaning still, and so on *ad infinitum,* so that interpretation becomes impossible, as being an infinite process? Moreover, these "meanings of poems" are at best something very trivial, prosaic, and obvious: *Œdipus* means that man walks in darkness, *Hamlet* that man is utterly alone, the *Ancient Mariner* that life is one and that the imagination revenges itself, etc. Such interpretation springs from the use of a very arid grammatical apparatus and wholly blinks the question of how powerfully we are affected by the spectacle of human fortunes, as well as that of how the situation, character, passion, and thought of the poetic *personae* affect their speech.

Nights tale," and so forth, Warren calmly says: "Nor did he [Coleridge] say or even imply that the poem would be better if there were *no* moral."

The refutation of Lowes is similarly facile. Lowes remarked that repentance, although it lightened the soul, did not absolve; this Warren takes as the "theme" and is astounded when Lowes goes on to say that this "law of life" appears merely to render the poem a more credible illusion, the moral being untenable outside the poem, because of the disproportion of cause to effect and of crime to punishment. This means, says Warren, that the moral is not to be taken seriously and, indeed, that it could not be; and this is unthinkable for Warren, for it means that poems are "in themselves meaningless and nothing but refined and ingenious toys for an idle hour." How Warren arrives at this conclusion is obvious; in his simple world poems either have a moral or they are mere toys, and no Puritan was ever so flat and dogmatic about the matter. Deny Warren's contention of a moral, and a trap opens to drop you into the abyss of absurdity. But, I protest, Griggs and Lowes are "refuted," not because of any absurdity in their statements or fallacy in their inferences; they are so only through Warren's introduction of a wholly untenable exclusive disjunction and through his complete distortion of their utterances.

Even so, how deep is this abyss of absurdity? Is it, after all, so utterly contemptible to regard poems as affording pleasure rather than truth? If so, Warren must contemn Coleridge as well; for, merely to quote Coleridge's famous definition of a poem:

> A poem is that species of composition, which is opposed to works of science by proposing for its *immediate* object pleasure, not truth; and from all other species—(having *this* object in common with it)—it is discriminated by proposing to itself such delight from the *whole,* as is compatible with a distinct gratification from each component *part.*[3]

[3] *Biographia literaria,* chap. xiv.

In other words, the differentia of the class *poem* is pleasure and the kinds and sources of pleasure; and, as Coleridge says, "The reader should be carried forward, not merely or chiefly by the mechanical impulse of curiosity, or by a restless desire to arrive at the final solution; but by the pleasurable activity of mind excited by the attractions of the journey itself." Nor is Warren's contention that imagination is cognitive pertinent here, for Coleridge sharply distinguished *poem* and *poetry*; it is to the latter that the imagination is relevant. The passage is well worth considering; having just defined "poem" as above, he continues:

> But if this should be admitted as a satisfactory character of a poem, we have still to seek for a definition of poetry. The writings of Plato and Jeremy Taylor, and Burnett's Theory of the Earth, furnish undeniable proofs that poetry of the highest kind may exist without metre, and even without the contra-distinguishing objects of a poem. The first chapter of Isaiah . . . is poetry in the most emphatic sense; yet it would be not less irrational than strange to assert that pleasure, and not truth, was the immediate object of the prophet. In short, whatever specific import we attach to the word, Poetry, there will be found involved in it, as a necessary consequence, that a poem of any length neither can be, nor ought to be, all poetry. Yet if an harmonious whole is to be produced, the remaining parts must be preserved in keeping with the poetry. . . .

And he continues, "What is poetry? . . . is so nearly the same question with, what is a poet?—that the answer to the one is involved in the solution of the other. . . . The poet, described in ideal perfection, brings the whole soul of man into activity." He unites and blends all the faculties "by that synthetic and magical power, to which I would exclusively appropriate the name of Imagination."

We may now ask: Was the action of the poem intended, as Warren seems to suppose, to be "real"? If so, in what sense? And how, since undoubtedly poems effect pleasure and since the *Ancient Mariner* is undoubtedly a poem, did

Coleridge propose to effect pleasure by it? But again Coleridge answers these questions for us:

> In the one [series of poems], the incidents and agents were to be, in part at least, supernatural; and the excellence aimed at was to consist in the interesting of the affections by the dramatic truth of such emotions, as would naturally accompany such situations supposing them real. And real in this sense they have been to every human being who, from whatever source of delusion, has at any time believed himself under supernatural agency.

These persons and characters, "supernatural or at least romantic," were to be so treated "as to transfer from our inward nature a human interest and a semblance of truth sufficient to procure for these shadows of the imagination that willing suspension of disbelief for the moment which constitutes poetic faith."

Seldom has a poet so clearly indicated his intentions and method, and the case is clear: Griggs and Lowes have followed Coleridge, and it is Warren who has misread, or read with insufficient care, "his text." They have held that, as a poem, the *Ancient Mariner* proposed as its end pleasure and not truth and that the "reality" of the poem is a *reality by supposition*—something which, though unreal, we may suppose to be real by a "willing suspension of disbelief." Nor are they incorrect in calling the poem "dreamlike"; Coleridge himself could use the expression in precisely the same sense:

> You will take especial note of the marvellous independence and true imaginative absence of all particular space or time in the Faery Queene. It is in the domains neither of history nor of geography; it is ignorant of all artificial boundary, all material obstacles; it is truly in land of Faery, that is, of mental space. The poet has placed you in a dream, a charmed sleep, and you neither wish, nor have the power, to inquire where you are, or how you got there.[4]

[4] *Coleridge's Miscellaneous Criticism,* ed. T. M. Raysor (Cambridge, 1936), p. 36; from *Literary Remains.*

Ignoring these *loci classici* of Coleridgeans, Warren in effect supposes (1) that the poem does not have the effect which Coleridge says it was to have and (2) that it has some other end which Coleridge denies it to have; and on this latter supposition his whole chimerical interpretation is predicated.

In the first place, despite the argument that the poem is symbolic and not allegorical, Warren's interpretation clearly makes the poem what Coleridge calls "allegory." The "true sense" of the word *allegory*, says Coleridge, "is this,—the employment of one set of agents and images to convey in disguise a moral meaning, with a likeness to the imagination, but with a difference to the understanding,—those agents and images being so combined as to form a homogeneous whole. . . ."[5] But, secondly, is the *Mariner* a "symbolic" poem? Here we must make a distinction. If by "symbolic" we refer to the imitative or participative relations of the One and the Many, familiar enough in the Platonic and Neo-Platonic philosophers with whom Coleridge associated himself, doubtless the poem is symbolic. It is this, in a Coleridgean sense, because in so far as it is also *poetry*, it reflects the particular activity of the imagination which produced that poetry; because that activity, in turn, images the imagination; and because the imagination, in turn, images the creative activity of God. Again, if by "symbolic" we mean merely the more particular as revealing the more universal, which is all that Coleridge seems to intend,[6] we need not quarrel. But if by any interpretation of the term we commit ourselves, as does Warren, to an exegesis of how one thing in Coleridge must always mean something

[5] Raysor, *op. cit.*, pp. 32–33; cf. pp. 28–32, also pp. 98–103, where Coleridge discusses symbol and allegory, and *Don Quixote* in terms of them.

[6] "I adopt with full faith, the principle of Aristotle, that poetry, as poetry, is essentially ideal, that it avoids and excludes all accident; that its apparent individualities of rank, character, or occupation must be representative of a class; and that the persons of poetry must be clothed with generic attributes, with the common attributes of the class: Not with such as one gifted individual might possibly possess, but such as from his situation it is most probable before-hand that he would possess" (*Biographia literaria*, chap. xvii).

else, we are exceeding our evidence. Coleridge's discussion of
the origin of the *Lyrical Ballads,* already cited in part, offers
no hint of symbolism in this sense. I can recall no use by
Coleridge—certainly, no crucial use—of the term "symbol" as
interpreted by Warren, even in such major critical flights as
Coleridge's discussion of Wordsworth and of Shakespeare;
nor, indeed, does the term "symbol" bear Warren's meaning
even when it is central to the discussion, as in Coleridge's
remarks on *Don Quixote.* Undoubtedly, Coleridge's conception of the imagination influenced his criticism and his creation; but it was a profoundly philosophical conception; and
Warren's refusal to treat its profounder aspects is responsible,
in part, for his interpretation of the term "symbol."

Thirdly, supposing the poem were symbolic, as it clearly is
not, on what basis does Warren determine the referents of
the symbols? How is the moon, for instance—the key-symbol
according to him—equated with the imagination? We are told
that the moon, or if not the moon, some sort of half-light,
frequently appears in Coleridge's work; that it is sometimes
symbolic; that it and sunset and other accidents of light and
shade diffuse a sudden novelty over the familiar, not unlike
"the modifying colors of the imagination," according to Coleridge. That is sufficient to make the moon the symbol of the
imagination for Warren. The crime now is "a crime against
the imagination." In vain we ask why. Warren simply says:
"Of course." One should rather have supposed that, if the
crime is one against the imagination, the Polar Spirit would
have represented the imagination, for certainly it is the Polar
Spirit, and not the moon, who loves the bird, who is offended
by its slaughter, and who exacts revenge. Why is the wind
the symbol of the creative urge? Why, particularly, is it a
symbol of the necessary kind, "rooted in our universal natural
experience," as are all phallic symbols? Does that mean that
the wind can never symbolize anything else? All that Warren
says here amounts to this: the wind is inimical, and so is the
creative urge, to complacent man. Why is the sun the light of
natural prudence? Because, says Warren, "the sun is, sym-

bolically speaking, the cause of their [the other mariners']
acceptance of the crime . . . they repudiate the luminous
haze, the other light, and consider it an evil, though we know
that the fog and mist are associated with the moon in the
wind-bird-moon cluster." And in their fortunes—Warren suggests—we have perhaps some fable of the Enlightenment
which terminated in the blood-bath of the French Revolution. So amid generous assumptions, undistributed middles,
inconsistencies, misinterpretations, ignorationes elenchi, post
hoc ergo propter hoc's, etc., Warren makes his way by the
light, or shall we say the half-light, of a vague supposition
which he terms the "symbolic cluster"—a supposition that
"symbols" simultaneously presented are henceforth linked (cf.
p. 90). Here is an illustration of one of the crucial points in
the interpretation:

> The Albatross, the sacramental bird, is also, as it were, a
> moon-bird. For here, with the bird, the moon first enters the
> poem, and the two are intimately associated. . . . The sun is
> kept entirely out of the matter. The lighting is always in-
> direct, for even in the day we have only "mist or cloud,"—
> the luminous haze, the symbolic equivalent of moonlight.
> But not only is the moon associated with the bird, but the
> wind also. Upon the bird's advent a "good south wind
> sprung up behind." And so we have the creative wind, the
> friendly bird, the moonlight of imagination all together in
> one symbolic cluster [p. 91].

Since Warren has been at pains to show a symbol to be,
for Coleridge, "focal, massive, and not arbitrary," one would
imagine that his demonstration would follow these lines; that,
for example, he would argue that the moon is the symbol of
the imagination because it is the focal, massive, and non-
arbitrary representative of the imagination; but he does not
—and, in fact, it is not. All such interpretation is really un-
controlled analogy; the double themes, their fusions, and the
multivalent symbols permit anyone to make of the poem
whatever he may choose.

In short, we may say to Warren what Coleridge himself once quoted. We shall not descend the dark cave of Trophonius with you, there to rub our own eyes, in order to make the sparks and figured flashes, which we are required to see. And more pertinently, perhaps, we may say, again with Coleridge:

Apollo be praised! Not a thought like it would ever enter of its own accord into any mortal mind; and what is an additional good feature, when put there, it will not stay, having the very opposite quality that snakes have—they come out of their holes into open view at the sound of sweet music, while the allegoric meaning slinks off at the very first notes and lurks in murkiest oblivion—an utter invisibility.

Adolescence and Maturity in the American Novel

LESLIE A. FIEDLER

THE YEARS SINCE 1940 have been for writers and critics in America a time of disenchantment, marking, one hopes, the passage from the easy enthusiasms and approximate ambitions of adolescence to the juster self-appraisal of maturity. We have been obliged to recognize not only that we have had most recently a narrowing down, if not an actual exhaustion, of the vein of invention and experiment in the novel; but also that much of the work of the earlier twentieth century which seemed a little while ago so exciting and important actually had only a temporary appeal and a parochial interest. It is not that we have not had in the last thirty years at least two novelists of major stature, but that our sense of a full-scale renaissance, of a continually dazzling level of accomplishment, has turned out to be an illusion. Ironically enough, we have come to a realization of our own limitations during the same period in which many Europeans have embraced the illusion we are leaving behind; so that we find ourselves often in the embarrassing position of having to insist upon the inadequacies of American work which critics abroad find it politic to overpraise.

One of the chief disenchantments of American criticism has been the disconcerting way in which the "great" novels of ten or fifteen years back have tended to disappear. Year by year we have greeted new works with enthusiasm, we have remembered them fondly; but looking back for them over our shoulders we have found them inexplicably turned to dust. The novels of Sherwood Anderson, for example, appear to us now incoherent and unconvincing; his diminished reputation rests on a handful of short stories which survive their sentimentality by fixing it precisely, and which can still move us though they seem alien to what we are at present doing.

Sinclair Lewis we find it harder and harder to believe we could ever have taken for a serious writer. The figure of Babbitt remains in our mind, a caricature of attitudes to which we no longer respond; but Lewis himself we remember as a cartoonist, a journalist with neither poetic nor psychological depth, the author of a curiously provincial parody of *Madame Bovary*. John Steinbeck we continue to find appealing only where he is least ambitious: his stories about animals touch us, and his sentimental entertainment *Tortilla Flat* we recall with affection; but his attempts to deal with adult human beings in all their complexity, to judge society (in such a book as *Grapes of Wrath*), seem to us marred by maudlin social piety and turgid symbolism.

John Dos Passos has recently been writing books that no one reads; and even turning back to *1919* or *The 42nd Parallel* we feel that all the famous technical devices are no more than mechanical substitutes for poetry, subterfuges to conceal from us the fact that he cannot create a convincing character. James T. Farrell strikes us as a writer who attains occasional passages of genuinely passionate insight almost by mistake, swathing them in such endless stretches of doughy, earnest documentation that we find it hard to remember them. Thomas Wolfe appears to us now as appallingly overblown, a writer still to be responded to enthusiastically, but only at the one moment of adolescence to which his frantic rhetoric is appropriate; certainly he is not a writer for the mature. We tend now to see him backwards through *Raintree County*, that illuminating failure arising from what Wolfe had made of Joyce and Kinsey had made of sex. The early deaths of Lockridge and Wolfe, self-inflicted or merely endured, blur into a single symbol of the plight of the American writer who does not know how to grow old.

Another such symbolic death is that of F. Scott Fitzgerald, leaving unfinished what might have been his only completely adult book. Even our best writers appear unable to mature; after one or two inexpert attempts, they find a style, a subject and tone, usually anchored in their adolescent experience—and these they repeat compulsively, like a songbird his single tune. Ring Lardner is an especially pathetic example, trying to make of his ballplayers occasions adequate to his bitter vision.

In general, our writers have no history, no development; their themes belong to a pre-adult world, and the experience of growing old tends to remain for them intractable. It is merely one aspect of that compulsive veneration of youth, that fear of all which is not simply strong and beautiful, so important in our total culture. When our novelists do not manage to die young or to stop writing completely (plunging into alcoholism as into a dream of the Garden), they are likely simply to get worse, ending often in intolerable parodies of their own best work. Ernest Hemingway is the classic instance of such a development. One of the best writers of the twentieth century, a novelist of immense technical means, and indeed the inventor of a style that has changed the writing of fiction in the whole Western world, Hemingway has still been unable to progress. When he has attempted to move from evocations of lost youth, from studies of impotence and the failure of love, to be "positive" or socially aware, he has seemed merely unconvincing and forced. It is almost as impossible to imagine a Hemingway character having a child (dying in childbed is another matter) as it is to conceive of one of them going to a ballot box. His characters seem never really old enough to vote, merely to blow up bridges; as they seem never old enough to reproduce, merely sufficiently mature to make the motions of the act of love. In every sense except the genital one, they remain children; so that the controlling values of his books are a boy's notion of bravery and honor and devotion, tricked out in the child's images of bullfighting and big-game hunting and playing war. In the earliest and best work, *The Sun Also Rises, A Farewell to Arms,* and some of the short stories, these notions and these images are turned into a nostalgic, desolate poetry, bare and mannered at the same time. But all the novels since *To Have and Have Not* (which enjoys the singular distinction of having had *two* bad movies made from it—and richly deserves the honor) have been failures, more and more disheartening up to the complete fiasco of *Across the River and Into the Trees.*

The Old Man and the Sea returns to a level of technical accomplishment almost equal to the earlier work by stripping away all social implications and any attempt to deal with mature emotions. Hemingway is always less embarrassing when he is not attempting to deal with women; and he returns with relief (with what we as readers at least feel as relief) to that "safe" American Romance of the boy and the old man. The single flaw in *The Old Man and the Sea* is the constant sense that Hemingway is no longer creating, but merely imitating the marvelous spare style that was once a revelation; that what was once an anti-rhetoric has become now merely another rhetoric, perhaps our most familiar one, and that even its inventor cannot revive it for us.

For the youngest American readers, writers barely beginning, the brighter college students, Hemingway has come to seem irrelevant, a little boring; though his immense, diffused influence continues to manifest itself in all American prose writing—and indeed in our speech itself. An occasional direct imitation (Chandler Brossard's *Who Walk in Darkness,* for example) only makes the point more firmly with its inescapably old-fashioned impact. The youngsters of today are disgusted not only by the dated and ridiculous role which Hemingway, more and more frantically, plays in his own life, but also by his failure to project an adult love, an adult commitment, an adult courage—from which they might at least revolt with dignity. His breathless pursuit of wars, swordfish, and lions leaves cold a generation born older than he will ever get.

Generally speaking, our writers no longer go to Africa or the left bank to escape from the dullness of America to a world of pure Experience; they are tourists or art historians or government officials or the holders of grants and fellowships, but they are not Exiles. They may get drunk in Paris or find mistresses in Rome, but they no longer consider their drunkenness a utopia or their sexual adventures a blow for freedom. In the same way, Bohemia has died for them; I do not mean that there are no bohemias, but that they are now escapes *from* writing, not escapes to it from the pressures of bourgeois life. It is for this reason that F. Scott Fitzgerald, who represents the world of bohemia and expatriation as something done with, who presents the world of the 'twenties with the pathos of something already outgrown, with a sense of how naïvely, how *innocently* lost that generation must appear to our post-Dachau vision, is more sympathetic to us than the much more talented Hemingway, to whom the Cult of Experience remains not a lost frenzy of the years after the First World War, but his only faith.

I suppose it is the death of the adolescent faith in Life as Experience which has led to a complementary loss of the ingenuous faith in Literature as Experience. It was once enough for us to know, or believe (it turns out that we were dealing with a legend), that Sherwood Anderson one day suddenly walked out of the office in which he worked, throwing aside bourgeois security for Art and Life. This seemed then a sufficient guarantee of his "integrity" (it was once our favorite word) and of his excellence as an artist. And, alas, this Anderson believed along with the rest of us, so that much of his work remains abortive, because, trusting to Experience to do the whole job, he stopped precisely where he should have begun in real earnest. There was in those days a hopeless confusion between what made a man "good" (i.e., everything his bourgeois parents would have believed bad) and what made a work of art good; "social consciousness," "sincerity," "progressivism" were taken for aesthetic terms. To such a muddled understanding of the relationship between the truth of art, the truth of conscience, and the truth of facts, writers like Upton Sinclair, Sinclair Lewis, and Farrell owe their former successes and their present waning popularity. Hemingway himself, though primarily a stylist and interested only at a second remove in "life," was victimized by similar assumptions, which have led to his continuing pose as a *naïf*, a latter-day Mark Twain; and he has felt obliged to invent with great pains a style which seems to take no pains; as some American politicians invest a great deal of art in seeming to speak like the artless common man.

Even so important and courageous a literary pioneer as Theodore Dreiser appears to us now of drastically limited value, despite his ability to create a milieu with all the thick substance of reality itself. It is not merely a matter of his sentimental subjects, those eternally seduced women, or of the gross style interlarded with ladies'-magazine elegancies, nor even of his profound and utterly unsuspected stupidity (intelligence and style alike are optional for the writer— and any subject can be redeemed); but of his failure to develop, his entrapment by the belief that a work of art is equal to its raw materials, and that its moral value is equal to the code its author professes rather than what is *realized* in the text.

It is tempting to say that the central fact of our period is the death of "naturalism" and the decline in reputation of the novelists associated with its seeming triumph. But what has died is only a small part of what is commonly associated with the term: a certain moral obtuseness, political sentimentality and naïve faith in documentation. Much has survived: the breaking of certain taboos about subject matter; the demonstration that no experience is too humble or trivial for the novel; the elevation of a solidly specified environment to equal importance with plot or character; the revolution in the conventions of writing dialogue—all these will never be lost. Yet the contemporary American author no longer believes that a work of art can be judged primarily by its accuracy in reproducing ordinary speech or rendering literally the horrors of Chicago slums; for us, the reality, the value, of a work of art lies in its symbolic depth and resonance, not in the exhaustiveness of its data.

It is for this reason that a vital influence on the contemporary novel is Henry James, who not long since was disowned as too aristocratic, too elaborately trivial to be either a good writer or a true American. In his own day, of course, James was felt, indeed felt himself, in the forefront of the movement toward "realism," while we relish in him what is least like such fellow-realists as William Dean Howells. Our James is the impressionist, the conscious artist, who dared assert that a concern with form is not immoral; and in whom we have come to recognize great poetry, profound images of good and evil, under the slowly elaborated accounts of people who apparently never sweat or blow their noses, and who manage to make love over teacups rather than in bed. From James, our younger novelists (even the ones most impatient with him, most insistent on all he ignores) have learned that a novel is not what its author *says* happened in it, but what is really *rendered*. It is possible to feel now that the Jamesian example has been assimilated, even institutionalized, and that we must be moving on; but there is no way to go except through Henry James, and no writer among us can ever doubt again that a book is made of words rather than facts.

For technique, the newer writers have been able to find a master no further back than the beginnings of realism; but, for an exemplar of the poetic subject, they have had to search behind the Civil War, to the Melville of *Moby Dick,* in whom they have found a blend of secularized puritanism, factual solidity, and symbolic resonance, an erudition and naïveté that point beyond realism. There is a Melville whom one scarcely knows whether to call the discovery or invention of our time, our truest contemporary, who has revealed to us the traditional theme of the deepest American mind, the ambiguity of innocence, "the mystery of iniquity," which we had traded for the progressive melodrama of a good outcast (artist, rebel, whore, proletarian) against an evil bourgeoisie. In James, too, a similar theme is suggested and then almost lost in the embroidery of sensibility; but, having seen once our theme, we do not willingly surrender it or the attitudes proper to it: "the blackness ten times black," the obligation to say *no,* the practice of irony and the acceptance that does not cancel it out. In these, there is the possibility of development and fulfillment, a way out of adolescence.

Guilt and innocence, the mystery of iniquity—most of our present-day writers are not in any orthodox sense religious (though a few are, and many enjoy playing poetically with the counters of orthodoxy: Original Sin and Salvation and the Dark Night of the Soul), but almost all of them feel that there are deeper perceptions of man's plight than the brash optimism of a Rousseau. We remember only too well the generations who tried to convince us that all metaphors of human evil were mystifications, the inventions of priests and aesthetes afraid of "real life." Indeed, during the 'thirties, when American "realism" was captured by the Marxists, such concerns were banned by the exponents of the "proletarian," who preached that the only criterion of good and evil, as well as the true subject of fiction, was the Class Struggle. The record of the so-called "proletarian novel" in the United States is one of the most absurd episodes of our literary history. The names of the "revolutionary" writers who seemed to us in 1935 about to make a new culture are hard to remember: Robert Cantwell, Grace Lumpkin, Jack Conroy, William Rollins—one sees them occasionally in a list of witnesses before a Congressional investigating committee, or on the masthead of a Luce publication. Merely to recite the half-forgotten names and to invoke our old enthusiasm is to learn the lesson which makes us smile a little when we see in Europe today attempts at social realism, at what the French call *littérature engagée.*

Yet once, even established writers rushed to give assurances that they had graduated from post-war cynicism, Hemingway writing *To Have and Have Not,* and Fitzgerald himself toying with the idea of having Dick Diver become a Communist; and those who would not conform were disowned. It is symptomatic of our new turning that the favorite writer of most of our young novelists now is precisely the author most despised, during the "proletarian" period, as reactionary, ghoulish, and cheaply spectacular—namely, William Faulkner.

We do not, to be sure, read his grotesque poems of comedy and horror as realistic reports on the South; for us the truth of Faulkner's world is a symbolic truth; and across his gothic landscape is fought not the historical war between North and South, but the eternal war between the dream of nobility and order and the fact of disorder and failure and sorrow. Naturally, his images are American images and even regional ones: the Negro, the Indian, the ravaged and forgotten wilderness, the miserable mountain farm, the riderless horse disappearing into the night—but their meanings are the meanings of such objects in dreams and not in history, meanings immediately translatable for anyone anywhere. Beyond this, there is Faulkner's concern with rhetoric and form which intrigues us; his stubborn insistence on finding for each book (*The Sound and the Fury* is perhaps the best example) a language and structure so nearly impossible that he is always risking absurdity.

Faulkner and Melville and James: these are the American novelists who function as living influences today. There are others whom we honor, Hawthorne and Mark Twain and Hemingway, for instance; but they do not so directly determine the ambitions of the beginning writer, except as they also contribute to the psychological, symbolic, gothic tradition these define. The strengths of contemporary writing correspond to the strengths of this tradition, boldness of imagery, subtlety of insight, and especially the willingness to plunge deep below the lintel of consciousness; and the weaknesses to its weaknesses, a tendency to involution and hysteria, to a rhetoric that becomes pseudo-poetry at its weakest; and a weakness in dealing with women. The tradition which stems from Melville, James, and Faulkner combines an overall moral maturity with a failure to achieve mature attitudes toward sex; there is a vacuum at the heart of American fiction that James's nervous indirection, Melville's underground homosexuality, and Faulkner's comic anti-feminism cannot fill. But at least there is a tradition at last, compounded ironically by three traditionless and lonely writers; and, beyond them, our newer novelists look to European sources: to the Russian novel of the nineteenth century, especially to Dostoevsky; to Marcel Proust, whose influence blends with that of James; to James Joyce and Thomas Mann; and more recently to Franz Kafka, who seems almost an American writer in his symbolic gothicism and who projected, before we knew we needed it, a style able to reproduce the logical insanity of a German concentration camp or a Russian political trial.

It is a point worth noting that most of our younger writers do not insist upon their *difference* as Americans, feeling themselves sharers in the general development of Western culture; indeed, one of the things that makes us feel alienated from an Anderson, a Dreiser, a Sinclair Lewis is their almost willful cultural naïveté, their fear of the traditional. For we have come to believe that an ignorance of the past and of Europe is the poorest way to ensure our own particularity. In homemade, degenerate form all the clichés of post-Enlightenment thought appear in the work of those writers most set on reproducing "pure" American experience; while in James and Melville the fruit of reading and study is an approach at once new and enriched by older sources.

Not all recent American writers, of course, fall into the post-naturalist camp I have been describing. The writers of books describing the Second World War have apparently felt themselves immune to the shifts I have tried to indicate, and with creditable diligence and woeful lack of invention they have rewritten the typical novels of the war of 1917, changing only dates and place names; while, a few years back, another atavistic novel, James Jones's *From Here to Eternity*, won considerable critical acclaim by reviving and exemplifying the pseudo-realist theory that to write honestly one must write badly, that Art and Truth are mutually exclusive. There survives and flourishes, in addition, the slick sentimental-realist school, represented by John Hersey's *The Wall* and the novels of Irwin Shaw, which manage to combine a banal liberal optimism with a commercially successful style based on watered-down Hemingway.

But among those writers who, in the phrase of Henry James, have "no ambitions except the highest" the majority are more concerned with symbol than with statement, more drawn toward poetry than toward journalism. Their work tends to be the opposite of naïve—in fact, rather difficult; and they are read, therefore, by a relatively small audience as compared not only with the readers of historical romances, but even with those who admire the tough or sentimental pseudo-realists. It is one of the ironies of the present situation in writing that our better novelists are at the same time un-popular and un-experimental. Nobody nowadays is doing any-thing startling or new; the techniques that are being exploited are those that were revolutionary in the 'twenties; but the mass audience has stubbornly refused to catch up. This is hardly cheering to our younger authors, who tend to be a melancholy lot, having neither the comfort of commercial success nor the thrill of feeling themselves a gallant vanguard. They have tended, in self-defense, to find themselves special audiences for whom they specifically write and by whose ac-claim they live; and while this strategy serves a purpose in sustaining them, financially and spiritually, it has tended to create a situation in which we have a series of competing "academies" rather than a conflict of the academic and the anti-academic.

Since it would be impossible to mention more than a few writers of the younger generation without simply compiling a catalogue, I shall limit myself to discussing particularly only two of the competing "academies," the two which seem to me in certain ways most important: one associated with *Harper's Bazaar,* the other with *Partisan Review.* I pick *Harper's Bazaar* to stand for a whole group which includes *Mademoiselle* and *Vogue* and the ill-fated *Flair,* which attempted to be de-liberately and whole-heartedly what the others had become partially and almost by accident, and which ended as a parody of itself and of the others. *Harper's Bazaar* is, of course, not primarily a literary magazine at all, but an elegant fashion magazine for women, read not only by those who can

afford the goods it advertises but by many who cannot and
who participate vicariously in its world of values, picking it
up on the table of a beauty-parlor waiting room. Finding a
story by, say, Truman Capote tucked away between the picture of a determinedly unbeautiful model and an ad for a
brassiere, most of the readers of *Harper's Bazaar,* one assumes, must simply skip the meaningless pages; and, knowing
this, the editors (writers, themselves, or friends of writers)
know that they can print anything they please.

But the conjunction of Capote and high style is not as accidental as it seems at first glance. We have been evolving in
recent years a new sort of sensibility, defined by a taste for
haute couture, classical ballet, baroque opera, the rites and
vestments of Catholicism—and above all for a kind of literature at once elegantly delicate and bitterly grotesque. This
new kind of sensibility, although (or perhaps because) it is
quite frankly a homosexual one, appeals profoundly to certain rich American women with cultural aspirations, and is
therefore sponsored in their salons and published decoratively
in magazines that cater to their tastes. The development of
new markets for the young writer with this sort of sensibility
has gone hand in hand with the development of a kind of
high bohemia, which moves freely from New York to Venice
to Capri to establish a world that is international and anti-
bourgeois without being political or sordid or sullen, like the
older bohemias.

The most important writer of this group is Carson McCullers, the most typical Truman Capote (or his latest version,
called Speed Lamkin or whatever, since in this world of eva-
nescent youth the hungry generations tread each other down
with astonishing rapidity). One can take the latter as almost
a caricature of the type: the "queen" as American author,
possessing a kind of beauty, both in person and as an artist,
which belongs to childhood and early adolescence, and which
withers before it can ripen; Southern in origin and allegiance;
and gothic (a very refined gothic) in style, blending Edgar
Allan Poe and Ronald Firbank in an improbable grafting.

Such writers also descend in a strange way from Faulkner, who provides them with a ready-made *paysage moralisée*, the landscape of the South as a natural symbol for decay and brooding evil. To the distrust and fear of woman in Faulkner, they respond according to their own lights; and what there is in the older writer of the agonizedly male has already been transmuted for them by two transitional writers, both women and both immensely talented, Katherine Anne Porter and Eudora Welty—who began the process of taming and feminizing Faulkner (he has had only one truly male follower, Robert Penn Warren, who falls outside the scope of my present essay), making possible the ingrafting of Henry James which produces the true Magnolia Blossom or Southern Homosexual style: pseudo-magical, pseudo-religious, counterfeiting the symbolism of Faulkner in a rhetoric and rhythm derived from James.

I have used the word "counterfeiting" because I find this kind of fiction often merely chic behind its pretense of being subtle and advanced. Even Capote, who possesses considerable talent, has come more and more to *play* at being an author, to act out for the benefit of his own kind of society the role of the elegant, sad, futile androgyne—half reigning beauty and half freak. His novel *Other Voices, Other Rooms* already represents a falling away from the slight authentic music of such an early story as "Children on Their Birthdays," and some of his most recent work seems more and more just décor—like the quasi-surrealist window dressings of certain Fifth Avenue shops.

There has been a tendency for this school at its periphery, where it touches, let us say, Princeton, to combine in a perhaps foreseeable way with the formal emphasis of the "New Criticism," and to find expression in the more studied Jamesian effects of a writer like Frederick Buechner; but its realest triumphs are achieved in the fiction of Carson McCullers. Her first novel, *The Heart Is a Lonely Hunter,* published when she was only twenty-two, is heartbreakingly wonderful; the melancholy Southern town, the deaf-and-dumb protagonists all make their meanings precisely, scene and symbol fused into a single poetry without strain. The subject of Miss Mc-Cullers' work is the subject of her whole group: the impossibility of reciprocal love, the sadness of a world in which growing up means only learning that isolation is the fate of every one of us. Her central characters, those ambiguous boyish girls (Frankie and Mick: the names make the point) who stand outside of everything, even their own sex, lost in a world of freaks—these are strange new heroes of our time.

The *Partisan Review,* around which the second "academy" tends to polarize, is quite another matter, though, indeed, its typical contributors sometimes appear (though not usually with their best or most characteristic work) in *Harper's Bazaar;* while a sensibility, shriller or icier, but not fundamentally different from that which informs the fiction of the ladies' magazines, manifests itself in such *Partisan Review* contributors as Tennessee Williams and Paul Bowles. But the impact, the very appearance of *Partisan* indicate a fundamental difference. It is not an advertising journal that has stumbled into printing advanced fiction, but a review which began as a "little magazine" and has managed (thanks in part to angels, but chiefly to the stubborn devotion of its editors) to become an institution without ever having achieved a large circulation. One of the strangest things about *Partisan Review* is that, though its readers have never numbered more than about 10,000, its name is confidently used in journals with 100,000 and 2,000,000 readers as a symbol for certain values which do not have to be further defined. Certainly, it is resented, hated, and sullenly respected by a much larger number of people than have ever read it.

In its beginnings, it attempted to combine an allegiance to *avant-garde* aesthetic ideals and radical politics; at first, it was quite frankly a Communist publication, though its editors quite soon broke from orthodox Stalinism as the enemy of free culture. Its contributors are characteristically unhappy with each other and with the magazine itself; and they would resent to a man being spoken of as a group, as I am doing now. But they *do* have a good deal in common, not the least of which is their uneasy feeling of independence from each other, the sense that it is only their past which binds them unwillingly together. In politics, for instance, they have grown far apart, becoming variously Anarchists, Trotskyites, Social Democrats, New Dealers, and even Republicans—but they have all of them the complicated political awareness of those who once lived inside of or close to the Communist movement.

They are "political" in the European sense of the word, a sense that does not even exist for most Americans. Not only do they have Marx, accepted or denied, in their blood, but also Freud in much the same way, as well as contemporary sociology, anthropology, and philosophy in general—so that they are likely to take sides passionately in arguments about, say, existentialism or other recent European ideologies. They share the fondness of the Southern group for James and Faulkner, but in some ways Kafka is closer to their hearts (Isaac Rosenfeld, for instance, made a major, not quite successful effort, to create a body of American work in his image), and they feel a real kinship with Dostoevsky and Tolstoy. Precisely because their cultural background is so complex, and also because they have almost all been forced somewhere between 1935 and 1940 to make a radical shift in their political allegiances and aesthetic ambitions, it has taken these writers a long time to grow up. Some critics have even found it comical or disheartening to learn that many *Partisan* writers spoken of as "young" are thirty or thirty-five or forty. But they are in truth, for the reasons I have tried to suggest, still young as writers when middle-aged as men, still *beginning*—not dazzling successes at twenty like Truman Capote. They have matured slowly, but they have matured; and this is exceptional in the American scene.

The best of the group is Saul Bellow, a novelist of exceptional talent and in many ways a typical figure. Like most of the writers I am describing, he is a second-generation Jew (this is important, for the Jews are just now taking a place of peculiar significance in American cultural life; and, as a history-ridden people in a history-less land, they stand in a different relationship to the past and to Europe than any other American group), an urban type, whose world is not the archetypal small town that from Twain to Sherwood Anderson and on to Faulkner has been the world *par excellence* of our fiction. Nor is his city the Big Town seen by the provincial, the bewildering un-home that has haunted the American literary mind from the moment of Pierre's wild trip to New York. Saul Bellow's Chicago (like the New York of Delmore Schwartz) is the only home of the essentially homeless, remembered not idyllically as the Garden but as the desert to which one woke at the moment of the Great Depression.

Bellow's controlling images and myths tend to be social ones; ideas, political and philosophical, are not something intrusive in his work, but the atmosphere, the very condition of life. He feels most deeply where his thought is most deeply involved, and his characters come alive where they are touched by ideas. It is for this reason that the most moving passages in his books are discussions, the interchange of opinions and theories as vividly presented as a love scene or a fight. But his books are never "problem" novels in the sense of the socially conscious 'twenties. Even *The Victim* (which remains in many respects my favorite), though it takes off from the problem of anti-Semitism, does not aim at establishing the smug sense of our own innocence and the other's guilt, but suggests in its muted fable the difficulty of being human, much less innocent, in a world of injustice.

With *The Adventures of Augie March,* Bellow has won for the first time the general recognition he has long deserved, though his two earlier books had won at least equal critical acclaim. Writers of this school have, I think, a special problem in reaching a mass audience to whom the commonplaces of their experience have an inevitable tinge of the remote and abstruse; and *Augie* is a deliberate attempt to break through to such a group out of the parochial world in which Bellow began. *Augie* itself is an uneven book, redundant and

untidy, full of a strange tough-abstract poetry that becomes
sometimes merely mannered; but it is held together finally by
a versatile irony that moves from barely quizzical tenderness
to wild burlesque. Ideally, the book should be read after the
gray, tight, orderly *Victim* in order to understand the self-
imposed limitations against which it is in revolt. In everything
but self-understanding and control, it is a better book, richer,
more ambitious, funnier, the saga of an improbable Huckleberry Finn: Huck as a metropolitan Jew, a wanderer through
cities, fallen among Trotskyites and comedians of ideas as
well as grafters and minor machiavellians—but Huck still, the
apostle of non-commitment, moving uncertainly but inevitably
toward the "happy ending" of un-success. It is an explosive
book, a novel powered by the atomization of its own world;
and the world fragmented in its humor and violence is the
world of the *Partisan Review*, which Augie may never have
had time to read.

There are other lesser, but still interesting, writers in this
constellation: Lionel Trilling, whose single novel was not
quite successful, but who in two short stories perfected a new
kind of moral-critical fiction; Delmore Schwartz, a poet and
fictionist who evokes the Jewish-American milieu with a
studied limpness, half-irritating, half-intriguing; Mary Mc-
Carthy, the most wickedly witty of the group, who satirizes
the ideas of the *Partisan Review* itself at the point where they
tend to die into banalities.

It is because the fictionists of this group are capable of
seeing themselves with a characteristic irony, sad or brittle,
because their world is complex and troubled enough to pro-
tect them from nostalgia and self-pity, that I see in them evidence of a movement toward a literature of maturity. Yet certain flaws endemic to the whole American scene reappear
disconcertingly in the *Partisan* group and mar *Augie* itself. One
feels sometimes that only the weaknesses of American literature survive from generation to generation; that the heritage
of our writers is a series of vacuums, which by evasion or
strategy they must bridge or by-pass.

One waits still, for instance, for the American writer who can render as successfully as, say, any second-rank French novelist of the nineteenth century the complexities and ambiguities of sexual passion, of—(how absurdly hard it is for the American writer to say simply "love") of *love*. The sentimental-love religion has died out of our serious fiction, leaving only a blank, a blank that the nympholeptic stereotypes which play the women's roles in Saul Bellow's book surely do not fill. Among certain *Partisan* writers, there has recently been an attempt to make out of Laurentian reminiscences and Reichian doctrines a new religion—not of love, of course, but of "full genitality"; yet this seems anything but mature.

Moreover, there appears to be a growing impatience inside the *Partisan* academy, superficially directed at the excesses of the newer criticism but actually aimed at the whole Jamesian cult of sensibility, and this threatens to end in a general scalping of all Paleface writers. Yet the urge toward this polar split between "honest crudity" and "elegant introspection" represents as deep a wound in the American aesthetic sense as the analogous distinction of Dark Lady and Fair Lady stands for in terms of our sexual consciousness. There is a kind of tough-minded provincialism implicit in the whole position: an impulse toward "moral realism," a fear of "mystification" (i.e., of religion and metaphysics), which may at any moment explode in a reversion to the simplest Redskin celebration of pure experience.

Against this temptation, Dostoevsky and Tolstoy and Kafka might well be expected to serve as antidotes; but it is hard to say how seriously these writers are finally taken and how far they are merely "culture" in the vulgarest sense of the word, the souvenirs of literary tourism. The "tradition" which sustains the *Partisan Review* remains, in a characteristically American way, partial and *willed*. Its canon develops not organically out of a given cultural past, but by forced breeding out of what a few strong-minded men *happen to know*. It is hard to see how such a situation can be avoided in a society distinguished by the indifference of the many to the making of its taste, and by an unbridgeable gap between its productive present and its only viable literary past.

The America which has survived westward expansion and the mass immigration of the last century can no longer live, except nostalgically, on the puritan-colored metaphysical tradition that was still able to nurture Hawthorne and Melville and Henry James. It is not only that America is comparatively young, but that it no longer possesses even the meager past it has lived; that it has, indeed, deliberately and joyously cast off that burden, so that each new generation must improvise not only its fate but its history. This is, on the one hand, an opportunity but, on the other, a curse; and, opportunity or curse, it cuts us off from the European alternatives of Tradition and Revolt. To be sure, we use these terms frequently but somewhat comically to describe our pious allegiance to or disavowal of values some ten or fifteen years old; and our failure to confess this leads to the constant counterfeiting of new pasts and the restless revaluations that succeed each other among us with bewildering speed.

There has been in recent times a notorious attempt to invent a full-scale synthetic myth of an America of the Open Road to replace the defunct New England version of our country; but this was born as unreal as its predecessor has become, and, as it has grown less and less sympathetic to a second-generation, urbanized world, its sponsors have grown shriller and shriller. The sentimentality of the wholesale American Legend and its corresponding dream of an unlimited mass audience have not directly influenced most serious American writers; but, in their self-satisfaction at having resisted so second-rate a temptation, they are likely to fall prey to the subtler allures embodied in the exclusive little audience with its conviction of the superiority of its special taste. To write deliberately for the few, we have been learning, is as dangerous as writing for the many in a mass society. To shift from the latter aim to the former is to move from the child's desire to buy universal love with perfect obedience to the adolescent's resolve to compel universal recognition with perfect non-cooperation, a resolve that ends typically in complete submission to the mores of one's gang.

The mature writer must write, as he has always written, for neither mass nor sect but for that pure fiction, the ideal understander, for whom we no longer have a name but who was once called the "gentle reader." In traditional cultures, that non-existent perfect reader was postulated in a set of values represented imperfectly but hopefully by a self-perpetuating body of critics. In America, he has never been institutionalized, surviving only in the unwitting parody of the "genteel reader," which at the end of the nineteenth century we rejected with scorn in favor of a more democratic but less useful concept, the "average reader."

The plight of the American writer is at best difficult; aware that the greatest books of our literature remain somehow boys' books, he seeks a way toward maturity. But between him and a mature relationship with his past lies our contempt for what is left behind, the discontinuity of our history; between him and a mature relationship with his public lies the impossibility of institutionalizing values in a democracy which regards taste as a vestige of aristocratic privilege; between him and a mature relationship with experience lies the fact that the only universally *felt* American morality arises from the ersatz religion of sentimentalism.

It is no wonder that our novelists have shuttled between the utopias of form and formlessness, pretending alternately that a technical point-of-view is a sufficient substitute for a moral viewpoint and that reported fact is the equivalent of judged experience. The images of childhood and adolescence haunt our greatest works as an unintended symbolic confession of the inadequacy we sense but cannot remedy. Perhaps it is impossible to attain a mature literature without a continuing tradition in the European sense; for it may be that no individual author alone and in a single lifetime can achieve an adult relationship to his culture and his vision of it. But we can, of course, never have such a tradition, only the disabling nostalgia for one; and quite rapidly the whole world is coming to resemble us in this regard. The essential fact of literature in our age is its inevitable "Americanization," as mass culture advances and the old systems of evaluation go down with the political structures into which they were ingrafted.

In this sense, the Continental vogue of American fiction, which seems otherwise a merely fashionable exoticism or even sometimes a gesture of self-contempt and anti-intellectualism, represents the search of Western literature for its future. Even now, the writers of many other countries begin to stand to their own past in a relation as uneasy as our own; and in our novel they find raised nakedly at last the question that underlay the experimentation of the 'twenties, the "social consciousness" of the 'thirties, the search for formal security of the 'forties: "Can the lonely individual, unsustained by tradition in an atomized society, achieve a poetry adult and complicated enough to be the consciousness of its age?" To have posed that question for the world is the achievement of the American novel at the present moment.

The Stone and the Crucifixion:
Faulkner's *Light in August*

RICHARD CHASE

WITHOUT ado I wish to direct attention to the symbolic texture of *Light in August*. This texture is very much a matter of mechanics and dynamics—a poetry of physics. Repeatedly Faulkner presents appearance, event, and even character in the images of stasis, motion, velocity, weight, lightness, mass, line, relative position, circle, sphere, emptiness, fullness, light, and dark. The phrase "light in August" has at least two meanings. As Mr. Malcolm Cowley informs us in his *Portable Faulkner*, the phrase means "light" as opposed to "heavy" and refers to a pregnant woman who will give birth in August. And it also means "light" as opposed to "dark"—an affirmation of life and human spirit. *Light in August* may be described, in Faulkner's own words (though he is describing something else), as "the mechanics, the theatring of evil." This is not a complete or fully fair description of Faulkner's novel, but it is complete and fair enough to demand that we look at the novel from this point of view—and that we finally ask, How successful is the author in extending his account of the mechanics and theatring of evil into an account of the human situation?

The reader of *Light in August* will be puzzled in the first few pages by what may be called "the string of beads image." We read that the wagon in which Lena Grove rides through the August afternoon is like "a shabby bead upon a mild red string of road" and that the village beside the railroad, from which she begins her long journey, is like "a forgotten bead from a broken string." Later our attention is called to the row of iron bars in the fence which surrounds the orphanage of Joe Christmas' childhood, to the identical windows of a street car, to a picket fence, and to the rows of identical white houses in which the lower-middle-class whites live. To these images of linear discreteness Faulkner opposes images of the curve. Lena Grove—searching for Lucas Burch, the father of her unborn child—passes through "a long monotonous succession of peaceful and undeviating changes from day to dark and dark to day"; but her mode of action and of consciousness is not of the order of the "string of beads." She is "like something moving forever and without progress across an urn." For her the road is not linear but like a string "being rewound onto a spool." These images of linear discreteness and curve are extended into one of the central images of the book: flight and pursuit.

We have already encountered the symbolic representation of two realms of being which are counterposed throughout the novel. The linear discrete image stands for "modernism": abstraction, rationalism, applied science, capitalism, progressivism, emasculation, the atomized consciousness and its pathological extensions. The curve image stands for holistic consciousness, a containing culture and tradition, the cyclical life and death of all the creatures of earth. Throughout the novel, Lena retains her holistic consciousness and she is strong, enduring, hopeful. All the other characters in one way or another are victims of the linear delusion. For Joe Christmas, in whom the linear consciousness becomes pathological, the curve image is a "cage" or a "prison" to be broken out of. Or it is something to be gashed from the outside so that whatever it contains will be spilled meaninglessly out. Joe gashes the whiskey tins he and Burch have buried in the woods as he has a vision of trees in the moonlight, standing like "a row of suavely shaped urns," each one cracked and extruding "something liquid, deathcolored, and foul." At the end, when Joe can no longer perform this symbolic act of even smashing, the curve image becomes the fateful circle of repetition which he has never really either escaped or broken and which is the only path to the only kind of holism he will ever find: death. "I have never got outside that circle. I have never broken out of the ring of what I have already done and cannot ever undo." The tragic irony of the linear consciousness, Faulkner seems to say, is that it is an illusion; all consciousness is holistic, but it may be the holism of life (Lena) or of death (Joe). The remarkable symbol of the wheel in the passage describing the final madness of the Reverend Mr. Hightower presumably coincides with Joe's circle of doom, though here it may symbolize the completion in death of a cycle of legendary family history.

Faulkner's counterposing of motionlessness and motion seems to imply a fairly consistent deploying of polarity of character. Lena, Joe, and Hightower each has a certain kind of motionlessness. Lena, "her voice quite grave now, quite quiet," sitting "quite still, her hands motionless upon her lap," has the inner quiet of the wheel's axle, a stillness within movement. The stillness behind Joe's cold, contemptuous mask is the abstract stillness of separation, a schizoid disengagement from outer action. The motionlessness of Hightower, sitting "rigidly" behind his desk, his "forearms parallel upon the armrests of the chair," is the negation of the will and action by fear, "denial," and impotence.

The quality of Joe's action is simply a willed translation of his separateness. Whenever he is in motion, in fantasy or actuality, he is in flight; and this is true even of his many connections with women—these also he must turn into the pattern of flight whenever they threaten to bring him too close to the kind of central and holistic place represented by Lena. Although Burch is throughout the book in a sense in flight from Lena, Byron Bunch, or the sheriff, his movements entirely lack Joe's willed abstract control. He is pure aimless motion, a rural poor white uprooted and cast adrift in an industrial-urban society. "He puts me in mind," says Byron Bunch, "of one of these cars running along the street with a radio in it. You can't make out what it is saying and the car ain't going anywhere in particular and when you look at it close you see that there ain't even anybody in it." A friend of Bunch's replies, "Yes, he puts me in mind of a horse. Not a mean horse. Just a worthless horse." This rude progression of metaphors will serve to indicate that Faulkner's imagination very frequently approaches the level of human character and consciousness beginning with the mechanical, and proceeding to the animal level through an intermediate level of dynamics.

The denouement of the novel can be conceived as the final resolution of several kinds of motion. Byron Bunch separates himself from his spiritual kinship with Hightower and his hitherto meaningless life finds its repose in Lena. Burch moves away from Lena, dooming himself, as it were, to aimless perpetual motion. The final flight of Joe to Hightower's house may seem too little explained as part of the plot. But it has a symbolic significance, since Joe, turning away for the last time from the realm of being which is represented by Lena and which he has tried to find in his various women, finds his ultimate refuge in the castration and death vouchsafed to him by Percy Grimm (only the last of all the symbolic castrations and deaths he has first sought and then endured). Hightower himself had turned away from the Lena-holism when years earlier he had in effect pursued his wife out of existence by believing in his fantasy that his "seed" had died with his grandfather in the Civil War.

II

Mr. Robert Penn Warren suggests that Faulkner's objection to the modern world is that it lacks the ability to set up "codes, concepts of virtue, obligations" by which man can "define himself as human" and "accept the risks of his humanity." In *Light in August,* Faulkner seems to be concerned with showing that the codes modern man *does* set up do *not* allow him to define himself as human—that codes have become compulsive patterns which man clings to in fear and trembling while the pattern emasculates him. Byron Bunch, wondering why he lives to the split second by his big silver watch and works alone in the planing mill every Saturday afternoon and why the Reverend Mr. Hightower has refused to leave Jefferson, the scene of his ruin and disgrace, reflects, "It is because a fellow is more afraid of the trouble he might have than he ever is of the trouble he's already got. He'll cling to trouble he's used to before he'll risk a change." Byron and Hightower have for years been sustaining one another in their "patterns." Their relationship ends over the question of Bunch's aiding and courting Lena, pregnant with another man's child. The dilemma for each is whether to stick to a pattern of behavior which prohibits accepting "the risks of his humanity" or to become involved responsibly in a human situation. Byron chooses to break the pattern and accept the consequences of intervention. Hightower remains in the pattern (though he makes certain senile excursions from it), choosing to conspire in closing the circle of his destiny, choosing separation and madness. It is not true, as has been said, that all of Faulkner's characters are rigidly controlled by fate: Byron, for one, is left free to choose his own fate.

Joe Christmas is in many ways a masterful portrait of a man whose earliest years have been spent in an institution—an experience, as the psychiatrists show, which definitively affects not only the emotional centers of the victim but also the character of his conceptual thinking. In the forbidding orphanage (a true symbol of the conditions of modern life) Joe finds a surrogate mother—a cynical, suspicious and indeed almost paranoiac dietitian, a mockery of the Nursing Mother of the myths. His surrogate father is an obscenely fanatical inquisitor and peeping tom who functions as the janitor of the orphanage and who later turns out to be Joe's grandfather. The pattern of Joe's life is inexorably formed when the dietitian finds that he has been hiding in her closet eating tooth paste while she has been entertaining an interne on her bed (the tube of tooth paste is another urn symbol). The definitive event is not that Joe has seen the dietitian in the act but that she fails to punish him and instead offers him money not to tell. Having felt terribly guilty, having expected and even wanted to be punished, and having had no idea of giving away the secret, he is irretrievably shocked when she offers him the money. He had wanted the woman to engross him in her life, if only by beating him. Instead she denies him this engrossment and gives him a silver dollar, whose shining circumference forms a circle Joe will never break through. Joe's homo-sexualism is another theme symbolized by the "string of beads" image. The relationship between Joe and his guardian, Mc-Eachern, a fanatical apostle of a parochial and degenerate Presbyterianism who beats Joe with the impersonal violence of a machine, has for both McEachern and Joe the uneasy satis-faction of an abnormal but vehemently pure sexual alliance. McEachern has succeeded with Joe where the dietitian failed. Joe finds the relationship "perfectly logical and reasonable and inescapable," and he quickly learns to hate Mrs. Mc-Eachern because her proffered feminine kindnesses always threaten to taint an abstract and predictable relationship—just as the food she offers him makes him sick (all the women in Joe's life try to feed him; one of them is a waitress in a restaurant).

Joe's many adventures with women are attempts to escape the abstract quality of a latently homosexual life. As Joe pauses outside Miss Burden's house before keeping a tryst with her, Faulkner says, "The dark was filled with the voices, myr-iad, out of all time that he had known, as though all the past was a flat pattern. And going on: tomorrow night, all the tomorrows, to be part of the flat pattern, going on." "Then," says Faulkner, "it was time"—which seems to be a pun (the same one occurs in *The Sound and the Fury*) meaning that now Joe's existence can be measured by time (the urn con-sciousness) rather than by the abstraction of eternity. But the connection with Miss Burden, like all of Joe's connections with women, turns into a ritual reaffirmation that no such connec-tion is possible, a circular path back to the compulsive pattern —as we see when after various ingenious phases of sexual flight and pursuit, Miss Burden, before Joe kills her, is transmuted in appearance and behavior into a mocking likeness of Mc-Eachern. The sexual dilemma of Joe's life is nicely symbolized in the episode where he lolls in the woods (and gashes the whiskey tins) reading a magazine "of that type whose covers bear either pictures of young women in underclothes or pic-tures of men shooting one another with pistols." He reads as a man "walking along the street might count the cracks in the pavement, to the last final page, the last and final word." He goes through life with this same attachment to his pattern, hating the women in underclothes, longing for a purely masculine annihilation.

In symbolic polarity to the compulsive pattern we have Lena, who does not need to flee from involvement in human life, and Lucas Burch. Distantly adumbrating all the polarities of *Light in August,* the gay, irresponsible, aimless Burch symbolizes pure Chaos. Perhaps through the child in Lena's womb, Burch symbolizes the undetermined possibility of a future the direction of which will be decided by the final resolution of forces among the other characters. If so, we may say that *Light in August* is a "hopeful" book. For the future is in the hands of Lena and Byron Bunch—a woman who endures and loves and a man who has decided to "accept the risks of his humanity."

III

Mr. Warren suggests that we ought not to think of Faulkner as an exclusively Southern writer but as a writer concerned with modern times in general. To this, one might add that Faulkner has many affinities with both Hawthorne and Melville. As Malcolm Cowley has said, the myth of a Southern society which emerges from Faulkner's work as a whole can be compared with Hawthorne's myth of New England. One might add that the dilemma with which Faulkner confronts Bunch and Hightower—whether to take the responsibility of moral intervention in human affairs—is the same dilemma which confronts many of Hawthorne's characters (for example, the painter in "Prophetic Pictures"). Joe Christmas would be recognized by Hawthorne; for he is frightened and obsessed by the inescapable stain on every human life. There is never any real proof that Joe is part Negro, but Joe's gratuitous assumption that he is tainted is at the root of all his actions. He becomes as obsessed with his stain as does Aylmer with the blemish on his wife's face in Hawthorne's "The Birthmark" and with a purpose as relentless and immoral as Aylmer's he goes about removing the stain—an impulse which arises in the central figures of both "The Birthmark" and *Light in August* from what is, in the final moral terms, simply their inability to bear the burden of being human. (The word "burden," by the way, seems to have the same significance for the Southern writers as the pack of the peddler had for Hawthorne and Melville: the "burden" of one's history or of one's continually self-annihilating humanity. Miss Burden, in *Light in August,* is not the only character in Southern fiction so named.)

Faulkner and Melville share a liking for physical, dynamic, and animal images. Both abound in images of light and dark. In Faulkner's novel there is a persistent reference to white "blood" and black "blood," and Joe's ambiguous character is symbolized by the dark serge trousers and white shirt he invariably wears. Both Ahab and Joe Christmas are seeking an elusive *purity,* symbolized by whiteness. Both shape their doom by their sharp rejections of their own humanity. Both are "unmanned," to use Melville's word, by fate or by their own moral acts. Faulkner's manner of handling symbols and themes is like Melville's. His downright spiritual vehemence often produces a wonderful lyric or epic sense of life; but sometimes the symbols are crudely imagined or imperfectly assimilated in context. For example, the uneasy connection of Joe Christmas with Christ: several of Joe's acts take place on Friday, or "on the third day"; Mrs. McEachern washes his feet; Burch betrays him for a thousand pieces of silver; Hines, his grandfather and the only father Joe knows, imagines that he is God. Faulkner seems not to sense exactly how the Christ theme should be handled, sometimes making it too overt and sometimes not overt enough. His attempts to enlarge Joe's character by adducing a willed mythology remind one of Melville's similar attempts in *Pierre.* It may finally seem to us that Faulkner and Melville are most in control of their work when they approach the epic form, as in *As I Lay Dying* and *Moby-Dick;* but that when they try novels of complex symbolic human relationships, their effort suffers from their uncertain power of grouping symbols into a close coherent statement.

IV

It has been said of Faulkner that his rhetoric and the actions it expresses are so terrific that they annihilate his characters, that his characters become mere targets for violent emotive bombardments. The measure of truth in this criticism does not destroy Faulkner as an artist. It simply indicates that he is one kind of artist—surely he is not a novelist of manners in quite the way that such a phrase as "the Balzac of the South" would imply. As if in self-criticism, Faulkner writes of Hines and his fanatical sermons: "So they believed that he was a little crazy. . . . It was not that he was trying to conceal one thing by telling another. It was that his words, his telling, just did not synchronize with what his hearers believed would (and must) be the scope of a single individual." Yet in one of the utterances of the Reverend Mr. Hightower we find this idea translated into a true definition of tragedy: "Too much happens. That's it. Man performs, engenders, more than he can or should have to bear. That's how he finds that he can bear anything. That's it. That's what is so terrible." In such a statement as this Faulkner begins to justify the overplus of superhuman and subhuman violence in his novels. Nevertheless there remains a discrepancy between the theoretical justification and the artistic practice. We cannot avoid phrasing the aesthetic implication of Hightower's words in some such way as this: "Faulkner attributes more action and emotion to his characters than can meaningfully be attributed to them."

The alienation of man *via* language is a common theme in *Light in August*. The people who have beaten and robbed Joe and left him on the floor of a cheap boarding house speak "in a language which he did not understand." The sermons of Hightower seem to have been expressly contrived to separate him from his congregation. As for Lena, her separation-by-language is always maintained only to the degree necessary to her total purpose. When she asks along the road for Burch, people direct her to "Bunch," but to her they always seem to say "Burch." She is purposefully separated from irrelevance and relaxed in her vision of reality. Separation by language is surely a fact of human life. But is Faulkner entirely in control of this theme? In the orphanage the dietitian and Hines meet "calm and quiet and terse as two conspirators" and then proceed to discourse in some pseudo-Old Testament language which is anything but calm, quiet, or terse. But perhaps it is another form of dissociation which makes this putatively powerful situation seem defective. Perhaps—in order that the dissociation might be in *his* mind, for it needs to be in *someone's* mind—the five-year-old Joe should have been present, watching and listening in awe to the terrible creatures, his mythical father and mother. It is simply a novelist's mistake to present us with a sharp dislocation between his characters and what they say, without accounting in context for the dislocation. One feels that Faulkner has missed a chance in this scene to form a profound associative human situation.

This leads us to a general question: What is the quality of consciousness displayed in *Light in August?* Surely, it is not a consciousness which broods over the whole range of action, associating people with each other or with a culture, establishing their manners and morals in a whole containment. It is a consciousness in flight and pursuit, wonderfully aware of fact, the physical and animal fact, wonderfully in possession of extreme emotions and the ecstasy of violence, cognizant too of the tender humorousness of love, and in general wonderfully fantastic and magical. *Par excellence*, it is the American folk-literary consciousness. When it seeks to interpret or enlighten the human situation, when Faulkner breaks off the humorous-tragical flow of rhetorical poetry and ventures an observation on human manners, he is likely to sound naïve. He will speak in the manner of the folk proverb: "Yes, sir. You just let one of them get married or get into trouble without being married, and right then and there is where she secedes from the woman race and spends the balance of her life trying to get joined up with the man race. That's why they dip snuff and smoke and want to vote." Or he will attempt a more intellectually formulated observation, with the following unhappy result: "the faces of the old men lined by that sheer accumulation of frustration and doubt which is so often the other side of the picture of hale and respected full years"—What a piece of philosophy! One can hardly help sensing an uncomfortable hiatus between Faulkner's poetic portrayal of manners and his explicit consciousness of them.[1]

Probably the episodes of family and cultural history which accompany Faulkner's account of Miss Burden and Hightower would mean more to a Southerner than they do to me. But especially in the case of Hightower there seems to be a failure of consciousness precisely at the point where we should understand the quality of the association between Hightower and his own history. Hightower has projected his sexual and spiritual impotence back upon a myth of his grandfather. Faulkner goes along with Hightower on this point, assuming too much that a fantasy projected from some center of real causation is the cause itself. He nearly allows Hightower to determine the quality of his (Faulkner's) consciousness. On the other hand, he is capable of involving Burch in a situation which calls for a degree of consciousness far above what seems possible, and then arbitrarily giving him the necessary consciousness; so that we have a dull country lout whose "rage and impotence is now almost ecstatic. He seems to muse now upon a sort of timeless and beautiful infallibility in his unpredictable frustrations" (the qualifiers "almost," "seems to," "a sort of" are significant). And a moment later we find Burch (so it seems) reflecting that a Negro he is talking with "does not appear to have enough ratiocinative power to find the town." In *Anna Karenina* a dog conducts a humorous and anxious conversation with himself. But unlike the Burch episode, this does not seem in the least out of place, because Tolstoy with his great associative consciousness always gives one the feeling that he knows exactly when and how much to withdraw or extend his mind in the universe of his novel. I do not mean to imply that Faulkner's novel *lacks* consciousness, but only that the consciousness it displays is sometimes unhappily biassed, bardic, parochial, and, in the societal or cultural

[1] But the observations I have made in this paragraph would be substantially less true if applied to *The Sound and the Fury*.

sense, unmannered. Davy Crockett still screams in the Southern wilderness.

But of course any discussion which compares Faulkner unfavorably with a writer like Tolstoy must not be guilty of the assumption that Faulkner's Southern culture is as cohesive and knowable as Tolstoy's Russian culture was; obviously it is not. And Faulkner's claim to be the novelist of a culture (if that is his claim) must be judged on the basis of his whole work. Nevertheless the evidence of *Light in August,* though it shows that Faulkner is capable of very fine and very extensive and complex fictional constructions, also seems to indicate that he can fail us exactly at that level of existence where the subtle complications of human behavior have to be established. Faulkner works inward from the extremities, from the mechanics and the ecstasy of life. And this relentless, bardic-American bias often makes us wish he would reverse the procedure, that his consciousness would work through human manners into the human character and then outward toward the extremities it can contain or fail to contain. Human life submits itself to die at the hands of the artist so that it may be reborn in art, somewhat as Joe Christmas submits himself to the beatings of McEachern: "The boy's body might have been wood or stone; a post or a tower upon which the sentient part of him mused like a hermit, contemplative and remote with ecstasy and self-crucifixion." One wants to know finally, What manner of man is this *between* the stone and the crucifixion?

V

But it is only one's high estimation of Faulkner which raises these questions at all. Like the author of *Moby-Dick* Faulkner might say of himself, "I try everything; I achieve what I can." In these bad times, a serious venturesomeness must count heavily with us. But it is also a sense of Faulkner's achievement which makes me think him the equal of any American novelist of his generation. Perhaps *The Great Gatsby* is the only novel of the time which can be defended as superior to Faulkner's best work.

In the nineteen-thirties the liberal-progressive culture turned away from Faulkner for many of the same bad reasons which caused it, eighty years before, to turn away from Melville. If our liberal thought now begins to return from its disastrous wanderings of the last decades—that era of the great rejections —and to recover its vitality, it is because it grows capable of coming to terms with Faulkner, as it already learns again to come to terms with Hawthorne and Melville.

Fallen from Time:
The Mythic Rip Van Winkle

PHILIP YOUNG

> *Black wing, brown wing, hover over;*
> *Twenty years and the spring is over;*
> *To-day grieves, to-morrow grieves,*
> *Cover me over, light-in-leaves . . .*
> —T. S. ELIOT

WASHINGTON IRVING is reported to have spent a June evening in 1818 talking with his brother-in-law about the old days in Sleepy Hollow. Melancholy of late, the writer was pleased to find himself laughing. Suddenly he got up and went to his room. By morning he had the manuscript of the first and most famous American short story, and his best single claim to a permanent reputation.

Nearly a century and a half have elapsed, and the name of Rip Van Winkle, one of the oldest in our fiction, is as alive as ever. The subject of innumerable representations—among them some of the country's finest paintings—America's archetypal sleeper is almost equally well known abroad. Nor is his fame simply popular, or commercial. The most complex of poets, as well as the least sophisticated of children, are attracted to him.

But there is something ironic here, for at its center Rip's story is every bit as enigmatic as it is renowned, and the usual understanding of Rip himself, spread so wide, is shallow. Very few of the millions of people who have enjoyed his tale would be comfortable for long if pressed to say exactly what "happened" to him, or if asked to explain what there is about the "poor, simple fellow" that has exerted so general and deep a fascination. Thanks to Irving, the thunder Rip heard is still rolling out of the Catskills. And it is pregnant thunder, charged with meaning. Perhaps it is time someone tried to make out what it has to say.

284

Irving's story may not be an easy one, but it can easily be told in such a way as to refresh the memories of those who have not encountered it of late. The hero of the tale was a good-natured, middle-aged fellow, and a hen-pecked husband, who lived with his Dutch neighbors in a peaceful village in the Catskill Mountains along the Hudson River in the period immediately preceding the American Revolution. The trouble with Rip was that although he would hunt and fish all day, or even do odd jobs for the neighborhood women, and entertain their children, he was "insuperably averse" to exerting himself for his own practical benefit. He had lost an inheritance, his farm was in the worst condition of any in the vicinity and, worst of all, his termagant wife was always upbraiding him about these things. He had only one "domestic adherent," his dog Wolf, and one comfortable retreat, a bench outside the local inn, where under the sign of His Majesty George the Third met a kind of "perpetual club." But he was driven eventually even from this refuge, and forced to the woods for peace. On a fine fall day it happened.

Rip was shooting squirrels in a high part of the mountains. Tiring in the late afternoon he rested on a green knoll beside a deep glen, with a sleepy view of miles of forest and the Hudson moving drowsily through it. Suddenly he heard the distant sound of his name. He saw a crow winging its way across the mountain, and Wolf bristling, and then he made out an odd figure, a short old fellow in antique Dutch clothes, coming up from the ravine with a heavy keg on his back. Rip quickly gave him a hand, and as they labored he heard distant thunder coming from a cleft in the rocks. They passed through this crevice, and came into a kind of amphitheatre, walled by prec-ipices. Stunned with awe, Rip saw in the middle of the space a group of odd-looking men playing at nine-pins. They had peculiar, long-nosed faces; all wore beards; one man, stout and old, appeared to be their commander. "What seemed particu-larly odd," however, was that "although these folk were evi-dently amusing themselves, yet they maintained the gravest faces, the most mysterious silence, and were, withal, the most melancholy party of pleasure he had ever witnessed." The only sound was the thunder of the balls as they rolled.

When the men saw Rip they stopped their play and stared at him as if they were statues. His heart turned within him; trembling, he obeyed his guide and waited on the company. They drank from the keg in silence, and then went on with their game. Soon Rip was trying the liquor, but he drank more than he could hold, and passed into a profound sleep.

When he woke he was back on the green knoll. It was morning and an eagle wheeled aloft. His gun was rusted away, Wolf was gone, and there was no sign of the opening in the cliffs. He called his dog, but the cawing of crows high in the air was the only answer, and he headed lamely for home. As he approached his village he saw no one he knew. People kept stroking their chins when they looked at him, and when he picked up the gesture from them he discovered that his beard was now gray and a foot long. As he entered town he saw that the village itself had grown. But his own house was in ruins, and a half-starved dog that looked like Wolf skulked about the wreckage and snarled at him. In town the inn was gone, replaced by an ugly building called Jonathan Doolittle's Union Hotel, and on the old sign King George's portrait had new clothes, and beneath it a new legend: George Washington. Even the nature of the people seemed changed: their drowsy ways had become disputatious. Rudely challenged to state his affiliations, "Federal or Democrat," Rip can only protest that he is loyal to his king, whereupon he is taken by some for a spy. No one knows him, the friends he asks for are dead, and he comes to doubt his own identity, until his daughter Judith's recognition confirms it. Now he is welcomed home, learns that his wife is dead ("in a fit of passion at a New England peddler"), and that he has unaccountably been gone for twenty years. The oldest and most learned member of the community is able to throw a little light on the story he tells: it is every twenty years that Hendrik Hudson, the river's discoverer, keeps a sort of vigil in the Catskills with the crew of the *Half-Moon*, and playing at nine-pins they make the mountains ring with the distant peals of thunder. And so Rip—idle, revered

and happy—retires to his place on the bench at the door of
the inn.

To be sure this story, though a fine one, is not perfect. For
one thing, although Irving's Federalism enables him to jab in
mildly amusing fashion at the shabby and pretentious repub-
licanism of Rip's new village, such pleasantries come at the
expense of our being wholly convinced of what he is trying to
tell us—that Rip at the end is in clover. But the village is no
longer entirely the place for him, and the fine old inn where
he sits is just not there any more.

That this is, however, the rare sort of story that both satisfies and stimulates is shown by the fact that it has been so
often retold, chiefly for the stage. There have been at least five
plays—beginning with John Kerr's, which first appeared in
Washington in 1829—and three operas, and several children's
versions. But none has added anything important to our understanding of the story. Joseph Jefferson, who played the role of
Rip for forty-five years in his own extraordinarily popular interpretation, had a few sensible ideas about the material, but
he also failed to throw out much of the nineteenth century
baggage handed down from Kerr.

Though Joyce and Dylan Thomas have punned elaborately
on Rip's name, most of the poets who have invoked him have
done nothing much either to interpret the story or the character, and only Hart Crane has given him serious and extended attention. *The Bridge* (1930) has a section called
"Van Winkle," whom Crane thought of as "the muse of
memory"—or, as he put it to his sponsor, Otto Kahn, "the
guardian angel of the trip to the past." Here Rip is a figure
evoked from recollection of the poet's childhood and the nation's; since this is to introduce Rip in a thoughtful and promising way, it is too bad that very little is really done with him
in the poem.

This is unfortunate partly for the reason that Rip is, potentially, a truly mythic figure. He is conceivably even more: *ur-*
mythic. At any rate a primal, primeval myth has been postulated (by Joseph Campbell in his *Hero with a Thousand
Faces*), and has been described—as "a separation from **the**

world, a penetration to some source of power, and a life-enhancing return." And this is a most excellent description of what happens in "Rip Van Winkle." But no one has elevated the story to this status. As Constance Rourke wrote of it twenty-five years ago, the tale "has never been finished, and still awaits a final imaginative re-creation." If then we are to be helped to understand the story more deeply by considering what has been done with it, we had better consider what had been done with it before Irving wrote it.

II

In 1912 an eminent Dutch historian, Tieman De Vries by name, published under the title of *Dutch History, Art and Literature for Americans* a series of lectures he had delivered at the University of Chicago. A large part of this book is devoted to a monumentally inept attack on Washington Irving for having, in "Rip Van Winkle," characterized the Dutch people as stupid, lazy and credulous. For his overwhelming blow the author, protesting great reluctance and sadness, brings forth the revelation that "Rip" is not the "original" story that Irving is "generally given credit for," anyway. The bitter truth, he discloses, is that the tale had been told before: its embryo is a myth about an ancient Greek named Epimenides, and this germ was "fully developed" by Erasmus (a citizen of Rotterdam) in 1496. In the myth Epimenides was sent to look for a sheep, lay down in a cave, slept for fifty-seven years and waked to find everything changed and himself unrecognized until a brother identified him. Erasmus used this story, then, to attack the Scotist theologians of his day (whom he thought asleep) as Irving used it on the Dutch. The fact that Irving never admitted knowing Erasmus's story, says De Vries, "touches too much the character of our beloved young author to be decided in a few words," and thus, having written the words, he drops the subject.

Quite aside from the foolishness about the Dutch, who are fondly treated in the story, there are two real blunders here. First, Irving's indebtedness was so widely recognized when the story first appeared as to be a subject for newspaper comment and, second, his source was not Erasmus, whose tale is in no sense "fully developed," but an old German tale published by Otmar, the Grimm of his period, in his *Volke-Sagen* of 1800. Actually Irving was on this occasion very noisily accused of plagiarism. At the end of his story he had appended a note in which he hinted that Rip's origin was "a little German superstition about Frederick *der Rothbart* and the Kypphauser mountain," but this has always been regarded as a red herring—so freely had he borrowed from another, and adjacent, story in Otmar: the folk tale of Peter Klaus. About the only thing Irving could do when this was pointed out he did: threw up his hands and said that of course he knew the tale of Peter Klaus; he had seen it in *three* collections of German legends.

There were probably still other sources for "Rip Van Winkle." We know for instance that in 1817 Sir Walter Scott told Irving the story of Thomas of Erceldoune ("Thomas the Rhymer"), who was bewitched by the Queen of the Fairies for seven years. "Doldrum"—a farce about a man's surprise at the changes he found after waking from a seven-year slumber —was played in New York when Irving was fourteen. It is almost certain, moreover, that Irving knew at least a couple of the other versions of the old tradition.

The idea of persons sleeping for long periods is of course very common in myth, legend and folk-lore. So sleep Arthur and Merlin and John the Divine, and Charlemagne and Frederick Barbarossa (or Rothbart, or Redbeard) and Wilhelm Tell, and Odin (or Woden), the Norse (or Teutonic) god, and Endymion the shepherd, and Siegfried and Oisin and several dozen other heroes of many lands, as well as Sleeping Beauty and Bruennhilde and other mythical ladies—and also the protagonists of many novels, who wake to their author's vision of utopia, or hell. And there are several myths and legends about these sleepers which come pretty close to the story Irving told. Probably the best known of these concerns the Seven Sleepers. These men were natives of Ephesus, and early Christians persecuted by the Emperor Decius. They hid in a mountain and fell asleep. On waking they assumed that a night had passed, and one of them slipped into town to buy bread. When he got there he was stunned to see a cross over the gate, and then to hear the Lord's name spoken freely. When he paid for the bread his coins, now archaic, gave him away, and he discovered he had slept for 360 years.

This myth has spread widely, and found its way into books so different as the Koran, where Mohammed adapted it and introduced a dog who sleeps with the seven men, and Mark Twain's *Innocents Abroad,* where Twain tells the story at considerable length (and says he knows it to be a true story, as he personally has visited the cave). Somewhat similar myths are also known in the religious literature of the Jews. In a section on fasting in the Babylonian Talmud, to choose a single instance, appears one of several stories about Honi the Circle Drawer, lately thrust into prominence as a candidate for identification with the Teacher of Righteousness of the Dead Sea Scrolls. One day Honi sat down to eat, the story goes, and sleep came; a rocky formation enclosed him, and he slept for seventy years. When he went home nobody would believe he was Honi; greatly hurt, he prayed for death and died.

The thing that is really vital to "Rip Van Winkle," but missing from all these other stories, is a revelation—some kind of mysterious activity witnessed by the sleeper. But such tales also exist—for instance, the Chinese story of Wang Chih, who comes upon some aged men playing chess in a mountain grotto, is given a date-stone to put in his mouth, and sleeps for centuries, finally waking to return home to practice Taoist rites and attain immortality.

More akin to Rip's is the misadventure of Herla, King of the Britons. He is approached by an ugly dwarf, somewhat resembling Pan, who tells him that he will grace Herla's wedding to the daughter of the King of France, and that Herla will in turn attend the wedding of the dwarf-king. At the Briton's marriage ceremony, the dwarf-guests serve food and drink from precious vessels. A year later, at the wedding of the dwarf-king in a mountain cavern, Herla takes a bloodhound in his arms, and he and his men are enjoined not to dismount until the bloodhound jumps. Some who try are turned to dust, but the hound never jumps and Herla thus wanders hopelessly and "maketh mad marches" with his army for the space of two hundred years. At last he reaches the sunlight and meets a shepherd who can scarcely understand the language the king speaks.[1]

Closer still, in one way, is the story of a blacksmith recorded in the Grimms' *Teutonic Mythology*. While trying to find wood to make a handle for his hammer, he gets lost; there are the familiar rift in the mountains, some mysterious bowlers, and a magic gift—this time a bowling ball that turns to gold. (Others who have entered this cliff have seen an old man with a long white beard holding a goblet.)

The most detailed precedent for Irving, however, and beyond a doubt his principal source, is the tale of Peter Klaus, which appeared in Otmar's collection.[2] This is a story of a goatherd from Sittendorf who used to pasture his sheep on the Kyfhauser mountain in Thuringia. One day he discovered that a goat had disappeared into a crack in a cliff, and following her he came to a cave where he found her eating oats that fell from a ceiling which shook with the stamping of horses. While Peter stood there in astonishment a groom appeared and beckoned him to follow; soon they came to a hollow, surrounded by high walls into which, through the thick overhang-

---

[1] This is the only story of its kind, except for "Rip," that can be attributed to anyone—in this case to Walter Map, author of the early thirteenth century *De Nugis Curialium* ("Courtier's Trifles"), in which it appears. An intolerant but witty feudal aristocrat, probably Welsh, Map is best known for his "Dissuasion from Matrimony," long attributed to a Latin writer of a thousand years before him. In this essay he counsels young men that women are monsters and vipers (do not look for exceptions, he says: "Friend, fear all the sex"). Thus Map provides a precedent both for Rip's adventure and for Irving's whimsical anti-feminism. It is very doubtful, however, if not impossible, that Irving knew of him; Herla's story has been cited as the true source of "Rip Van Winkle," but Map's book was not available to Irving until some three decades after the Irving story had been published.

[2] Otmar's book is very hard to come by, but Henry A. Pochmann's "Irving's German Sources in *The Sketch Book*," *Studies in Philology*, XXVII (July, 1930), 489–94, prints the most relevant portions of it.

ing branches, a dim light fell. Here there was a rich, well-graded lawn, where twelve serious knights were bowling. None of them said a word. Peter was put to work setting pins.

At first his knees shook as he stole glimpses of the silent, long-bearded knights, but gradually his fear left him, and finally he took a drink from a tankard. This was rejuvenating, and as often as he felt tired he drank from the vessel, which never emptied. This gave him strength, but sleep overcame him nonetheless, and when he woke he was back at the green spot where he grazed his goats. The goats, however, were gone, and so was his dog. There were trees and bushes he couldn't remember, and in bewilderment he went into Sittendorf, below him, to ask about his herd.

Outside the village the people were unfamiliar, differently dressed and strange-spoken. They stared at him and stroked their chins as he asked for his sheep; when involuntarily he stroked his own chin he found that his beard had grown a foot long. He went to his house, which was in decay, and there he saw an emaciated dog which snarled at him. He staggered off, calling vainly for his wife and children. The villagers crowded around him, demanding to know what he was looking for, and when he asked about old friends he learned that they were dead. Then he saw a pretty young woman, who exactly resembled his wife, and when he asked her father's name she answered, "Peter Klaus, God rest his soul. It is more than twenty years since . . . his sheep came back without him." Then he shouted, "I am Peter Klaus, and no other," and was warmly welcomed home.

Since this elaborate parallel with Irving epitomizes the process whereby a national literature adapted foreign materials and began to function, it is somewhat appropriate that our first short story should owe so large a debt to a European source. But it is not at all clear why this *particular* story should have come down to us across a span of some twenty-five centuries—from the time, say, of Epimenides. Some of its charm is obvious; the idea of falling clean out of time, for instance, must be universally fascinating. But the very heart of "Rip Van Winkle," and of "Peter Klaus"—the strange pageant in the mountain—is still, from whatever version of it may be the earliest on down to the present time, enigmatic.

In the scene with the "dwarfs"—to focus again on Irving— it is not even clear what is going on. When the silent men of outlandish appearance and their leader go through their motions, the feeling is very strong that their actions are intended to convey something. But what? They are bowling, of course, and producing the sound of thunder, but why are they doing this? Why are they so sad and silent as they do it? Why so odd-looking? And why does Rip's participation cost him a generation of his life? The action is fairly pulsing with overtones: the men are speaking in signs; their motions cry out for translation as vigorously as if this were, as it seems, some strangely solemn charade. The question, which seems never even to have been asked, is what are we to make of this thundering pantomime? What have the gods to impart?

The notion that somewhere in the story lurks a secondary, or symbolic, meaning is by no means new. Walter Map, for instance, intended the latter part of his story about Herla to be a satire on the court of King Henry II, which he thought unstable. Erasmus, as already noted, attacked the Scotists through his; and the Talmud draws a moral from Honi's lonely end: "Either companionship or death." More interesting, however, is Arnold Toynbee's interpretation of "Rip Van Winkle" in the third volume of his *Study of History*. There is likely to be, he feels, something "old-fashioned" about any given colonial ethos, and his theory comes to a generalization: "geographical expansion [of a civilization] produces social retardation." Toynbee thinks Rip an expression of his principle, the long sleep symbolizing the slumber of social progress in a newly settled place. Irving "was really expressing in mythological imagery the essence of the overseas experience. . . ."

The trouble with the interpretations of Map, Erasmus and the Talmud is that they are forced and arbitrary, and the trouble with Toynbee's is that the story doesn't fit the theory it is supposed to express. If we ever had a period during which social progress was not retarded then it was exactly the period Rip slept through. In that generation we were transformed from a group of loosely bound and often provincial colonies into a cocky and independent republic with a new kind of government and—as the story itself makes clear enough—a whole new and new-fashioned spirit. In order to fit the thesis Irving must have had Rip return to a village where nothing much had happened or changed, and thus he must have written a different story. But he chose instead to write a story on the order of the myth about Honi the Circle Drawer who, according to one tradition, slept through the destruction of the First Temple and the building of the second, or like the one about the Seven Sleepers, who slept through the Christian revolution.[3] In all these tales the startling developments that have taken place during the sleep are a large part of the "point." And even if to Toynbee nationalism is—and was even in eighteenth century America—a thoroughly deplorable thing, it was not a sign of social retardation.

Since such explanations as these will not help much more than the poets and playwrights have done to show us what is going on in "Rip Van Winkle," and since there is nowhere else to look, we are forced at long last to squint for ourselves through that crevice in the mountain. In the shadows there, lurk figures and images which take us back, along a chronological line, to a time before the beginnings of recorded history. And if we could identify and understand these figures and images we should have, finally, the answers to most of our questions.

Many editions of Irving's story carry as an epigraph some lines he took from the seventeenth century poet William Cartwright:

[3] Indeed Irving may have got some specific ideas from the Seven Sleepers myth, for there the surprising changes in the speech of the people, and the prominent new sign over the gate of the town, are precedents for two of the very few important details to be found in "Rip" but not in "Peter Klaus." Elsewhere there is an exact precedent for the form Irving's change of signs took: in the famous *New England Primer,* with its alphabetical rimes ("In Adam's fall we sinned all"), a woodcut of King George that appeared in early editions eventually became very smudged; when this happened the portrait began to carry the name of our first President ("By Washington, great deeds were done").

By Woden, God of Saxons,
From whence comes Wensday, that is Wodensday,
Truth is a thing that ever I will keep
Until thylke day in which I creep into
My sepulchre—.

The most plausible reading of these lines is: "By God it's a true story I'm telling." But this makes Irving's two notes—in which he calls this a true tale—redundant. Less simply read, it might be the story itself saying, "By God, I'll keep to myself the truth about this thing as long as I live." At any rate, it is either a curious coincidence or an obscure clue that in swearing by Woden Irving has pointed to the remotest origins of his story that can be uncovered. To bare these origins would be to force the story, at last, to give up its secrets.

Here is a grab-bag of traditional elements—folk, legendary, and mythic. The green knoll on which Rip sits when he hears his name has behind it the Green Mounds of Irish fairy tales— often prehistoric burial mounds. It is an appropriate spot for his bewitching and approximate to the "buried men" he is about to visit. Magic potions and sacred drinks are so standard in mythology, folk-lore and religion as to suggest parallels automatically as Rip plays Ganymede, wine-pourer to the gods. A less familiar little tradition lies behind those dogs, which Rip and Peter find barely and implausibly alive after so many years—this takes us all the way back to Odysseus, returning after a generation's absence to find his dog Argos in Ithaca, still half-alive and lying on a heap of dung.

But the most important recognition in Irving's story concerns the identity of the men Rip meets in the mountain, and of their leader. These are "Hendrik Hudson" and his crew.[4]

---

[4] It should, of course, be "Henry": Hudson sailed from Holland but was English. Of all the people Irving could have put in the Catskills, however, Hudson was a fine choice, not only because the river below him was named for him and discovered by him, but because he was (in 1611 on another trip) the victim of a mutiny near Hudson Bay, was abandoned there, and disappeared for good. Thus he is like the heroes of myth and legend who sleep in mountains; no one knows where, or if, he was buried, and it is easier to think of him as not entirely dead.

The blacksmith and Peter Klaus never identify their strange mountain men, and the unnamed leaders never appear. Nevertheless it is not hard to guess with considerable assurance of being right both who they are and by whom they are led. It was the Odensberg that the blacksmith entered, and the Kyfhauser that Peter wormed his way into; it is in the Odensberg, according to legend, that Charlemagne and his knights are sleeping, and the Kyfhauser where sleep Frederick Barbarossa and his.[5] Hudson, then, is playing the role of the great kings of European countries, as Arthur plays it in England, and is a survival of this tradition. This recognition opens the door.

Part of the Barbarossa legend, which is better known and more detailed than the one of Charlemagne, concerns the conditions under which he can return to active life. Around the Kyfhauser a flock of ravens is said to fly, and each time the king wakes he asks if they are still there (they are, and this means the time has not come). Another important detail of the story is his beard: it is extraordinarily long already, and when it has grown three times around the table where he sits his time will have come. It is very likely, then, that the black wings hovering over Rip just before he enters the mountain, and just after he emerges into consciousness, are the ravens of Barbarossa—just as the beards which are prominent in his story and Peter's (although the natural-enough consequences of not shaving for twenty years) come down to us from this legend.

But the most important detail of all is a game, common to so many of these stories—the Chinese and Japanese versions, and Peter Klaus and the blacksmith and Rip. And the fact that the game in the stories that primarily concern us here is always bowling, which makes the sound of thunder, gives the whole show away: we are dealing, ultimately, with the gods, and in the farthest recess of this cave the figure with the red

[5] This is clear in the story that lies, in Otmar's collection, adjacent to the one of Peter Klaus—the "little German Superstition about Frederick *der Rothbart*" that Irving claimed as the origin of "Rip." It is almost certain, then, that Irving knew who led the knights Peter saw, and who Hudson's most immediate ancestor was. How much more he may have known about the origins of the materials he was borrowing is very difficult to say.

beard (to represent lightning), that helped to identify him with Frederick the Redbeard, is the god of thunder—Thor, God of Saxons, whence comes Thorsday, that is Thursday.

More clearly the prototype of all these sleeping heroes, however, is the magnificently white-bearded Woden, or Odin, the god of the dead whom Cartwright swore by. In the legend about Charlemagne the people who saw the king described him as a man with a white beard, and the name of the mountain Charlemagne inhabits, the Odensberg, suggests all by itself his ancestor. But the fact that the blacksmith on the Odensberg is in search of wood for a handle to an instrument of power which was the very emblem of the god of thunder, a hammer, suggests Thor just as strongly. So thoroughly have the two gods been confused in these myths that the king who is buried in Odin's mountain has in some stories the red coloring and the red horse that are really appropriate to Thor. On this horse the god issues from the mountain with his men, every so-many years, and in this activity he is again Odin, the leader of the Wild Hunt.

These confusions between Thor and Odin are not surprising, since the two figures are confused in Norse mythology itself. Although Thor was the son of Odin he was also sometimes an older god than Odin; often he was a god superior to Odin, and sometimes they were thought of as exactly the same god. The direct ancestor of the Hudson Rip saw, then, was a Thor who has many of the attributes of Odin, and recognizing this takes us to the source of the traditions out of which Irving's scene is principally compounded. Recognizing these traditions, in turn, enables us to understand the subliminal richness of its materials, buried under the detritus of centuries.

The ravens which fly about the Kyfhauser, and the crows and eagle of the Catskills, are lineal descendants of the ravens Thought and Memory who sat on Odin's shoulder and kept him informed, or of the eagle that hovered over Odin's own retreat, or of the flight of ravens, "Odin's messengers" (without whose message Frederick cannot emerge)—or of all three. The dogs in the stories, mixing Greek myth with Teutonic, are progeny of the wolves Geri and Freki who sat at Odin's feet, or of the totem wolf which hung over the west door of his residence—in honor of which ancestry Rip's dog gets his name, Wolf. The drink which both invigorated and overpowered Rip is the same drink Barbarossa's knights gave Peter; it belongs also in the goblet Charlemagne was seen holding, and, despite all the magic drinks of folk-lore and myth, it is ultimately "Odin's mead," from which Odin got wisdom, and inspired poets; it was a magic draft related to the drink always available in the Abode of the Blest, the drink that rejuvenates, and obliterates all sorrow.

In a like manner, consider the odd appearance of Hudson's crew: those ugly, drab, short and curious creatures (one fellow's face is comprised entirely of his nose) are echoes of the dwarfs Herla met—although those dwarfs also looked like Pan, mixing Greek and Teutonic (and probably Welsh) mythology again. But Hudson's men get their appearance from the Night-Elves who made Thor's hammer—those ugly little long-nosed people, dirty-brown in color, who lived in caves and clefts. Beneath this effective disguise the crew-men of the *Half-Moon* are really the knights of Barbarossa and Charlemagne, who are the brave dead warriors brought back from the battlefields by the Valkyries to Odin's hall of the dead: Rip has really been in Valhalla and seen the slain collected around their god, who by the old confusion is now Thor, whose men they have become. The reason for the oddness of their behavior—their melancholy and their lacklustre stares—has become completely obvious, if indeed it was not before: they are dead. And one of Odin's chief characteristics, his extreme aloofness, accounts for the fact that Rip got but a glimpse of their leader, while neither Peter or the blacksmith ever saw him at all.

Why such pagan gods should have been imagined as sleeping in mountains can be plausibly explained. When converted to Christianity, the people who had worshipped these figures could not quickly and completely reject the faith of their fathers. To them the outmoded gods lingered on, wandering, sleeping, and appearing infrequently. Later, vanished but actual heroes like Charlemagne, Frederick, Sir Francis Drake, Prince Sebastian of Portugal, and Arthur, were given attributes of the earlier gods. It was most common as well to place them in a mountain, where they were in earth, like the dead, but not under it—not under level ground, that is—like the really dead. Here they are sequestered in their slumbers, but the gods can be thought of as not entirely departed, and the heroes as in a position to return.

Occasionally mortals get to visit the legendary heroes who have taken over the attributes of vanished gods. When this happens, the visitor suffers a magic sleep and a long lacuna in his life: he has lapsed into a pagan world, got himself bewitched, and trafficked with a forbidden god. The punishment is severe. Thus Herla lost everything and Peter lost his flock, wife, home, and twenty years of life—though Rip, to be sure, in Irving's half-convincing happy ending, doesn't suffer so badly. The reason for the punishment is nevertheless clear: it is Christianity's dire objection to traffic with such cults as attached to these gods, as with any intercourse with fairies. This centuries-old element of the story is an historical, symbolic, and didactic expression of the church's long struggle with paganism—and has nothing to do with any social retardation of progress in colonies. Look what happened to Herla and Peter, Christian instruction could say. They were kind and ingenuous men. What then could happen to you? And then because the story is compelling in its own right it survives past the need for it, even after the knowledge of its purpose is centuries forgotten.

Is there any other connection between the visit and the great changes that follow in the life of the man who made it? And what are these visitors doing where they are not supposed to be? The sleeping gods and heroes could be described, and have been, without any mortal to intrude on them, and it doesn't look as though the mortals had just happened in: most of them appear to have been approached and led. And Rip was called by name.

Almost all of the protagonists of these stories, if they witnessed anything within the mountain, saw some kind of game. The fact that the origins of many games fade into ritual and ritual dance suggests that the games in these legends and myths might have their origin in some rite. And some authorities (Jane Harrison and Lord Raglan are notable examples) believe that all myths have their origin in ritual —that a myth is never a folk-explanation of natural phenomena, or anything of the sort, but a narrative that was once linked with a ritual—is the story, in other words, which has outlived the ritual, that the ritual once enacted. Frazer had a more moderate view, and felt that there is a *class* of myths which have been dramatized in ritual, and that these myths were enacted as magical ceremonies in order to produce the natural effects which they describe in figurative language. This hypothesis has it further that the core of such a myth traces back, finally, to the divinity who is imagined to have founded the rite. The actors are simply impersonating an activity of the originator and worshipping him in this way, his acts being the prototype of the rite. Gradually, then, the rite may be performed more out of piety than from any belief in its efficacy, and finally may be forgotten while the myth endures.

Whatever the merits of this theory one thing seems fairly sure: if it explains the origins of any myths, Rip descends from one of them. The bowlers of the Catskills are impersonating a disguised Thor, in a figurative or symbolic way, in his principal role as God of Thunder, and the actions of these resurrected men are the means of their worship. The solemnity Rip and Peter felt, in the presence of a mystery, is entirely appropriate to so sacred and secret an occasion. "Rip Van Winkle," then, is our version of a myth that survives as a description of a nearly forgotten ceremony in the worship of Thor for the production of rain. It proceeds by a symbolic imitation of how rain is made. The ritual is of the magical sort, and is intended to influence nature through the physical sympathy, or resemblance, between the ceremony and the effect it is supposed to produce.[6] Indeed the story is an example of what Robert Graves has called "true myth": it is an instance of "the reduction to narrative shorthand of ritual mime."

Exactly *why* Rip was allowed to witness this mystery is a secret which, since he was ignorant of the reason himself, he has been able to keep for many generations. So, in all likelihood, was Irving unaware of the original reason for the outsider's presence at the ceremony: even by Peter Klaus's time the myth had so badly deteriorated into folk-lore that only the fragments we are deciphering remained. But the secret is out by now: Rip and Peter were initiates. Rip goes right through the steps: while he sits dreamily and alone on the green knoll the period of preliminary isolation passes; then he is summoned by name. Helping to carry the heavy keg up the side of the ravine, which he may have had to volunteer to do, is a sort of test. There followed a kind of procession, and something like a vigil, and finally the experience of communication with the divinity and his disciples. Rip is even given a magic drink, which as a novice he is first required to serve, and after this he is plunged into the magic sleep. When he wakes he is in a new phase of life, and on this level the great changes he finds about him are symbols of the changes in him, and of the differences in his situation, now he is initiate.

Rip has also been reborn in another, reinforcing way, for the imagery of his emergence into a new life inevitably and

---

[6] The thunder that Thor made came ordinarily from the roar of his chariot, of course, but the method described in the myth Irving drew on is by no means unknown. Grimm reported that on hearing thunder North Germans were likely to remark, "the angels are playing at bowls"; and in our own country there is a close parallel in the mythology of the Zuñi Indians of New Mexico, whose warriors when they die go off to make lightning in the sky, where rainmakers cause thunder with great "gaming stones."

unavoidably suggests an issue "from the womb." This concept, which is often thrown about gratuitously, really urges itself here, for Irving's description of the entrance to the mountain, taken from "Peter Klaus," is extremely arresting —almost as pointed, say, as accounts anthropologists have given of pits dug in the ground by primitive tribesmen, and trimmed about the edges with over-hanging shrubbery (which ditches the men dance about in the spring, while brandishing their spears and chanting that these are no ditches, but what they were built to represent). The imagery is the same when Rip is led eerily through the ravine till he comes to the bottom of a hollow, surrounded by perpendicular precipices, over the brinks of which hang the branches of trees.

From this setting he is delivered into his old age. Ripe for escape before, he has experienced an escape only one step short of death. Apparently well into middle age, and saddled with a wife who had completely lost her desirability, he laid down his gun and entered the mountain. Here he witnessed some symbolical activity—which, in the severely censored form of the pins and bowling balls, has overtones of human, as well as vegetable, fertility—and he saw it all as joyless and melancholy. Magically confirmed in his own feeling about the matter, he drank, slept like a baby, and was released into the world he had longed for—into an all-male society, the perpetual men's club that used to meet at the inn, which his wife can no longer violate as, unforgivably, she had done before. His gun is ruined and useless, and his wife is gone. But it makes no difference now; he has slept painlessly through his "change of life."

The trouble with this story as some kind of "male-menopause myth" is that the reading is partly based on a misinterpretation attributed, perhaps unfairly, to Rip. Lacking the information we have, he made a mistake: the men were lifeless and unhappy at their bowling because they were dead. More than that, they were still the followers of Thor, whose sign was lightning and whose emblem was a hammer. Thor

was god of power, and of human fertility as well as vegetable. He was god of the vital moistures in general, an ithy-
phallic, not a detumescent, god. Even dead, his worshippers
made a great deal of noise in his service. In short, the bowling which sends thunder across the Catskills is violently
masculine symbolic activity in a very feminine mountain.
And in this last vague but massive symbol is a final irony, for
the mystery revealed to Rip had thus two aspects, animal or
human, and vegetable—one for each of Thor's two fertility
powers.

Of what pertinence were all these revelations to Rip?
What does it mean to him that the strange men he saw have
come down to us from the men of Thor, or that he was initi-
ated into an ancient mystery and shown the sacred secrets of
all life? No relevance at all to him and no meaning whatever.
And that is the ironical point. Befuddled, unwitting and likeable old Rip: no man in the valley, luxuriantly green already,
thought less or as little about the crops, and no man he knew
could have been chosen to witness the secrets of human fertility and found them more sleep-provoking.

III

What would have interested him, and what did he want?
Concentrating somewhat anthropologically on the story's central scene in an attempt to get at the bottom of it we have
not got to the bottom of the character. But if for a moment
we will think more as psychologists, and consider the story as
a sort of dream—as a product of the unconscious, itself a
kind of anthropologist—we open a whole new and remarkable
area of meaning. Suddenly everything seems illusive, unreal;
time goes into abeyance and the sense of history is lost; the
very identity of the central figure is shaken, and reason dis-
solves.

The easiest entry to the dream-level of "Rip Van Winkle"
passes through that inn where Rip once sat with his friends
—the inn which was "gone," and replaced by a hotel straight

out of nightmare: "a large rickety wooden building . . . with great gaping windows . . . mended with old hats and petti-coats"—and in front a sign with a familiar face all out of place in its setting. Soon, however, "idle with impunity" and "reverenced as one of the patriarchs of the village," Rip "took his place once more on the bench at the inn door." A conflict in Irving explains the confusion. He wanted to show the great changes a revolution had brought, but wished more deeply to feel, and wanted us to feel, that aside from the happy loss of his wife nothing had really happened to Rip. Toynbee, re-sponding fully to this absence of time and change, made what amounts to the same mistake. But it is a meaningful slip, and on one level they are both right. For Rip, time and history *have* ceased operation. Nothing *has* happened, and the inn is there to signal the fact.

What, then, are we to think when we come to the start of the very next paragraph and are told (in a kind of prelimi-nary postscript at the end of the tale-proper) that Rip is now telling his story "to every stranger that arrived at Mr. Doo-little's hotel"? The inn is there, is gone and replaced, is there again, is gone again. Reality is slithering away; and so it must eventually do, for this is not ultimately its world. Nor is this truly the world of fiction, unless of Kafka's. It is the world of the unconscious, where time and history are not suspended, exactly, but do not exist—where everything exists at once. It is the region where people and things are always appearing in unreasonable places, and everything is passing strange: but distorted toward some hard-to-recognize truth. The recurring transformation of Irving's hostelry belongs in this night-world. It represents a "willful accident," and as such makes its own kind of sense. Irving was groping very darkly in a world of symbol, myth and dream for meanings beyond awareness.

In this strange new world Rip's identity is harder to estab-lish than the identity of that shifting meeting place. Removed as he is from time, the confusion of generations is appalling, and he is hard-pressed to know in which of at least three generations he really "belongs." It will be next to impossible to know for sure, for the truth is he had almost as little part in his own generation as the one he slept through. This was entirely clear, had we the wit to see it, when we first met him. He was not an adult, but a child playing with children, a kid with a dog. He lived with his wife, to be sure, but only in a manner of speaking, for he accepted instead his "only alternative": "to take gun in hand and stroll away into the wood." Or, more striking, he would escape her by sitting on a wet rock with a rod in his hand "as long and heavy as a Tartar's lance, and fish all day . . . even though he should not be encouraged by a single nibble." "A great favorite among all the good wives of the village," he ran their errands and did "such little jobs as their less obliging husbands would not do for them"—not, by pointed implication, what their husbands would do: "as to doing family duty . . . he found it impossible."

At the inn with the men-folk, Rip shows that he wants to be a father. But at home he is a son, and not up to it: he is the son who wants to be the father but his mother won't let him. He represents, to be technical for a moment, the ego arrested at the infantile level in an Oedipal situation; under pressure he reverts all the way back to the sleep of the womb.

The scene in the mountain now takes on a new and different suggestiveness. It is at once the dream of a child and an adult dream reflecting Rip's own predicament. The great noses of the mountain men give the next phallic clue, as they must likewise have done in the ancient Teutonic mythology (the psychoanalytic and the anthropological mix well: they are both—the first personally, the second culturally—"regressive"). From this viewpoint the dwarfs are really disguised little boys with pins and balls practicing, in highly activated silence, a forbidden rite; Rip is not invited to play too and they make him work, so he sneaks their drink and goes off to sleep. On the other hand the dwarfs are also so many mirrors to the "adult" Rip, held up as revelations which his consciousness is not likely to read: they are aged little men playing games, who have grown old but not up. Our protagonist, then, is both gerontion and child—or is neither, precisely. He has nor youth nor age, but as it were an after-dinner's sleep, dreaming on both.

On his return to the village, the sense of the decomposition of his "self" becomes even more awesome. His wife-mother is gone, but he is still a child as much as he is anything, and as such he must find his role in a relationship to someone else. But now it is completely bewildering. He is soon confronted with the very "ditto of himself," a negligent loafer named Rip —actually his son. Worse, he faces a woman who seems both strange and, as his poor mind struggles into recollection, hauntingly familiar. She had, she says, a father named Rip, and she carries in her arms a child of that name. Who, then, is our protagonist? His own unaccepted and "impossible" self, or the son of his wife that he used to be and emotionally remains? Or his own son, the loafer leaning there against the tree and, after the ravages of twenty years that passed as a night, looking more like the man Rip impersonated than he suddenly does himself? Or perhaps another Rip, the child of his daughter, now surrogate for his departed wife, and the sign of his true emotional state? Or even, conceivably, the husband of this replacement-wife-mother, and the father of this son—or of that one, or of himself? The sense of generation is shattered; his daughter's house, in which he lives, is a whole house of mirrors, and everywhere he looks he sees a different distortion. He has one moment of panicked insight: "God knows . . . I'm not myself—I'm somebody else—that's me yonder—no—that's somebody else got into my shoes. . . ." Small wonder he departs all the sons Rip and the rejuvenated mother for the security of the role he can play at Mr. Doolittle's.

It is clear now that Rip escaped no change of life, but his very manhood—went from childhood to second childhood with next to nothing in between. It is not just his wife he has dodged, either, but all the obligations of maturity: occupation, domestic and financial responsibility, a political position, duty to society in a time of war. His relation to history is so ambiguous that—ridiculous suspicion—he is thought a spy.

Charming and infantile, he narcissistically prefers himself; he will tell his tale of twenty years' sleep at Mr. Do-little's, where Irving leaves him for the last time. It has become a symbol for the sleep that has been his life.

Considering the universality of his fame, it is a wonder that no European, say, has pointed gleefully to this figure as a symbol of America, for he presents a near-perfect image of the way a large part of the world looks at us: likeable enough, up to a point and at times, but essentially immature, self-centered, careless and above all—and perhaps dangerously—innocent. Even more pointedly Rip is a stereotype of the American male as seen from abroad, or in some jaundiced quarters at home: he is perfectly the jolly overgrown child, abysmally ignorant of his own wife and the whole world of adult men—perpetually "one of the boys," hanging around what they are pleased to think of as a "perpetual men's club"; a disguised Rotarian who simply will not and cannot grow up. In moments of candor we will probably admit that a stereotype with no germ of truth in it could not exist: some such mythic America, some such mythic American, exist both actually and in the consciousness of the world. Rip will do very well as their prototype.

"Rip Van Winkle" is then, and finally, a wonderfully rich tale—the richest in our literature—and an astonishingly complex experience arising from a struggle among many kinds of meaning. On the "prehistoric" level we are dimly aware of immemorial ritual significance, on the psychological of an extraordinary picture of the self arrested in a timeless infancy—rich appeals, both, to the child and primitive in everyone that never grow up and never die in anyone. These awarenesses conflict in the story, as they do in life, with the adult and rational perception that we do indeed grow old, that time and history never stop. In much the same way our affection for Rip himself must oppose our reluctant discovery that as a man we cannot fully respect him.

But in addition to all his other sides, this remarkable Van Winkle also, of course, projects and personifies our sense of the flight—and more: the ravages—of time. And this is what wins us ultimately to his side. We know perfectly well that as an adult this darling of generations of Americans will not entirely do. But if he does seem, finally, meek, blessed, pure in heart, and if we mock him for what he has missed we do it tenderly —partly because it is something hidden in ourselves we mock. And this is not just our own hidden childishness. It is all our own lost lives and roles, the lives and roles that once seemed possible and are possible no more. In twenty years all springs are over; without mockery it might be too sad to bear. To-day would grieve, and to-morrow would grieve; best cover it over lightly.

And so here is Rip at the end: Lazarus come from the dead, come back to tell us all. He will tell us all, and, badgering any who will listen, he tries: Well now!—have you heard what happened to *me*? But it won't do; he doesn't know. And that is a pity, truly. Here is a man in whom rest complexities and deficiencies a lifetime might contemplate, as the world has done; a man who has peered toward the dawn of civilization, witnessed ancient mysteries, and stared at his essential nature; a man who now in town is looking at the future and realizing a dream of the ages. And he cannot communicate his visions.

But supposing that he could, that he could tell us all: would it have been worthwhile? Visions, revelations like these are private. To translate what the thunder meant, to confront the meaning of life and the future of all our childish selves, we all have to go up into our own mountains.

DUTTON PAPERBACKS

DUTTON PAPERBACKS